I0147785

Contemporary Native Fiction of the U.S. and Canada:
A Postcolonial Study

Punyashree Panda

Library of Congress Cataloging-in-Publication Data

Panda, Punyashree

Contemporary Native Fiction of the U.S. and Canada:
A Postcolonial Study

p.cm

Includes bibliographic references and index.

Literature – Native Americans. 2. Literature – Comparative. 3. Native Americans – Literature. 4. United States – Literature. 5. Canada – Literature.

ISBN 13: 978-0-9820467-9-1

Bäuu Press
PO Box 4445
Boulder, Colorado

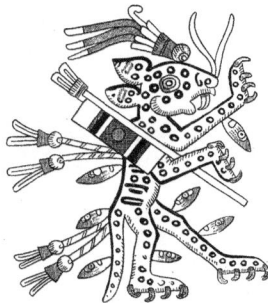

Printed in the United States of America
All Rights Reserved

Jitu & Naman

My Two Loves,

For both of you...

TABLE OF CONTENTS

Chapter I

Introduction: The Dominant Characteristics of Contemporary Native Fiction

This book makes an attempt to study the writings of the Native authors of both the United States and Canada from a postcolonial perspective. The Native authors chosen for the purpose are namely Louise Erdrich and Leslie Marmon Silko from the United States and Thomas King and Maria Campbell from Canada. Since the Native culture has for ages been dismissed as the Other, as an uncivilized culture, there is obviously a return of the repressed on the part of the Native authors in which case these authors are very often prone to celebrating their aborigine culture with their definite dimensions. Though the authors who celebrate their culture are plenty in the Native writing tradition, this book concentrates on one such specimen namely Louise Erdrich who is at the apex of Native cultural leaders. Apart from the glorification of their cultures, the contemporary Native authors are no less aware of the cannibalization of their culture by the mainstream through the obvious strategy of binary opposition. Playing the role of the colonizers, the majority whites looked down upon the Native culture and history which needed a rewriting in the hands of the Native writers. Here comes the role of postcolonialism of which the Native authors of both the United States and Canada are very much aware. They have very often taken recourse to the postcolonial and poststructural theories which have opened up new vistas to reappriciate and reinterpret their marginalized world. The thesis establishes the fact that the Native writers have their own storytelling tradition. On the top of it, in their attempt to right the wrong, they have adopted the strategy of mimicry and subversion in their writings. The writings of such authors as Leslie Marmon Silko emphasize their indigenous storytelling tradition. The free structure of autobiographical narrative has been chosen by Maria Campbell to mythicize the Halfbreed culture of the Natives. Such authors as Thomas King point out the inadequacy of the canonical strategy of narration and create a genre which is a mélange of multiple voices and diverse narrative techniques.

This part of the book, namely "Introduction: The Dominant Characteristics of Contemporary Native Fiction" has been divided into two parts. The first part has accepted as its onus to show how contemporary theories such as postcolonialism, poststructuralism, and postmodernism which have a bearing on the contemporary Native writing are mutually influencing each other. It has been argued how the Natives as subalterns have taken advantage of these literary theories and have tried to establish themselves as a Nation of their own. The second part of the Introduction makes an analysis of the

7

chief cultural ingredients of the Native culture which make them a proud people. This Introduction also gives a brief picture of the subsequent chapters which deal with the different nuances of the Native culture, including its resistance to revision of the canonical strategies of literature of the dominant group. It also makes a reference to the conclusion which has made a bold attempt to make a comparative study of the U.S. and Canadian authors with reference to the four texts taken up for study in this book.

I

Having grown as an offshoot of Franz Fanon's *The Wretched of the Earth* (1961), Postcolonialism has come to gather a place of prime importance in contemporary critical arena. Postcolonialism has been variously ascribed to and associated with cultural representations, identity issues, nativity, rewriting of history and such like. Postcolonialism as a concept thus has been understood to deal with a variety of aspects of not merely literature but also of life. Because of its inherent heterogeneity, it is not only difficult but almost implausible to reach at a comprehensive, all-encompassing definition of postcolonialism. However, an attempt could be made to define colonialism, so that it would be easy to gauge the objective of "post" in "postcolonialism." Aimé Césaire in his essay "Discourse on Colonialism" strikes at the root of "*colonization*" (emphasis mine) when he says:

> ... the essential thing here is to see clearly, to think clearly – that is, dangerously-and to answer the innocent first question: what, fundamentally, is colonization: To agree on what it is not: neither evangelization, nor a philanthropic enterprise, nor a desire to push back the frontiers of ignorance, disease, and tyranny, not a project undertaken for the greater glory of God, not an attempt to extend the rule of law. To admit once and for all without flinching at the consequences, that the decisive actors here are the adventurer and the pirate, the wholesale grocer and the ship owner, the gold digger and the merchant, apetite and force, and behind them, the baleful projected shadow of a form of civilization which, at a certain point in its history, finds itself obliged, for internal reasons, to extend to a world scale the competition of its antagonistic economies (Césaire 33).

Césaire rightly observes that colonization has never been for charity or for the betterment of humankind. That is, inherent in it has been an economic desire to exploit the resources (people included) of the yet 'uninhabited' 'places' of the earth and further the interests of different agents who would do anything to exploit others in the name of "educating the savages."

Now coming to the term "postcolonialism," the 'post' in postcolonialism can perhaps be interpreted as 'after' colonialism. This is tricky. When does this 'after' come to play? Is it after the intrusion of the colonizing forces into the hitherto indigenous landmasses or is it 'after' the colonizing forces have already 'left' the 'colonized' people? Questions of similar kind had been raised in the context of postcolonialism earlier too. However, what we need to focus on is, is it important or even necessary to assign a particular temporality to the concept of postcolonial? Doesn't it then become essential that we give a thought or two to 'precolonialism' if such a concept can be rationalized? What would then be the ramifications of the 'New literatures' or 'World literatures' that are already doing rounds of the contemporary critical circle? And most importantly, for this particular study, where should we *place* (emphasis mine) Native literatures of the U.S. and Canada?

Finding answers to all these questions and more would not be an easy task, taking into consideration the vast scope it involves and the possibilities of the cropping up of multifarious points of view. Donna Bennet, in her article "English Canada's Postcolonial complexities," gives a wholesome idea of what postcolonialism is all about. She writes:

> *Postcolonial* is thus a description that can be applied to a body of already existing literary responses to, and critical dialogues about, colonialism and its cultural effects ... and that postcolonial writing is therefore also a way of referring to the political, social and cultural developments characteristic of previously colonized regions as they sought for, and took on, varying degrees of self-recognition and an autonomous status (Bennet 169).

Thus, Bennet rightly refers to the sedimentation of ideas about a particular subject which needs to be thrashed out by discovering the loopholes in its discourses.

However, raising concerns about the uneasiness most postcolonial critics find themselves in, Arun Mukherjee argues against an attempt to establish a homogenizing "post-colonial writing, regardless of the differences of gender, race, class, caste, ethnicity and sexual orientation" (Vautier 4). The very essence of postcolonialism lies in its differentiating viewpoints and multifacetedness. It respects the fact that the world is not the same everywhere nor are the practices of the people who inhabit various parts of it. Robert Young, on the other hand, emphasizes what is common to the postcolonial people. He asserts "the right of all people on this earth to the same material and cultural   9 well-being" (Young 2) which holds good for different places and times. Postcolonialism, thus, serves the dual purposes of recognizing the differences as well as underlining the verisimilitude.

If postcolonialism deals with representation of the unrepresented, identity creation of the underprivileged and the recovering of a 'voice' of the hitherto voiceless, anticolonialism which is often confused with postcolonialism doesn't discharge any such function. It operates comparatively in a limited canvas, only catering to the needs of a die-hard nationalist. While dealing with "anti-colonialism," Young in his seminal book *Postcolonialism: An Historical Introduction* observes:

> Whereas postcolonialism has become associated with diaspora, transnational migration and internationalism, anti-colonialism is often identified exclusively, too exclusively, with a provincial nationalism (Young 2).

Young, thus, in the most laconic manner, brilliantly focuses on how postcolonialism in general and postcolonial writing in particular, put ample emphasis on what have been variously termed as issues pertaining to 'independence,' 'autonomy,' and 'cultural politics'. Franz Fanon, in *The Wretched of the Earth*, discusses the binary oppositions that exist in the cultural matrix. As the whites are often critical of the blacks, the latter become intolerant of the whites. Fanon is very much conscious of the construction of the binaries in the society if the blacks only react against the white hegemony. He terms the resultant configuration as "Menichean delirium" which is nothing but "counter racism" (Fanon 48). Hereupon, we should be careful not to indulge in binary thinking such as that of colonizer/colonized, religion/secularity, black/white, evil/good etc. as postcolonialism derives much of its soul from poststructuralism, which debunks binary patterns of thinking and worldview. Poststructuralism with its accent on the principles of "difference" helps in establishing the notions of postcolonialism.

According to Catherine Belsey, poststructuralism "...names a theory, or a group of theories concerning the relationship between human beings, the world, and the practice of making and reproducing meanings" (Belsey 5). Poststructuralism, thus creates meanings of words in a sense different, many a times radically, from what these words previously meant or further; it creates yet unheard of words and contextualizes them with hidden texts and sub-texts to bring out the true meaning of such words in the contemporary context. Thus it shatters the earlier convention that we, human beings, being the only 'organisms' of earth with the 'power' of language are in 'control' of it. Rather, we are continuously controlled and shaped by the language we use and the meanings they produce.

Poststructuralism, thus throws a challenge to all our previous understandings of the world and creates a layered universe where meanings are multifarious and powerful.

Saussure's inference that meaning is differential and not referential has generated a lot of debate and raised a million questions about the way language functioned till date. His idea of the signifier and the signified broke down all rules of linguistics and made the world rethink what it wants from language. It is this quality of poststructuralism that helps postcolonialism establish its credentials. Using the very language of the colonizer, postcolonial writers break the rules set forth by colonials in the act of their writing.

Postcolonial writing makes a conscious effort to demur the stereotypes and reestablish their identities. Dealing as it does with the production of knowledge, poststructuralism enables re-production of the same knowledge in a significantly different way. It helps look at the other side of the story. In doing so, postcolonial writing negates the colonial production of knowledge and subverts the power►►knowledge nexus. "To name the world is to 'understand' it, to know it and to have control over it" (Ashcroft 283). Postcolonialism, thus, with ample help from poststructuralism, creates a counter-discourse and by subverting the earlier 'knowledge' uncreates the master-narratives of the past.

Drawing from Althusser's notion of the *subject*, Poststructuralism challenges the power structures and the ideologies it adheres to by the act of speech and writing and thus creates waves, initiates action and generates a possibility of choices which had not existed in the past for the subject. Speaking from the podium of the subject, postcolonialism thus uses tools of subversion like parody and irony to decolonize the 'colonialized' mind and almost boastfully reconstructs the 'consciousness' of the community. Speaking from the position of subject, thus, postcolonial writers write not merely to assert their individual decolonization but rather to take back what has been denied to them for ages, their sense of worth and a 'dignity' hitherto denied because of colonization.

Poststructuralism thus connotes that one is not the controller of meaning; Rather words mean for themselves in such a way that unconsciously and many a times unwillingly one is controlled by the very words one utters or writes and the meaning that thus comes forth. Taking it further, Penny Petrone in the context of Native Literatures opines: "Words did not merely represent meaning. They possessed the power to change reality itself" (Petrone 10).

The colonial masters used language to produce meanings and images of Native cultures and people in a negativist manner. Terry Goldie in his essay "Semiotic Control: Native peoples in Canadian Literature in English" says that "The native is a semiotic pawn on a chessboard controlled by the white signmaker" (Goldie 112) and by saying so subverts the 'superiority' of the colonizing race. The application of poststructuralism helps the postcolonial writer position herself in the place of the signmaker and appropriate the signs previously produced. One of the tasks of the postcolonial writer is thus to write and right the wrongs. This involves replacing the myths

11

created by the colonizing forces by deliberately twisting the indigenous myths, putting back on track the derailed history of the communities and resisting further damage to the cultural matrix. To quote Bennet, "To describe a country as *postcolonial* in this sense could simply be to imply a coming of age, or a coming into identity" (emphasis mine) (Bennet 169).

Postcolonial writing has often emphasized a national identity. To focus merely on "national identity" is to create a trap of territorialization, which is seemingly the contour of postcolonialism. But, as a matter of fact, postcolonialism goes beyond such limited dimensions and enters into the arena of "hybridity" which respects differences of both the majority and minority cultures (Fanon 78-80). Thus, postcolonialism, so far as the play of differences is concerned, catches up with the Saussurean poststructuralism which gets a premium on the difference of meanings to the given words.

As noted earlier, poststructuralism engages itself to find out what happens when language is twisted and turned and also to understand who is the 'authority' behind it, if any exists at all. For the poststructuralist, the world is very much here; what is important is to see how much of it one knows and whether one 'really' knows it! Truth is truth but what needs to be examined is whose truth it is, as no ideology can be free from truth and vice versa. Language is dynamic and potent; power structures and dominance can be altered and subverted with the use of language, as is evident in the body of postcolonial writing.

Discarding binary practices such as that of the self and the other, poststructuralism essentially dismantles existing rules and thus alludes to another concept of 'post' i.e. postmodernism. Gallagher's doubt that a poststructuralist approach to postcolonial literature would result in an 'unnecessarily restricted canon' (Gallagher 16), seems to be ill founded as the very nature of poststructuralism is posited on the play of meaning with differences.

Postmodernism, as a literary theory, is rather young. Though it would be difficult to put a temporal marker to the origin of it, its origins are referred to art and architecture of the early twentieth century. Taking its cue from such varied disciplines as art, architecture, human philosophy and industrial economies, postmodernism has now come to occupy its pride of place in all the aforementioned disciplines as well as film, music, literature, sociology, fashion and science. According to the postmodern thought, "Ideas such as God, freedom, immortality, the world, first beginning, and final end have only a regulative function for knowledge, since they cannot find fulfilling instances among objects of experience" (net article np). In other words, the essentialist notions of an object or an individual have ceased to exist. Both animate and inanimate objects enjoy a free play of meaning.

The relevance and usefulness of postmodernism in the context of postcolonial literature comes from the rejection of the authority and the negligibility with which the postmodern

12

literary artist views the 'centre.' Self-reflexive as it is, postmodernism has often been confused with and paraded as a sub-head of poststructuralism. While similarities abound in the sense that both theoretical concepts try to break preexisting rules and bring forth new (dis) order, they differ in that while the latter is obsessed with language and meaning, the former delves deep into mindsets, space and time. According to Jean-Francois Lyotard:

> A postmodern artist or writer is in the position of a philosopher: the text he writes, the work he produces are not in principle governed by pre-established rules, and they cannot be judged according to a determining judgment by applying familiar categories to the text or to the work. Those rules and categories are what the work of art is looking for (Lyotard 81).

It is evident from the quote above that the postmodern text questions all sorts of hierarchy, power structures and close-ended operations, thus bringing the chaos back to the text. Whereas both modernism and postmodernism have been cultural phenomena, the 'post' in postmodernism makes all the difference and helps arrive at the conclusion that the two ideologies are poles apart. While modernism depended on absolutist concepts, postmodernism questions the very meaning of these ideals. As M. F. Salat brilliantly simplifies, modernism exemplified "order, authority and universality" while contrarily postmodernism "endorses notions of heterogeneity, multiplicity and particularity" (Salat 24).

Thus postmodernism makes everything relative. As there can be no single authority, there can be no single truth either. Hence, we often come across appropriation of the 'official' versions of truth in postmodern writings. To achieve this purpose, postmodern writers often use the techniques of irony, parody, intertextuality, metafiction, self-reflexivity and such like, shrouding everything in doubt and suspicion. In mimicking the existing notions of all givens, the postmodern denies the possibility of a singular worldview. Hence, the postmodern always perforce becomes a Bakhtinian dialogue. The discourse in the fictional art itself becomes dialogic, with a language that simultaneously represents and is represented. As Bakhtin points out, in the hands of the artist, the language is made "to sound simultaneously both outside it and within it, to talk about it and at the same time talk in and with it" (Bakhtin 358). Unlike theories of criticism of previous times and like postcolonialism, postmodernism is political in nature. As it questions the existing power structures, it creates jitters down the spine of the powerful, resulting in the generation of a noise that ultimately gives way to the *voice* from the margins (emphasis mine). Inherent in it, thus, is a possibility to change the status 13 quo and bring about a radical change. Moreover, though postmodernism raises questions, it does not always, nor is it bound to, provide the answer. This makes things even more interesting as this leads the reader to a chance and a process of invention and discovery. Owing to its affinity towards multiplicity and certain disinterestedness towards existing close-ended structures, postmodern writing often comes up in a manner where borders and boundaries are blurred and old forms are appropriated for new purposes. Hence, in a postmodern text the unexpected could be expected to happen in terms of technique, form, style, language, narrative as well as the story itself.

In such a scenario, it is difficult to appreciate Ihab Hassan's statement that "we are all, I suspect, a little Victorian, Modern and Post Modern, at once" (Hassan 589). It is this very generalization that postmodernism opposes. As in postcolonialism and poststructuralism, postmodernism, too, appreciates heterogeneity and multiplicity. As far as postmodernism is concerned, there is no space for singular versions of truth and history and the authority does not necessarily have the last say in matters concerning communities.

This results in a contempt for history, or the 'official' version of it; because, according to the concept of postmodernism, history, like fiction, is nothing more than a 'construct' and hence can be changed, altered, subverted or replaced altogether. Discarding the notion of 'original', 'natural' or 'logical,' postmodernism problematizes a clear-cut distinction between fact and fiction. This results in the postmodernist re-writing of history, not in a singular version but in multiple versions depending on the number and variety of readers. In this context, the only 'truth' that can emerge is interpretation and anybody's interpretation is as good or bad and as true or false as anybody else's. Even when 'organisms' share the same 'history,' their individual interpretation of and presentation of that history are bound to be different. Postmodernism thus gives rise to identity politics where questions such as "who can write," "for whom," and "from what point of view" are inadvertently raised.

Postmodernism thus discards the grand narrative or master narrative of the modern era to generate a multiplicity of metanarratives. In an anonymous article, the author is of the opinion that postmodernism suggests that:

> ...history has been written by the victor, the suppressor and the idea of history as a single narrative has now become defunct. The opinion today is more likely to side with petite histories instead of one grand historie. It is generally accepted that there is more than one way to see things, including history and which complicates, but makes more necessary, the process of uncovering

14

the truth, a process which can be slow and painful but will inevitably lead to a clearer understanding of ourselves and our world (Net article np).

History thus loses its status as the 'only' truth or the universal narrative. Thus, history as is commonly understood as a monolithic document of truth has lost its veracity. Since the local remained concealed under the universal, the local at present comes up with a thumping noise claiming its ingenuity. There is more truth in the local, the 'petite' than that meets the eye. Barbara Godard hence rightly underlines: "What is foregrounded is history as narrative, history as telling, history as a process of unfolding of local stories, or provisional truths- narratives that make no claims to universal truth" (Godard 200).

From the above discussion, it can be agreed upon that postcolonial literature functions with the conceptual vocabularies of postmodernism and poststructuralism. One can easily discern what are the different threads which rung along through postcolonialism, poststructuralism and postmodernism. First, any kind of authority or hierarchy principle is an anathema to all of them. They do not accept history as truth as much as it is the workmanship of the vested interests. Nor do they believe in the binary structures which only result in the counter-reaction or counter-racism. Hence, all the three- postcolonialism, poststructuralism and postmodernism adopt texts which have disbanded 'closure' and are more prone to having 'open-enededness.' To quote Gallagher in this context:

> A conjunction of similar writing strategies and forms lends credence to the comparisons among poststructuralism, postmodernism, and postcolonialism: much postcolonial literature, like poststructrualist criticism, rests upon dismantling, unmasking or questioning the concepts of hierarchy and otherness. Proclaiming the value of the marginal in its very existence, much postcolonial literature challenges the master-narratives of history. These shared concerns result in many similar formal techniques: much postcolonial literature, along with postmodernism, rejects realism, employs irony and allegory in a reconfiguration of history, refuses textual closure, and attacks the binary constructions of concept and language (Gallagher 13).

II

For any discussion on the Native Literatures of the U.S and Canada within the ambit of the contemporary theoretical frameworks, it is required to first take a glance at who these 'Natives' are, where they come from, what defines them and how. According to N. Scott Momaday, "An Indian is an idea which a given man has of himself" (emphasis mine) (Simard 244). A "Native" in the true sense of the term is more than his nomenclature. He is so diverse that he cannot be contained by any single definition. He is more often than not fluid in his nature. Any attempt to tie him down to a label is like doing injustice to him. Emma LaRocque in the seemingly simplistic description brings out the richness of a Native through the use of the conspicuous "absence." In her words:

> through the reading
> of a friend's poetry
> I learned about you
> About us
> us who don't belong
> us
> us brown people------
> (LaRocque 130)

The 'Native' peoples of the U.S. and Canada have been variously described in terms of "nativity,' 'blood-quantum,' 'Indianness,' 'communityhood,' so on and so forth, and they have been variously named as the 'First Nations people,' 'Natives,' 'Amerindian,' 'Aboriginal,' 'Indians,' 'Indigenous peoples' and more. These terms have, however, stayed on and have come to be used almost interchangeably. The Native peoples of the U.S. and Canada do not fit into any straight-jacket terms, nor are they fully defined by a ghettoizing term like "Native American" or "Canadian Indian." With such problematics of attaching a generic term to such a vast variety of people, and with their equally heterogeneous cultures and ways of life, "Native" peoples' definition in definite terms is an arduous task. However, Kenneth Lincoln, though he still uses the generic term "Native American," perhaps comes closest to defining what constitutes a 'Native' identity. In the words of Lincoln, *"Native Americans*: the stress falls on a hemispheric complex of original peoples, histories, languages, cultures, ecologies, radically diverse and no less than forty thousand years "native" to America." (emphasis original) (Lincoln 3). This is a Pan-Indian definition of the original peoples of the U.S. and Canada who could sustain themselves for thousands of years with a rich legacy of conflicting histories, diverse languages and varied places. The Natives, however, face a lot of difficulties in the contemporary world because of the radical changes that have taken place both in

16

the ecological and administrative level. As primitiveness has given place to modernity, the Natives had to change their own life styles, adopting newer versions of life. No wonder Drew Hayden Taylor lamentably argues:

> "As cliched as it may sound, I think everybody has his or her own unique definition of what being Native means. Very few of us exist in the world our grandparents lived in, where their *definition* was no doubt *far from ours*" (emphasis mine) (Taylor 59).

Taylor's argument about the changing definition of the Natives is a pointer to the obvious transformations that have recently taken place. The other hurdle which the Natives confront today is the regular intervention of the Governments with a view to giving them some new identity. The provincial and federal governments in both countries have more often than not depended on arbitrarily done up practices like the infamous Indian Act to 'recognize' the 'Natives.' Doing so, they have systematically neglected the cultural and sociological connotations of these people and this has led to fragmentation in the Native communities per se by having them divided and fractured over the various 'official' statuses and their impact on the day-to-day transactions of Native life, society and community.

A people called the Métis, or the mixed-bloods or the half-breeds are living on the fringes of the Native society. Neither White nor Indian, these in-between people "grew out of the symbiotic relationship that existed between Natives and the European immigrants to the New World" (Frideres 295). As soon as the French, English, Scottish explorers landed in America, they not only noticed the stout Native men but also the charming Native women, full of life and zest. Soon enough there occurred liaisons between them out of which were born these people now known as the 'Métis.' In this context, it is apt to quote Howard Adams from his classic *Prison of Grass*:

> Halfbreeds became a recognized separate racial group on the prairies during the last half of the 18th century. French, English, and Scottish men had mingled with the Indian population and from these relationships sprang a race of people distinct from both white and Indian society (Adams 46).

As sociologists today claim that miscegenation is the order of the day, originally Métis referred to categorize the Native people who had mixed French and Native ancestry. But today, the term 'Métis' symbolizes all those people who have some Indian ancestry to refer to. Thus, in the contemporary context, the Métis are a bonafide   17 people as they are the product of mixed blood.

It is now imperative to delve deep into the culture and traditions of these people, their lifestyles, and food habits. One may comfortably say that each culture has its own social significance, with its marriages and funerals, its deities and customs, its festivals and mournings, and its own boundaries of social interaction with people from 'other' cultures. Each culture maintains its own identity. It is ten to one that the boundaries of a minority culture are broken, when a dominant culture tries to subvert or underrate its values and systems. The Native peoples of the United States and Canada, though distinct in their own communal identities, share some common traits in their own culture and traditions, their lifestyles and social structures, their stories and myths. As Lincoln observes:

> Their cultures and histories differ as widely as terrain and climate, flora and fauna; but all tribes acknowledge ties distinct from those of other Americans-indigenous time on this "turtle island," as original myths relate, unified in an ancestral heritage (Lincoln 4).

One of the ways in which the Natives differ from the mainstream whites is the way they maintain their oral tradition. Whereas the majority culture heavily depends on the written tradition, the indigenous Natives find it easy to sustain their culture through the oral tradition. As an oral tradition is kept alive from generation to generation, through repeated tellings, Natives consider storytelling as much more than pastime, as it nurtures and furthers Native life. Storytellers in Native societies are hence accorded a lot of respect. And more often than not, these storytellers are the elders of the Native societies. Being the only bridge between the past and the present, the elders in Native societies are given much importance. In fact, figures like Silko's "Grandmother Storyteller" abound in Native mythology and oral tradition. To quote Hartmut Lutz in this context:

> Through the oral tradition, First Nations people learned who they are, where their ancestors came from, who all other beings around them are, how to behave, what to do and what not to do. In short: oral tradition, encompassing both the sacred and the profane, lies at the heart of the cultural identity of Native nations (Lutz 79).

Native oral tradition is always layered in meaning. There are stories about almost everything a Native child would require knowing to live in the land. There are origin stories, hunting stories, stories based on ceremonies and rituals, trickster tales and all these function with a dual motif to train the Native children for future and to upkeep the Native traditions and ways of life. Along with that, it creates a distinct sense of community and identity among the Natives. To quote Beth Cuthand in this context:

18

> We come from an oral tradition where our values, our worldview, and our system of beliefs are transmitted orally. In this process, there is something more than information being transmitted: there's energy, there's strength being transmitted from the storyteller to the listener and that is what's important in teaching young people about their identity (Cuthand 54).

Oral tradition being an essential and integral part of Native life, it is not enough to tell a story; *the way of telling* is important too (emphasis mine). The Natives of U.S. and Canada thus attach a lot of value to words. Words have power and words shape the consciousness of a people. According to Native beliefs, words are potent with energy and hence these must be used carefully and not wasted. As Lorelei Cederstorm rightly observes in her "Introduction to the Special Issue on Native Literature" of *The Canadian Journal of Native Studies*: "Unlike white man's words which scatter like leaves, the words of a Native Orator, once spoken, were granted an eternal life, a living presence that could be tapped by all those who heard the words" (Cedestorm 146).

A figure that occurs and reoccurs in many Native stories, ranging from the Southeast to the Plains, from the Northeast to Oklahoma, from the Rocky Mountains to California, from Alaska to the Canadian terrain, is that of the Trickster. The Trickster is everything one wants to be and does not want to be in the same breath. Trickster is both goodness personified and evil reincarnated. However, the most alluring characteristic of the Trickster is his "funkeism," an inherent ability to laugh at his own humiliation. Most often, he is an amalgamation of animal and human traits, which makes him funny and dangerous in the same vein. The Trickster appears in various forms as he can impersonate from animal to human and any other form with unequalled ease. The trickster is simultaneously a cheat and a helper, killer of life and giver of joy, tragic and comic, doer and done, and being so, this figure appears in origin myths as well as in hunting stories, in vision quests and ritualistic practices, on earth and in the sky, thus giving himself a range unthinkable in the canonical tradition. Appearing under various names such as Coyote or old man (Plains), Raven (Pacific coast), Nanabozho or Nanabush (Ojibwa), Wisakedjak (Cree and Saulteaux), Glooscap (Mi'kmaq), Wolverine and Jay in Canada, Spider (Sioux), the Trickster culture-hero of the Native peoples is both sinister and benevolent, thus creating in the listener's mind a laughter tinged with fear. One can laugh at him but one can be his victim too! To put it in David Williams' words: "Trickster, in postmodern terms, is meant to keep us free of the intolerable choice of who we are going to be" (William 267).

Without a fixed form or role, animal and human, capable and helpless, the Trickster is the ultimate paradox. 19 In many of the tales that he appears in, the Trickster lives outside the village or away from other beings, thus establishing his status as a marginal. However, he is not to be confused with a victim or a tragic hero. He, being the transformed and the transformer, is powerful and yet powerless. One is at agreement with Barbara Babcock's statement that the "trickster belongs to the comic modality or marginality where violation is generally the precondition for laughter and communitas, and there tends to be an incorporation of the outsider, a leveling of hierarchy, a reversal of statuses" (Babcock 158).

One of the broad characteristics of the Native societies is the community hunting. Community hunts are festive in mood and full of grandeur. All members of the community including women are welcome to these community hunts. In fact, it is the grandmothers who decide the time for the hunts, as their mapping of the land is considered to be more perfect. Community hunting is regarded as the privilege of each and every one of the community. Hence, if someone is sick or is obliged to attending a sick person because of which s/he would opt out of the hunt, s/he would still get her/his share when people come back from the hunt. Food is sacred too and in many ritualistic practices, it is offered to the Great Spirit and the Great Spirit is thanked by the people for the benevolence. What marks these Natives as a rich nation is their sense of special status for their women. Native women are accorded a high status in their communities. Owing to their cooperative view, Native peoples look at women as complementary to men and not as rivals. The master/slave relationship which existed between man and woman in the so-called civilized societies was never the case with the Natives. Almost all Native tribes believe in the female origins of the earth and its people. Women are regarded as the giver of life and the nurturer for continuance of traditions. To quote the Native Canadian poet, writer, storyteller Jeannette Armstrong in this context:

> In traditional Aboriginal society, it was woman who shaped the thinking of all its members in a loving, nurturing atmosphere within the base family unit. In such societies, the earliest instruments of governance and law to ensure social order came from *quality mothering* of children (emphasis mine) (Armstrong IX).

Many Native tribes were and still are matrilineal, showcasing the power and respect women once enjoyed in Native societies. Native women have played the role of the "insurers of the next generation" as Armstrong puts it (Armstrong XI). As far as Métis women are concerned, they bring forth and practice a beautiful blend of French-Canadian or English-Canadian tradition and aboriginal heritage. The women in the Native societies can be easily credited for keeping alive their traditions in a fast changing world.

20

The most glaring trait of the Natives is the 'worldview' they uphold so tenaciously in the wasteland of the twentieth century. The Native worldview has always judged all beings as equals in the universe which is the product of their unique religion and philosophy. In fact, Native tribes relate themselves to animals and claim them as their kin. Even while hunting the animals, the Natives never forget to thank the hunted ones for having given their lives so that their brethren can live. This worldview is a cooperative worldview where all beings on earth are equal and contribute to the functioning of the world equally. Compared to this tribal worldview, the Eurocentric worldview seems narrow and limited. While bringing about the sad contrast between these two worldviews and talking at length on their essential differences, Paula Gun Allen explains:

The notion that nature is somewhere over there while humanity is over here or that a great hierarchical ladder of being exists on which ground and trees occupy a very low rung, animals a slightly higher one, and man (never woman)—especially "civilized" man- a very high one indeed is antithetical to tribal thought. The American Indian sees all creatures as relatives (and in tribal systems relationship is central), as offspring of the Great Mystery, as co-creators, as children of our mother, and as necessary parts of an ordered, balanced and living whole (Allen 59).

In the legends, tales, and the myths of the Native languages, there is no clear-cut wall between what constitutes of *human* values and what constitutes of *animal* values.

While understanding the dominant traits of the Natives, one should mark their peculiar negative attitude to their sense of possessiveness which is similar to that of the East rather than the West. Living in and with Nature, the Natives never had any inclination for individual ownership of any of the resources Nature offered them. The habit of sharing is inculcated early in a Native child's education and a sense of community makes the world a pleasant place to live in. Individualism, the supreme virtue of the European thought process is regarded essentially negative to tribal life and society. As Kenneth Lincoln remarks, "Tribal life centers in a common blood, a shared and inherited body of tradition, a communal place, a mutual past and present" (Lincoln 21). Land for the Native is sacred and revered. Land is not inanimate. It is living too. It is, for them, the sacred mother, Mother Earth. The Native eye sees land and human beings as integral to and part of each other, not as separate units. Being the Mother, the land provided well enough for the Natives and there was no reason why they would view her otherwise. It is this strong feeling for the Mother Earth that led to the Native scorn of the white advice to till and farm the land. The following lines from a treaty speech by a Native Nez Perce Chief portray the Native sentiment for land:

"You ask me to plow the ground. Shall I take a knife and
tear my mother's breast? Then when I die she will not
take me to her bosom to rest" (Lincoln 28).

Championing the elders is one of the hallmarks of the Natives.
Native life being essentially a community life, the elders of the community
are respected for their knowledge of the flora and fauna, the forest and
the spirit people. Along with the respect for elders, comes a respect for
tradition. Its importance in Native life is evident in the various rituals
and ceremonies followed by the different tribes. If the Native life is a
community life, it is also a ritualistic life. Though manifested in a multitude
of ways, rituals and ceremonies undoubtedly carry a huge importance in
all the Native communities of the U.S. and Canada. Central to most Native
communities is a belief in the "Great Spirit." However, this "Great Spirit"
is not to be considered the same as the Christian individualistic God.
Native ceremonies are enactments of rituals to establish and further the
communal relationship all 'peoples' shared on this earth. There is evidence
that the Natives often associated themselves closest with one or another
'people' of the earth and this resulted in the Sun Clan, Moon Clan, Buffalo
Clan, Eagle Clan and so on. Most often the ceremonies are held with an
intention to integrate all these 'peoples' from different kingdoms and thus
ensure continuity of life and harmony in nature. The ceremonies, like
the Native world itself, are structured in a layered manner. Thus we find
prayer, song and dance altogether in Native ceremonies. The individual in
the Native society was allowed her/his sanctity, but as a communal being
linked together with other beings by means of a ritualistic life. To put it in
the words of the Native Laguna poet, novelist Leslie Marmon Silko:

In the ancient times, cohesiveness was all that stood
between extinction and survival, and, while the individual
certainly was recognized, it was always as an individual
simultaneously bonded to family and clan by a complex
bundle of custom and ritual (Silko 506).

Another important component is the Native sense of cyclical time
versus the western idea of linear time. The western tradition divides time
into three clear-cut distinctions, past, present and future and actions take
place in either this or that part of time. Things happen and are recorded in
a straightforward manner. This is not so for the Native peoples. Extending
its view of tribal life and culture as happening in a sacred circle, time too,
in the Native world, is cyclical and circular. Things happen continuously in
all times in the Native world. Even the storytellers, when they tell stories,
move back and forth in time. This might be confusing and frustrating
for the untrained ear but the Native tradition draws from
it the way to express its world and its experience. To quote

22

Cederstrom in this context: "This moment of Indian time sees past and present simultaneously and sees, at once, the physical present and the spiritual eternal" (Cederstrom 148).

Like all marginal people, the Natives too are burdened with a false account of history and the Native writers are very conscious of its damaging effects on their people. Columbus who came to the coast of America in 1492 was the first person to give an ambiguous picture of the 'Indians' as he called them, to the outside world. This European's contact with the Natives was more a curse than a blessing to the Natives. Instead of giving an objective picture of the Natives, he was giving to his Western brethren a black-and-white picture of the Natives. In the words of William W. Savage, Jr.:

> "The first ambiguous response to Indians belonged to Christopher Columbus, their discoverer and the man who misnamed them. Struggling to define for his employers just who and what these aborigines were, he described them as being "neither black nor white" (Savage, Jr. 3).

This initial report, we can assume, set the stage for the European's (mis)understanding of and (under)dealings with Native people. Europe found in the Natives exactly what it wanted to find, "non-white" subjects who practiced 'pagan' religions with a nomadic lifestyle, perfect beings to deserve a colony or two. The European colonial forces hence attempted war against the Natives. Though they were not armed, the Natives fought for their nations in bloody battles that antagonized them further against the white colonial onslaught. The Natives who initially hosted the white explorers were soon disillusioned. This antagonism between the original peoples and the people who came to take away their home and land raged four centuries of bloodshed and massacre that expanded from the fifteen century to the middle of twentieth century. The loss has been heavier on the Native side, obviously less powerful with their spears and knifes in comparison to the Europeans' guns and ammunitions. Some of the most infamous in Native-White history are the Trail of Tears, the Wounded Knee Massacre of 1890, the Métis Uprising in 1869, Seven Oaks massacre in 1816, Riel Rebellion in 1885 and so on. The list would be endless. Though voices were raised against these atrocities against Natives by some whites themselves, those were few and far between.

Treaties were posited by the Euroamerican forces as means for harmonious existence which were often dubious. Though trusted by the Natives as instruments of a healthy relationship between the two peoples, they were never intended to have a lasting relationship. Treaties were often signed only to be flouted and violated by the colonizing forces, thus leading to disillusionment and vibes of antagonism among the indigenous peoples.   23

The colonisers not only encroached upon the Natives' land, but also killed many of their people in bloody battles and massacres and wiped out entire communities. Thus, the Euroamerican forces looked forward to unleash the tools of colonization on these original peoples and subjugate them altogether, exploit their resources further and destroy their cultures and traditions, their ways of life. The first among these, as poststructuralism tells us, was the production of knowledge, knowledge suited to and serving the purposes of the powerful.

Systematically rejecting the Native peoples' religions, languages and ways of life, the colonizers paved the path for the total destruction of their culture. In order to authenticate the process of colonization, the colonizer subverted the indigenous knowledge and produced new knowledge that would help maintain the *status quo*. Turning the Natives into the Foucouldian Other, they made an attempt to obliterate the indigenous value systems, communities and in doing so they exercised the colonial power. For this purpose, images were manufactured to present the Natives in ways the dominant culture wanted to perceive them. To quote Daniel Francis in this issue:

> Lacking any real knowledge of Native people, non-Natives have felt free to imagine all manner of things about them. Indians were (are) savages; Indians were (are) natural mystics; Indians were (are) militant warriors; Indians were (are) disappearing; Indians were (are) the original environmentalists (Francis 10).

The primary intention of the colonizer being the acquisition of Native land, creating the stereotyped images of Natives as 'noble' or 'bloody' 'savages,' as 'nomadic' tribes without any 'proper' religion served them well. This stereotyping was a means towards an end, towards the justification of why the 'civilized' people have a right over Native land. By marginalizing the Native communities and their cultures, the colonizing masters created a master narrative that frequently reinforced the dominant culture's interpretation of indigenous life and cultures. To quote Susan V Gallagher in this context:

> As an economic practice, colonialism sought to control the production of wealth, but in so doing it also controlled the production of culture... Either by denying the existence of indigenous culture or by denigrating its value, colonialism marginalized the cultures of the colonized ... Without a recognized culture, colonized peoples were deemed less civilized, less advanced, perhaps even less human (Gallagher 7).

24

By such control over the production of culture, colonization not only affected the colonized physically and economically but also morally, psychologically and socially. The colonizer wanted the ultimate control, control over the mind of the colonized. And what better way to do this than in the realms of religion? The white belief in the superiority of Christianity and the white race manifested itself in the appropriation of the Native cultures through the eyes of the colonizer. To quote Young:

> The idea of imperialism, and the notion of a civilizing mission, presupposed racial superiority, for the fundamental difference between civilization and savagery that justified and required the civilizing mission assumed a basic differentiation between white and non-white races, and this was made in increasingly *absolute and derogatory terms* (emphasis mine) (Young 32).

To achieve this objective, it became necessary to degrade and demean the age-old Native cultural practices and to create a sense of inferiority in the Native Mind. To quote Morse in the same vein, "They were told that they should feel ashamed of their traditions and values. This message was repeated in the schools and churches" (Morse 2). Lincoln describes it as "Deicide" (Lincoln 7), or the definite death of the Native deities. This, combined with the introduction of materialistic goods and alcohol into their lifestyle, led to a double loss for the Native communities. Along with the loss of land came an additional sense of loss of identity. The missionary practices devalued the Native social practices. Native women, who till then enjoyed power and prestige in their communities, were now made to imitate the Euroamerican model of a submissive, demure woman. To quote noted poet, critic Emma LaRocque in this context:

> Racism and sexism found in the colonial process have served to dramatically undermine the place and value of women in Aboriginal cultures, leaving us vulnerable both within and outside of our communities. Not only have Native women been subjected to violence in both white and Native societies, but we have also been subjected to patriarchal policies that have dispossessed us of our inherited rights, lands, identities, and families (LaRocque 11).

The Natives not only suffered a terrible loss of their culture but were also subjected to the colonial apparatus. The schools meant for the Native Indians were veritable prison houses. The traditional Native pride was thus eroded by the Indian School system. Functioning under the European missionaries, the Indian Boarding   25 schools often took away the Native children by force from the familiar surroundings of their families. In the process of "civilizing the Native children," they created a cultural and social vacuum in the Native child's mind and surrounding. Allen talks of this coercive education which had a debilitating effect on the children. To quote her:

> To use educational warfare effectively you have to have your enemy in captivity. Thus the Indian school system was developed to aid the military and 'legal' establishment in processing the resigned, defeated young Natives who fell into its hands. Schools that were little more than concentration camps for young people were erected all over the West, Midwest, and even in the East, where the star colonial establishment, Carlisle Indian School, was located (Allen 15).

Jeannette Armstrong, the fiery poet, novelist, critic tells us that most of the present day "Indian Problem" dates back to these ill-maintained residential schools, and traces the subsequent alienation of the young Natives to the same vile system. Armstrong observes:

> The ensuing nightmare of the effect of residential schooling on our communities has been what those "Indian problem" statistics are all about. The placement of our children in residential schools has been the single most devastating factor in the breakdown of our society. It is at the core of damage, beyond all the other mechanisms cleverly fashioned to subjugate, assimilate and annihilate (Armstrong X).

Furthermore, there has been on the part of the colonizing force, a continuous attempt to create stereotypes of the Natives. From Columbus's assessment of the Natives to the representation of indigenous culture and peoples in twentieth century popular culture like that of the Hollywood Western, images have been manufactured time and again to justify colonial presence and practice. From the early images of the "noble savage" to the more contemporary "vanishing race" theory, the Euroamerican oppressive forces have permanently hoodwinked the Natives. Juggling between these created images, the Native peoples have been subjugated to such a position that many young Natives now see themselves in the colonizer's image. By perpetuating the stereotypes, the white colonizing forces have made the Native look down upon themselves as a paradoxical figure, a mumbo jumbo, a mixture of opposites. In the words of Savage, Jr.:

26

> Thus, "the Indian"- a myth, a conceptual monolith
> ... appears in American culture in a series of paired
> images: he is both a noble savage and a brute, a bearer
> of gifts and a bloodthirsty killer of woman and children,
> a teacher without whose help survival is impossible and
> a ward incapable of survival without public or private
> assistance (Savage, Jr. 3).

The colonizer has thus reduced the Native into a reductive image, a good-for-nothing person who is a buffoon, an idiosyncratic figure. The Native is pitted in the past for a decorative value while their present value is almost zero. Summing up these characteristics of the Native, Healey comments:

> A variety of studies have documented continuing
> stereotyping of Indians in the popular press, textbooks,
> the media, cartoons, and various other places. Native
> Americans are often portrayed as stereotypical bucks
> and squaws, complete with headdresses, bows, tepees,
> and other such 'generic' Indian artifacts. These portrayals
> obliterate the diversity of Native American culture and
> lifestyles. Native Americans are often referred to more in
> the past than in the present, as if their present situation
> was of no importance or, worse, as if they no longer
> existed (Healy 158).

The image of the Natives in the celluloid is no better either as stereotypes are further reinforced in the films. The Westerns so popular in both the U.S. and Canada reinforce the myth of the "noble" or "bloody" "savage" in mainstream psyche and there has been little deviation, if any, from such portrayals of Native peoples, even in the contemporary times except for a rare one like *Dances with Wolves*, the 1991 Oscar winning movie which is about a white man's finding of identity through the practice of Native culture. The Native female, too, has suffered from such callous stereotyping as Emma LaRocque truthfully records: "The dehumanizing portrayal of the 'squaw' and the over sexualization of Native females such as in Walt Disney's *Pocahontas* surely render all Native female persons vulnerable" (LaRocque 12).

The oppression of the whites both in the United States and Canada has not come to an end even in the postcolonial period. The whites have almost thrust upon the Natives the choice of assimilation. Thus, giving the Natives the choice of either assimilation or annihilation, the colonizing forces have wiped out whole cultures and value systems and all the Native are left with now is "reservation life," a life sans hopes and dreams. As the Natives began to disappear as a result of these two choices, up came the myth of the "vanishing race." A   27

Lavonne Ruoff curtly talks about the white assumption of the Natives as a fast disintegrating and disappearing people, "as a noble red man, either safely dead or dying as fast as could reasonably be expected" (Allen 77).

Early writings both by and about Natives in the United States and Canada often played to or confirmed the aforementioned stereotyping. One of the reasons that came to be attributed to this conformist attitude was the predominantly white readership for whom the books were written. Influenced by the white colonial value systems and looking up to the western literary tradition for acceptance and inspiration, the early writings by Natives were often nostalgic, creating a sense of *deja vu* that presented the Natives as "noble savages" in need of or having woken up to the superior experiences of civilization and Christianity. The white authors who took up the cause of Natives in their writings often talked about the stoicism of the Native males or the natural charm of the Native females, who, more often than not, fell in love with a white woman/man. Apart from these, early anthropologists like Henry Rowe Schoolcraft and Roy Harvey Pearce worked towards the collection of Native myths, legends, stories, tales and ways of life, though for more scientific and less literary reasons.

The earliest known Native writers of the U.S. whose writings were published in English were generally the missionary educated clergy. Most of the times, the writings were either sermons or autobiographical accounts dealing with the life and times of the Natives.

As one moves from early Native American and Native Canadian writings to the contemporary Native Literary scene, we come to notice an upward surge, in terms of theme, scope and reach, especially the writings after the 1970's. While talking about postcolonial literatures of the world, one cannot move ahead without giving a thought to the process that gave rise to this phenomenon in the first place. Postcolonial literature, it has been often argued, brings forth hitherto non-existent voices to the forefront and shatters boundaries and conventions. It describes a vast range of experiences from various parts of the world, of heterogeneous societies belonging to widely varied cultures, ethnicities, religions and so on. Western literary conventions and critics, who practice a singular view of the world, have often failed to appreciate these diversities of postcolonial literature.

Postcolonial theory has emerged out of a dialectical process between power politics, imperialism and indigenous struggles to regain what has been lost over a period of centuries. Young remarks: "Postcolonial theory involves a political analysis of the cultural history of colonialism, and investigates its contemporary effects in western and transcontinental cultures, making connections between that past and the politics of the present" (Young 6). The postcolonial criticism brings to the surface the differences that lie underneath the marginal societies and also the varieties of their facets which are often ignored by the majority society. In this respect, what Gallagher states below is more relevant:

> Colonialism shows different faces in different parts of the globe, and its progeny come in different shapes, colours, and forms. Any discussion of Postcolonialism, then, is a *discussion of the difference* and multiplicity as well as the commonality of oppression and injustice (emphasis mine) (Gallagher 8).

In spite of their diverse community cultures, ways of life that varied from farming and fishing to hunting and food gathering, the variety in their languages and cultures, their lifestyles and religious practices, what makes the Natives of the United States and Canada stand on a common ground is the pan-Native experience of colonization. They share an experience of their cultures being uprooted, their ways of life being ridiculed, their communities being wiped out, their very humanity being questioned and it is these experiences from which the contemporary Native writing emerges. It is their resistance to what Cèsairè calls 'thingification' that resonates in their literature (Cèsairè 42). Because literature is a cultural dialogue and Native literature does not function in isolation, it draws from and gives to the vast arena of Native culture. Agnes Grant defines "Native Literature" in the following words:

> "Native Literature" means Native people telling their own stories, in their own way ... Native literature reveals the depth and status of the culture, expresses Native wisdom and points of view recognized by non-Native writers. Native literature records oral narratives, values, beliefs, traditions, humour and figures of speech. It emphasizes communal living and portrays a mingling and sharing ... (Grant 125).

The Native peoples from the U.S. and Canada are now raising their voices, not only to protest against the atrocities of the colonizer and demand their rightful place in the world but also to reclaim and reassert their ancient heritage. Native Canadian poet and critic Emma LaRocque defines "voice" as a "textual resistance technique" (LaRocque 13). To achieve this objective, the Native writers are going back to their own cultures and are building up their writing from their cultural resources. One such element is the rich oral tradition prevalent among Native cultures. The Native oral tradition inspires them to tell a story from their point of view, to reject the Judeo-Christian worldview and to establish the Native worldview.

29

Doing so, these Native writers are creating a historical tradition in order to recreate a lost identity. On the way, they are also deconstructing the stereotypes created by the colonial production of knowledge and creating new literary styles that rarely confirm to the western traditions of writing. This leads to a postmodernist debunking of the "master narratives" created by "white history." Barbara Godard puts it thus: "Narrative is a way of exploring history and questioning the historical narratives of the colonizer which have violently interposed themselves in place of the history of the colonized" (Godard 198).

Initially dismissed by the Euroamerican intellect as an "oral culture" and hence regressive, degraded and uncivilized, the Native peoples writing in English are subverting the previous assumptions. The Native writers are talking about their religions, beliefs, social structures, political practices, customs and rituals, languages and lifestyles, thanks largely to their vibrant oral tradition. To quote the Acoma writer critic Simon Ortiz:

> The oral tradition is not just speaking and listening, because what it means to me and to other people who have grown up in that tradition is that whole process... of that society in terms of its history, its culture, its languages, its values, and subsequently, its literature. So its not merely a simple matter of speaking and listening, but living that process (Ruoff 5).

One of the most fascinating aspects of Native writing has been its treatment of the feeling for land. Land and landscape play a central role in the telling of Native stories. The oral tradition too emerges out of the Native understanding of the land. For the Native writers, the whole universe is living and they are as much a part of it as any other. This participant view of the Native world manifests itself, among other things, in its perception of the land. It is with the loss of land that the Native cultures face an ultimate loss of identify; because colonialism, at its root, is about the appropriation of land.

Talking about the land and landscape, Allen has famously proclaimed that as Natives "we are the land" (Allen 3). Hence, land often spurts up as a central theme in Native Literatures. Richard Fleck observes in this context: "For this reader, one of the most compelling themes of Native American fiction is the sacredness of land... Our Earth mother is not only alive and sacred, but she also speaks to those who will watch and listen (Fleck 4).

Appropriation and rewriting of history is one of the major aspects of any postcolonial writing. Postcolonial authors often look back at the "official" versions of history as a tool of the larger

30

scheme of colonization and hence subvert it in their own writings. Robert Young's comments on postcolonial literary productions would validate the argument being made here:

> Postcolonial critique incorporates political and theoretical practices whose reach extends back into the history of the colonial past as well as the day-to-day realities of the postcolonial present, practices which seek to contest the legacies of that past as well as to challenge the priorities and assumptions of its political heirs. Postcolonialism, therefore, operates through the dimensions of time or history, and space, both geographical and the other, third space of cultural reconceptualization, the reordering of the world through forms of knowledge reworked from their entanglement in longstanding coercive power relations (Young 66).

Thus, the postcolonial writing helps the subaltern in reconstituting its histories and shaping its identities anew. Thus, the subaltern, in the postcolonial era takes the responsibility of giving new directions to its history and culture. This empowerment results in a rewriting of history in a way to present the Other side of the story. Poststructuralist and postmodernist theories tell us that meaning is always layered and subjective. By taking up the colonial version of history and looking at it from a Native perspective, the First Nations writers are questioning the authoritativeness of such a history. Breaking down the binary representations of good/bad, civilized/uncivilized, subject/object, profane/angelic, margin/centre, the Native writers are presenting an ex-centric viewpoint. Redefining "history," Rudy Wiebe tells us:

> History is often just the accidental data you happen to have. What is really crucial or important in what happened may have existed only in certain acts that were never recorded. No one ever saw. So there is always an assumption among historians that the most important things that happened are one you can find evidence for. That may not be true (Salat 33).

Native authors are hence coming up with postmodernist historiography where the core myths created by colonizers are re-presented from a Native perspective.

To reassert their cultures and identities, to debunk the established notions of history and rewrite it with their own versions of histories, Native writers use the language of the colonizer. Appropriating the language of the colonizer, the Native authors tell their own stories in essentially Native ways.   31

Postcolonial literature all over the world has witnessed this phenomenon of the appropriation of the invader's language by the once colonized to present localized viewpoints. Meaning is no longer what the hegemonic forces intend it to be. Language has ceased to be private and personal. In the poststructuralist era, the subaltern other's meaning is as valid and reasonable as the dominant other's. Meaning is subjective and hence the Native writer's writings in European languages such as English, French or Spanish are as much capable of bringing forth new meanings from the colonizers' language as the colonizer himself is. Native writers writing in English are thus changing the tongue of English itself. They are, it can be termed, *Nativizing* the English tongue (emphasis mine). To quote Arnold Krupat in this context:

> Even though contemporary Native writers write in English and configure their texts in apparent consonance with Western or Euroamerican literary forms- that is, they give us texts that look like novels, short stories, poems and autobiographies- they do so in ways that present an 'English' nonetheless 'powerfully affected by the foreign tongue,' not by Hindi, Greek, or German, of course, and not actually by a 'foreign' language, is as much as the 'tongue' and 'tongues' in question are indigenous to America (Krupat 77).

"Appropriation," Seiler tells us, is "the process by which the language is taken and made to 'bear the burden' of one's own cultural experience" (Seiler 53). And this appropriation is necessary as language on its own, within itself, consists of markers that are cultural, social and political in nature. To alter these markers is essential to represent a different way of life and a different worldview. The Native writers use English with the purpose of projecting, protecting, and defending their peoples, their cultures and their ways of life, because it is this language of the enemy that has been used in schools, in the church and in community gatherings to create in the Native mind a sense of loss and alienation.

Many first world critics have overlooked this aspect in their analysis of Native literature; They have gone on to opine that the very use of the dominant culture's language for cultural/literary expression speaks of assimilation on the part of the indigenous writers. It has also been argued that the Native writers write in English because of the market the language enjoys. One such critic, Wolfgang Horchbruck, commenting on indigenous fiction, tells that:

> Not only do they use language (English, Spanish, or
> French) not native to their groups of origin, but also, the
> idea that their literary productions constitute part of a
> "culture of resistance" is mostly romantic myth, as long
> as the texts are written for distribution in the dominate
> culture's marketpldace (Horchbruck 135).

While Horchbruck may not be exactly off the mark in observing that Native literature indeed seeks a place in the dominant culture's marketplace, it is difficult to agree with his assumption that the Native writing's functioning as a culture of resistance is a romantic myth. For how are they supposed to communicate to the world outside if they do not use English as a means of expression? Using the language of the colonizer can in fact be seen as a means to an end and not the end itself. Postmodernism tells us that it is the process that is more significant than the product. In that sense, the Native writers use the process of appropriating the colonizer's languages in order to recreate a Native view of the world. In the lack of a pan-Native language, using the colonizer's language for resistance, not assimilation, English is seen as a "gift" from the colonizer, because it acts as a bridge among the communities to communicate with each other. Beth Cuthand rightly observes:

> Maybe one of the most valuable gifts the colonizers gave us
> was the English language so that we could communicate
> with each other. I fully believe that we can use English
> words to Indian advantage and that as Indian writers it's
> our responsibility to do so (Cuthand 53).

English, the language of the colonizer, is thus used not merely to refer to and retell past experiences of colonialization but also as an activism to protest such misadventures in the contemporary world.

Appropriating the enemy's language, the Native writers thus establish their notions in contest with the dominant cultures' notions, rewriting thus, new codes of culture and values, virtues and vices. Thus writing even within the framework of the dominant discourse, the Native writers can subvert the said discourse from inside. Writing from two worlds and two cultures, Native writers thus use irony to show the paradoxes of the world they inhabit. Linda Hutcheon has this to say about irony:

> Its' inherent semantic and structural *doubleness* also
> makes it a most convenient trope for the paradoxical
> dualities of both postmodern complicious critique
> and post-colonial doubled identity and
> history. (emphasis mine) (Hutcheon 73).

33

Orality is another significant aspect which differentiates Native literature from the mainstream literature. Native authors and critics often cite the significance orality has in Native cultures and the "oral literature" reflects itself in their writings. This "oral literature" as a tradition is extremely conspicuous in Native literature. The conventional use of language has always kept a clear-cut wall between the oral and the written. The fusing of these two apparently bifurcated terminologies adds to the complexity of Native literature. Krupat suggests this explanation for "Oral literature":

> Because *littera-ture* in its earliest use meant the cultivation of letters (from Latin *Littera*, "letter"), just as *agriculture* meant the cultivation of fields, peoples who did not inscribe alphabetic characters on the page could not, by definition, produce a literature... It was the alteration in European consciousness generally referred to as "romanticism" that changed the emphasis in constituting the category of literature from the medium of expression, writing- literature as culture preserved in letters-to the *kind* of expression preserved, literature as imaginative and affective an oral literature can be conceived as other than a contradiction in terms and the unlettered Indians recognized as people capable of producing a "literature"(Krupat 76) (emphasis original).

While acknowledging the presence of "oral literature" and hence the indigenous people's capability to produce literature, Krupat simultaneously also refers to this recognition in European consciousness to as late as the eighteenth century. What needs to be noted here is that the non-recognition of indigenous oral cultures prior to eighteenth century need not necessarily mean that these did not exist *a priori*. It is only because they are coming to the forefront now, are they being given their pride of place in the literary scene. However, what is noteworthy is the fact that Native authors, while writing in an adopted tongue, also adapt their oral tradition to the nuances of their language of expression. This process hence includes a certain amount of translation from the Native cultural traditions to the dominant cultural tradition. Talking about North American indigenous peoples, Kenneth Lincoln remarks:

> They lived as oral cultures, traditions generating mouth to mouth, age to age, alive only as the people passed on a daily culture. Their literatures come down as remembered bodies of myth and ritual, song-poetry and narrative tales, legends and parables. Once these oral literatures carried through the double translation into English, onto the printed page,

34

literatures carried through the double translation into English, onto the printed page, America began to recognize, belatedly, the long presence of Native American Literatures (Lincoln 20).

As already discussed, contemporary Native writing often consists of the elements of resistance and activism. In such a scenario, "text" is not merely affected by but also affects politics. As far as Native literature is concerned, the "'literary text,'" then, "is not merely of secondary importance to political events but is a constitutive element in the political process," asserts Julia Emberley (Emberley 99). Oral literature, thus, assumes political connotations, and gives rise to a pan-Native Nationalism and tribalism. Having the paradoxical qualities of change and constancy, oral literatures thus incorporate the political as clearly and flowingly in themselves as any other aspect of Native life. Thus, if these speak of pre-contact tribal life in their tales and stories, they also reflect on colonialization of the past as well as the present-day nationalist activities by the tribes.

That the Native writers often take inspiration from their oral tradition for the theme, style and presentation of their fiction need not fathom a view that these literatures are "basic" or lacking in literary sophistication. In fact, as Rodney Simard tells us, oral literature, "is necessarily fragile, being always only one generation away from extinction; but it still is the basis for *all* literatures, and it is no less distinguished because of its orality" (emphasis original) (Simard 243).

The other sure trait of the Native literature is that the Community invariably occupies the center stage in the life of the fictional protagonists. Writing from a community perspective, Native writers reassert their communal cultural identities and this is one of the major differentiating factors between Native literature and western literature. To quote noted Native writer activist Kateri Akiwenzie-Damm in this context: "Family and community give us a knowledge base, a way of being, a worldview. This is provided to us through arts, language, ceremonies, songs, prayers, dances, customs, values, practices" (Akiwenzie-Damm 90).

Preoccupied with the recovery of lost myths, rituals, orality and a Native way of life, the Native authors are nevertheless equally conscious of the audience for their texts. Catering to pan-tribal, and the mainstream 'white' audience as well as non-Native, non-white readers and critics, the Native writers of the United States and Canada do not shy away from a manifestation of their mastery in the contemporary postmodern traits of fiction. Writing as they do from a postcolonial pedestal, these Native authors postmodernise their works of art both in terms of theme and technique. Drawing heavily from their own tribal traditions, the Native authors make comfortable use of the postmodern tools of irony, parody, sarcastic humor, intertextuality and thus slander the so-called sacrosanct canonical tradition.   35

Indulging themselves in a play of words and language, the Native writers from the United States and Canada, including the ones discussed in this study, achieve and establish their tribal identity in the language of English. In the Native fictional art, there are many voices, each with their own versions of stories as well as the pattern to tell these stories. The presence of multiple voices inside a single text points to the Native writer's use of the postmodern craft of writing that underlines hybridity in terms of theme, technique, form, genre as well as treatment.

Native writers often fuse and blur boundaries inside their textual productions so as to avoid monolithic norms of comprehension and discard 'territoriality' which is a virtue for the colonizers. The product of centuries of oppression and inferiorization, the Native text seeks to establish the contours of a Native point of view, a Native universe and hence tribal traditions of thought often enter the Native text. But along with it, the Native authors often being well-educated and well-informed scholars, their understanding of the contemporary fictional writing finds its way to their textual productions as well. Paying scanty respect to the rules laid down by the canon, Native writers cut across genres and sources to create the effects of a pastiché inside their texts. Thus, Silko does not mind opening her first novel *Ceremony* with a poem or intermingling prose and poetry throughout the text. Further, the poems can be prosaic and the prose lyrical in quality. Thomas King breaks all conventional norms of novel writing when the story in *Green Grass, Running Water* begins with tribal opening lines, many of which are unintelligible to readers outside the Cherokee world. Erdrich's appointment of two narrators in *Tracks* instead of the conventional one is to shock and baffle the non-Native reader trained in the canonical tradition. Maria Campbell's discourse of a Halfbreed way of life in her autobiographical novel *Halfbreed* not only creates new myths but also demolishes the earlier ones created by the colonizing forces.

This study shall hence also take into account the form and technique employed in Native fiction to comprehend a fuller appreciation of the postcolonial, postmodern Native work of art. It can be suggested that the use of such tools as self-reflexivity, magic realism, storytelling, and orality furthers the cause of the shaping up of a Native, tribal identity inside the fiction discussed here. Hence, it is apt to study their application in Native fiction as the theme of identity formation and cultural politics cannot be achieved without using appropriate form and techniques of expression. An analysis of Native fiction would then be incomplete without giving due weight to the use of various poststructural and postmodern tools of writing.

The year 1969 saw the emergence of what critics have called the "Native American Renaissance" with the Native American Kiowa writer N. Scott Momaday's winning of the Pulitzer Prize for fiction for his brilliant first novel *House Made of Dawn*. Simultaneous arrival of such books as Vine Deloria's *Custer Died for Your*

Sins (1969), Dee Brown's *Bury My Heart at Wounded Knee* (1971), Basil Johnston's *Indian School Days* (1989) on the Native American front and George Clutesi's *Son of Raven: Son of Deer, Fables on the Tse-shaht People* in 1967 and his *Potlatch* in 1969, Harold Cardinal's *The Unjust Society* (1969), Maria Campbell's *Halfbreed* (1973), Howard Adam's *Prison of Grass* (1975) and Lee Maracle's *Bobbi Lee: Indian Rebel* (1975) on the Canadian side announced the grand arrival of Native Literature on the world stage. Drawing from and continuing with the oral tradition, these contemporary Native writers deal with themes as varied as maintenance of tribal culture and identity to the political and social struggles of their communities in the current scenario. Even though written in English, these writings often depend on the ritualistic base of their original cultures. Allen opines thus:

> ...Native American writers are concerned with tribal and
> urban life and have taken up themes that characterize and
> define that life in Native American terms. Most of these
> contemporary novels are ritualistic in approach, structure,
> theme, symbol, and significance, even though they use an
> overlay of western narrative plotting (Allen 79).

Native American and Native Canadian literatures are now moving to a new phase of their representation where authors like Louise Erdrich, Michael Dorris, Leslie Marmon Silko, Gerald Vizenor, James Welch, Jeannette Armstrong, Beatrice Culleton, Thomas King, Rudy Slipperjack and more such tribal and mixed-breed writers are coming into prominence.

Keeping the preconditions in mind and at times moving beyond these, this study shall deal with four novels written by four Native authors from the United States and Canada. This study comprises of four chapters, each concentrating on a single text representing an integral and significant mode of Native fiction of the United States and Canada.

A common experience of colonization and a common but varitist search for a singular as well as communal identity mirror Native writings from the United States and Canada. Native culture as well as Native fiction derives much of its vitality from its layered dimensions. Louise Erdrich (1954-), a Native American Ojibwa poet and novelist, best known for her tetralogy *Love Medicine* (1984), *The Beet Queen* (1986), *Tracks* (1988), and *Bingo Palace* (1994) is highly acclaimed for her representation of the Ojibwa culture in her writings. Taking up her novel *Tracks* for discussion in the second chapter of this thesis, the interweaving of Native American traditions with the progress of the events in the novel shall be examined. This chapter shall analyze how Erdrich's text encodes the norms and values of tribal kinship system and cultural practices. This chapter shall also reflect on Erdrich's deep spiritual thought patterns as represented in the novel. The area of focus here is Erdrich's

37

portrayal of the definite dimensions of Native culture in the book. *Tracks* deals almost exclusively with the lives, stories and experiences of the Turtle Mountain Chippewa in the early decades of twentieth century, a time that witnessed allotments, land acts and fragmentation of the Native society as a result of the white imperialistic policies. The loss of land, the loss of Native religion, the intrusion of Christianity, inter-community conflicts, the breaking up of relationships, internal colonization and a subsequent confusion over one's own identity—all these themes feature prominently in *Tracks*. *Tracks* highlights the historical, political and cultural realities of the Chippewa nation. Characters in *Tracks* foreground both the clash of cultural codes, as in case of the fanatic Pauline as well as the survival and continuity of Native life and culture as in case of Nanapush and Fleur. As authorities stand challenged, centre decentered and master narratives of history and culture questioned in the postmodern era, authors like Louise Erdrich tell the yet untold stories, represent the unrepresented and rewrite history, politics, and culture. In such tellings, the stories from both traditions are retold and appropriated. Speaking as she does from two traditions, Erdrich's fiction in general and *Tracks* in particular communicates "what is unique and terrific about Indian culture without piety or scolding" (Disch 170).

The third chapter concentrates on Leslie Marmon Silko (1948-) a Laguna Pueblo Native American writer, who enjoys a much sought after reputation in the Native American literary arena. As with oration, storytelling is the manifestation of a living oral tradition in many Native cultures. The third chapter of this study shall focus on the storytelling tradition of Native American cultures with respect to Silko's novel *Ceremony*. Having gathered praise for its rich and abundant stories, Silko's *Ceremony* has been hailed as a new age Native American classic. This chapter shall analyze this novel from a postcolonial, poststructual, and postmodern perspective. It will deal with the stories of the individuals/characters that appear in *Ceremony*, their experiences with the stories and the reciprocal relationships the stories and the characters share. This part of the study shall also look into the various sub-stories or side-stories the novel has and their implications. This shall also include an analysis of the structure and form of the novel and their link with the stories. This chapter shall also focus on the narrative form and the much-documented multivocality of the text. Silko's style as a novelist, her use of mythical stories and her creation of layers and layers of meaning like the Spiderwoman's web shall be analyzed. This chapter shall also analyze the elements of postcolonialism, postmodernism and poststructuralism *Ceremony* consists of.

The fourth chapter veers round Thomas King, the Cree German Cherokee mixed-blood from Canada who has dismantled old conventions and traditions through his writings and has thus come face to face with the western literary traditions. It will discuss his second novel *Green Grass, Running Water* (henceforth

38

GGRW) to understand and analyze this brilliant Native authors' command and control over the dominant culture's language and literary traditions and his twisting of dominant culture's language and literary traditions for furthering the Native cause and creating an alternative discourse. Heralded as a landmark text on its own right, *GGRW* has received critical applause for its interfusional[1]and associational narrative style. The urge to have chosen *GGRW* for a postcolonial, poststructural, postmodern analysis stems from an observation that the text functions at multifarious levels of narrativity and representation, thus offering enormous challenge to the reader to comprehend and correlate. What is even more interesting is the fact that, *GGRW*, while focusing on the trials and tribulations of being Native in a hegemonic world, avoids dichotomizations in terms of victim/victor or center/margin. In fact, the subtle beauty of King's fiction takes its cue from a blurring of boundaries and a simultaneous appropriation of cultural difference. Even though he is a Cherokee himself, King's fiction, as also in *GGRW*, portrays Blackfoot characters thanks to his long time association with the Blackfoot people of Canada. While writing as a representative voice of the Native people of the United States and Canada, Kings' fiction perhaps would be expected to perform in the lines of resistance and militant writing. However, King, through the retelling of stories from history and the literary canon as well as religion and popular culture, confronts the falsifications the Natives of the land have been subjected to and at the same time stays away from the trap of depicting the Native peoples only in relation to their colonial masters.

The fifth chapter deals with Maria Campbell's *Halfbreed*. Maria Campbell is a significant Native Canadian Métis autobiographer, novelist, poet, activist whose autobiographical work *Halfbreed* is considered to be one of the landmark texts of contemporary Native Canadian writing. *Halfbreed* has been termed as a literary work par excellence with a purpose to break old myths and replace them with a multifaceted undercurrent. It will be dealt with to figure out how the practice of retelling the story from the Other side's perspective can change the understanding of history. Having been dispossessed of their land, their cultures, their religions, their livelihoods, their stories, and everything else that counted for them, these people have become alienated in their own world. Displaced from their universe, the Native peoples have lost their sense of identity and uniqueness. The condition of Native women is even worse, for they are the lowest on the sociological ladder of Canada. Worse than the plight of Native women is that of Métis women who find a representative voice in Maria Campbell and her book *Halfbreed*. Using writing as a tool to resist and to heal, Maria Campbell's *Halfbreed* establishes the uniqueness of a Métis identity.

The Conclusion to this study shall present an interpretation of the Native literatures of the United States and Canada from a postcolonial, poststructual, postmodern viewpoint. It will make an attempt to underline the thematic and stylistic

39

similarities and diversities exhibited by the four writers mentioned above. The Conclusion shall focus on the importance and influence of the indigenous traditions and sources on the writings the Native authors discussed here. It will also attempt to comprehend the findings of the study in a manner so as to go beyond the ethnocentric biases many of us still fall prey to while examining literatures from the margin.

Chapter II:
The 'Definite Dimensions' of Native Culture:
Louise Erdrich's *Tracks*

The postcolonial atmosphere has provided an opportunity to the marginal of the world to illuminate the definite dimensions of their own cultures. Surviving on the present day world in spite of repeated declarations of their doomsday by the hegemonic forces and an assorted five centuries of inflicted atrocities, the Native American people's primary concern in the contemporary era is the existence, continuance, and maintenance of their unique cultures and ways of life. The contemporary Native fiction from the United States thus works towards connecting the past and present through cultural experiences. Without indulging in a megalomaniac glorification of the past, the Native writers emphasize the uniqueness of their cultures. This chapter deals with noted Native American (Chippewa) novelist, critic, poet Louise Erdrich's brilliant novel Tracks, especially landing focus to Erdrich's portrayal of the "definite dimensions" of the Native culture. This chapter seeks to investigate how Erdrich focuses in her fictions on the different dimensions of Nature such as land, fire, water etc. which form the very essence of the Native American cultural life. As the Native tradition is posited on the wholesome life, it also tries to bring out the importance accorded to the feminine and motherhood in Native societies. It carefully underlines the devastating and erosive effects of the mainstream culture on the Native ways of life and the Native people's courageous face-off with such brute forces through the Native vitality. This chapter also briefly deals with Erdrich's narrative technique and its impact on the furtherance of the Native cause inside the text. It also delves into Erdrich's use of her Ojibwa language in order to enhance the Nativeness of her text.

I

Writing with an urge to put emphasis on their beautiful and unique cultures, Native writers are often concerned with establishing the contours of their ancient cultures in their textual productions. Working as the keeper of traditions, Native writers indulge in a celebration of the indigenous cultural ethos and hence this consciousness towards their own cultures is often manifested in their writings. Chippewa poet, writer Louise Erdrich is one such keeper of tradition. Born in Little Falls, Minnesota in June 1954 to a German American father and a French-Ojibwa mother, Louise Erdrich grew up near the

42

Turtle Mountain Chippewa Reservation in North Dakota. In her numerous visits to her maternal family home on the Chippewa reservation, where her grandfather was the tribal chairman, Erdrich gathered first-hand experience of the Chippewa world that she would later relate to in her works of poetry and fiction. And hence the Chippewa Reservation figures prominently in many of her novels, including *Tracks*.

Erdrich's first novel, *Love Medicine* was published in 1984. Set in the Chippewa Reservation near North Dakota, *Love Medicine* earned high praise for its innovative narrative technique and its emphasis on a Native (especially Chippewa) experience of the world. One of the most fascinating characters in the text is that of Lulu Lamartine, who as the mother of a brood of children fathered by different men, functions as a symbolic representation of the Native creatrix spirit, Native fertility and vitality. That Lulu has been educated in the Native tradition by Nanapush (in *Tracks*) also adds to her dynamic, tricksterish persona.

Erdrich's next novel *The Beet Queen* appeared in 1986 and as Erdrich becomes more open to the world outside, the German American community of her father's side also gains prominence in this novel along with the Chippewa characters. Erdrich's poetic prose, a Chippewa sense of the world and the foregrounding of the Native ways of life are further displayed in The *Bingo Palace* which deals with the Indian Gaming Industry. In the text, myth and reality fuse many a time as they would in the Chippewa land.

One of Erdrich's latest novels, *Four Souls* (2004) deals largely with the Anishinabe woman Fleur who is one of the central characters in *Tracks*. This chapter analyzes in detail the importance of Fleur to accord definite dimensions to the Native culture and the same determined Fleur reappears in *Four Souls* seeking revenge against John James Mauser, the white man who took away her land. Several other characters from *Tracks* like Nanapush and Margaret also reappear in the novel as husband and wife. Further, Nanapush's maternal qualities that are discussed in detail in this chapter are further strengthened in *Four Souls* where he appears in a woman's attire in a tribal meeting and as the leader of the community, addresses a gathering in that dress.

Erdrich's *The Last Report on the Miracles at Little No Horse* (2001) deals with Pauline Puyat who appears for the first time in *Tracks* and by the end of the novel gets transformed to Sister Leopolda. This novel deals with the imminent sainthood proposed by the church for Sister Leopolda and the secrets from her murderous past.

It is hence evident that Erdrich as a master storyteller not only blurs boundaries inside her text but also outside it. Her texts themselves are intertwined and hence are in the tradition of the cyclical Native worldview. Further, her insistence on defining the Native cultural ethos in almost all her writings stands good for *Tracks* as well. This chapter hence looks at Erdrich's portrayal of the Chippewa culture inside an English text.

43

II

The postcolonial literary production more often than not points to the marginals' attempt to preserve their cultures and ensure continuance of the same. Writing for cultural survival, the postcolonial authors variously focus on the celebration of their liminal status and in the process, deconstruct and reconstruct cultural codes and modes of representation. Native writers, writing from a postcolonial, postmodern space, thus shake the ontological and epistemological foundations of the western cultural discourse. In such a scenario, history, politics and culture itself are altered, rediscovered, reassessed and re-presented in the voice of the hitherto voiceless. As they contest and resist the colonial structures of power and hierarchy, Native authors emphasize on the presentation of the definite dimensions of indigenous cultures. Rejecting the unitary and monolithic versions of western textual and cultural discourse, Native authors stress on the polyphonic and heteroglossic concepts of poststructuralist discourse. The Native author thus writes with the intention "to restructure the problematics of ideology, of the unconscious and of desire, of representation of history, and of cultural production, around the all-forming process of narrative" (Darias-Beautell 30)

Without falling into the dual trap of western authority and the narrow ethnocentric notions of authenticity, Native writers tell their stories to reflect on and further continuance of their cultures, their ways of life and to reassert a Native identity lost in the bylines of colonialism. In their determined efforts to preserve the indigenous traditions, Native authors engage their literary productions to story history, to resuscitate orality in the written text and to counter the generalized notions and stereotypical constructs of the Native in the master-narratives. In doing so, they create texts that communicate the lived experiences of the Native peoples, from the past and their hopes and aspirations for the future. Their writings thus concentrate on the production and preservation of a Native worldview. As Meldan Tanrisal aptly puts it:

> Due to the "breakup of ancient orders of life" and the destruction of their family identities by Euroamerican domination, Native Americans need to formulate new concepts of self, family and continuity. Therefore, at the center of American Indian fiction is the attempt to recover an identity and to illustrate the continuity of Native culture (Tanrisal 71).

Writing for a postcolonial readership that comprises of both Native and non-Native readers and writing in English, the language of the hegemonic discourse, Native writers concern themselves with establishing definite dimensions of their cultures. They always remain conscious of the fact that the culture itself, being dynamic and living, undergoes constant modification by means of both inside and outside influences. Hence, they often faithfully reflect this ever-changing process of cultural evolution in their textual production with their focus on the here and now. The changing historical, political and cultural phenomena of the Native world obviously become the subject matter of their writing. The stories they tell may not look overtly historical, political or cultural but nevertheless their concerns lie very much with the history, politics and culture of their communities and their peoples.

Writing in the celebratory tone of a participant in two worlds and its additive experiences rather than in the accusatory mode of an oppressed victim, Native writers take into account the tragedies that have befallen their peoples. Moreover, by celebrating their communities and cultural life style, they, as representative voices of their peoples, foreground their resolve for cultural continuity and survival.

In Native literary productions, it then becomes obvious that the Native sense of Nature, time, religion, humor and experience finds expression. Alongside, history and politics are often appropriated in the process. As the Native writers reflect on their world, a world irrevocably changed by colonialism, they categorically celebrate the Native cultural ethos in the form of innumerable stories and experience. Louise Erdrich is one such writer who believes that Native writers "must tell the stories of contemporary survivors while protecting and celebrating the cores of cultures ..." (Towery 99).

As Nature occupies the centre stage in Native culture, the Native writers often focus on the role of Nature which plays a pivotal role in their life. While celebrating Nature, they dwell on the significant elements of Nature like water, fire and the land. It is usually seen that the Native writers often invoke the images of water, earth and fire in order to tell their stories. With their lakes taken away and converted to dams, their land snatched away from them with the help of treacherous policies, and their tribes subjected to genocide by means of modern weaponry, tribal authors are conscious of both the life-shaping and life-taking powers and effects of the troika of water, earth and fire.

Water and water related images appear throughout *Tracks*. One of the most prevalent and powerful images of *Tracks* is that of Missipeshu, the Chippewa water monster staying in Lake Machimanito. Pauline describes Missipeshu like this:

> Our mothers warn us that we'll think he's handsome,
> for he appears with green eyes, copper skin, a mouth
> tender as a child's. But if you fall into his arms, he sprouts
> horns, fangs, claws, fins. His feet are joined as one and
> his skin, brass scales, rings to the touch. You're
> fascinated, cannot move. He casts a shell necklace   45
> at your feet, weeps gleaming chips that harden into

mica on your breast. He holds you under. Then he takes
the body of a lion, a fat brown worm, or a familiar man.
He's made of gold. He's made of beach moss. He's a thing
of dry foam, a thing of death by drowning, the death a
Chippewa cannot survive (11).

Much of Pauline's warped sense of Christianity results from her
confused dis/belief of Missipeshu and the sacredness of Matchimanito.
The Native understanding of sacred, P.G. Allen asserts, is different from
the white binary understanding of sacred and profane (Allen 72-73). For
the Natives, sacred is something powerful, capable of both good and
evil. And hence Missipeshu and Matchimanito are sacred in the Native
sense of the term. Delicka points out the differences of significance of
Matchimanito for the Natives and the whites in the context of *Tracks*:

> For the Chippewa, Machimanito is a sacred place,
> inhabited by the ghosts of the dead Pillagers...The Indians
> avoid Machimanito and associate it with Misshepeshu,
> the water man...The white men, on the contrary, treat
> Machimanito as a land of opportunity for lumberjacks
> and bankers (Delicka 31).

By helping Fleur time and again, Missipeshu, as the cultural force
of the Chippewa, helps in the survival of the Chippewa culture through
Fleur. Though Fleur goes off the reservation at the end of the text, Lulu's
homecoming, with her eyes that "blazed bright as his" and her skin being
"the color of an old penny" could mean her being the child of Missipeshu
and thus the authorial hint that tribal culture and Missipeshu will
survive.

While Erdrich's portrayal of Missipeshu shows the use of a
Chippewa mythical water monster as an icon of Native cultural survival,
water seems to trouble Pauline, the voice of oppressed assimilation in
Tracks, more than it comforts her. Pauline's uncomfortableness in water
points to her being uncomfortable in the waters of Native culture. When
in a symbolic act of Native culture cleaning itself from the devastating
effects of colonialism and assimilation, Fleur cleans Pauline and washes
her, Pauline warns herself "not to experience any pleasure" (154). By
denying herself the pleasure of the "wash," Pauline negates enjoying
the experience of Native culture. Though she gives in to the soothing
experience of Native culture, it is but temporary:

> Fleur poured a pitcher of warm water over me and then
> began to shampoo my head and hair. I think I fell asleep,
> lost awareness, let the water course over me and let

46

the hands on my hips, my throat, my back, my breasts,
the cupped hands under my chin and around my feet,
break me down (emphasis mine) (154-155).

But soon after Pauline returns to the convent and thus to the colonized experience: "I [Pauline] felt no jealousy or zeal. I purified myself and then very quietly, returned" (155). Earlier in the text, Pauline would longingly watch Fleur's comfort with water but would herself maintain a distance from it. She notes:

Every night, Fleur bathed in the slaughtering tub, then
slept in the unused brick smokehouse behind the lockers. ...
When I brushed against her skin I noticed that she smelled
of the walls, rich and woody, slightly burnt (21-22).

On the contrary, Fleur is comfortable in the Native waters, as she is comfortable in surviving in Matchimanito when nobody else dares to even move close to the lake. With Missipeshu as her helper, Fleur can punish the men who do not respect the Native feminine. Fleur's first encounter with Missipeshu happens when she was a child. Though Pauline's reliability as a narrator is a matter of debate, she tells us that two men who went to save Fleur from drowning soon died. The second time Fleur drowned in Matchimanito was when she was fifteen years old. Though nobody went to save her this time, one man who had the misfortune of witnessing it, died by drowning in his bathtub, a death Missipeshu brings. Later in the novel, when Fleur becomes pregnant for the second time, Eli tells Nanapush that she had denied him relations, suggesting that the child could have been Missipeshu's. After Eli's adulterous lovemaking with Sophie, Fleur does not accept Eli's advances and Eli would often wake up from bed at the mid of night and find Fleur walking to the lake or sleeping in the room with her braids and dress wet from her visit to the lake.

Fleur's connection with Missipeshu, however, seems to be more than a merely sexual one. While Missipeshu punishes whoever makes a pass at Fleur, thus symbolically preserving Native culture, Fleur too goes to Missipeshu at her most difficult times. When the second child is lost to her, she goes to him for drawing power and courage from him who is the embodiment of the cultural life force. Moreover, by keeping her link with Missipeshu, Fleur connects the cultural present to the mythical past and thus ensures survival. Victoria Brehm observes:

When Erdrich takes up the matter of Micipijiu in her
novels, she creates in Fleur the rare woman who dares take
the water monster as a pawagan and uses his power to help

her people survive by recovering traditional culture... As
cultural hero she (Fleur) risks herself to mediate between
Micipijiu and her people (Brehm 693).

Even Lulu, whose likeness to Missipeshu is evident, could be a
gift that Fleur gets from Missipeshu for her daring act of continuing the
Chippewa culture in spite of great difficulties. With Fleur's land gone
at the end of *Tracks* and her daughter alienated from her, the power of
Native waters and Missipeshu, like that of Fleur, seem to be diminishing.
But Fleur has not died. She has only gone away. The waters inside her
body would continue to flow and thus the flesh and blood of Native culture
would not stop growing. The cultural destiny of the Chippewa is not bleak
though it won't be smooth flowing.

Nanapush, soaked in tradition like Fleur, is aware of the powers
of water. Being the incarnation of the Chippewa trickster, Nanapush is in
possession of the knowledge of how to use water for healing and rituals, for
authenticating Nativity and also for teaching a lesson to those who do not
understand the significance and power of water in Native life. Nanapush's
understanding of the power of water is evident from the very beginning
of his narration. Infected by the consumption and recovery being slow for
both Fleur and Nanapush, Nanapush has felt the water of death: "We were
filled with the water of the drowned, cold and black, airless water that
lapped against the seal of our tongues or leaked slowly from the corners
of our eyes" (6).

When Lulu suffers from frostbitten feet that have turned ice-cold,
Nanapush gives the warmth of his tradition so that the Chippewa blood/
water flows again inside Lulu's spirit. He cures Lulu by bathing "those
feet in water and pickling salt" and fanning them "With purifying smoke,"
thus taking the help of water and fire for the survival of Native future.
Later, when Fleur grows weak and is fast losing power after the death
of her second child, Nanapush conducts a ritual in which he has to "pull
meat from the bottom" of a "boiling stew kettle." Though he is unable
to complete the ritual because of Pauline's interference, Nanapush, as a
traditional Chippewa elder, demonstrates his control over both water and
fire. Nanapush also knows how to use water to teach a lesson to Pauline.
Being the Native scatological trickster, Nanapush tricks Pauline by a water
story and thus succeeds in breaking Pauline's comically crazy practice of
not relieving herself more than twice a day. Hughes thus comments on
the water imagery in *Tracks*:

At times it seems that Nanapush or Fleur might try to
help Pauline reintegrate to the Native community and
extended family they are reconstructing, even as they
recognize the threat she poses to this project. Because
water is a central image for all that is Native, oral, wild,

48

mutable, transformative, and life-giving in the novel, it is the medium used to attempt this reconciliation (Hughes np).

For the Natives, the land is their life. They draw the sustenance of their life from the land itself. Thus the land as integral to the Native cultural identity is another central image in Erdrich's *Tracks*. The origin of the Native-White conflict has undoubtedly been in the colonial thirst for occupying Native land. Unlike the western hegemonic forces who viewed land in terms of money, profit, and private prosperity, the land in the Native vision has been communal and not meant for exploitation. Erdrich dramatizes this conflict of viewing the land in *Tracks*. Much of the tragedies in *Tracks* result from the loss of land and the fight for keeping the land. Early on in his narrative, Nanapush, the Native figure of resistance in *Tracks*, prophesizes that the "land will go" and it will be "sold and measured" (8). Nanapush knows that with the rising inflow of the hegemonic forces, the Chippewa are set to lose their lands forever.

Allotment of the land to the Natives according to the rules of the white and its after effects figure throughout *Tracks*. Set in between the years of 1912 and 1924 when the North Dakota Chippewa had their lands fragmented and divided according to the 1887 Allotment Act, "*Tracks* is in part an autopsy of this process, whereby place becomes property, and an analysis of how the process affects innocent bystanders" (Larson 1). With no faith in government and contempt for the assimilationists, Nanapush, as a fighter in the Chippewa's increasingly losing struggle for the upkeep of Native land and culture, highlights the importance of land for the Native peoples. He tells Lulu:

> "Land is the only thing that lasts life to life. Money burns like tinder, flows off like water. And as for government promises, the wind is steadier" (33).

Nanapush is concerned that with the "wholesale purchase" of Chippewa land by the whites, the community's survival is challenged. Nanapush laments the fact that unable to understand the colonizer's language, the Anishinabe are signing away their lands "with thumbs and crosses" (99). Even while working inside the colonizer's systems, Nanapush remains loyal to his Indianness and resists the loss of land for the Chippewa. He tells Lulu:

> As a young man, I had made my reputation as a government interpreter, that is, until the Beauchamp Treaty signing, in which I said to Rift-In-A-Cloud, "Don't put your thumb in the ink." One of the officials understood and I lost my job (100).

49

But with elders like Nanapush losing their influence over "the young of the tribe" and the colonial forces' lure of money to the Natives for selling off their land, Native peoples are fragmented and divided, their ways of life, their traditions and cultures lost and forgotten in the wave of colonization. With the Europeans' introduction of paper money and alcohol, Native virtues are replaced by European vices. Nanapush laments:

> Our trouble came from living, from liquor and the dollar bill. We stumble towards the government bait, never looking down, never noticing how the land was snatched from under us at every step (4).

The trauma of losing land and culture is further precipitated by the colonizers' well-thought out plans of inter-community conflict. By dividing the Natives under various guises, the colonizers made it easy for themselves to acquire the Native lands. One of the most enduring friendships in *Tracks*, that of Fleur Pillager and Margaret Kashpaw, is lost in the struggle for keeping the land. Again, the feud between the full-blood Kashpaws and the mixed blood Morrisseys also results from their differing opinions on the ownership of land. While the Morrisseys, working as agents for the colonial authorities, are able to keep their own land as well as acquire more, full-bloods like the Kashpaws and Pillagers have to struggle hard and pay heavy taxes for keeping their allotment land. The loss or acquisition of land thus divides Native families and communities. Pauline, the mixed-blood narrator in *Tracks* too reasons out her joining the nunnery by saying that she has "no family" and "no land." Because she has no land of her own, Pauline's jealousy for Fleur also rises from Fleur's ownership of the Pillager land. Pauline is satisfied to find towards the end of the text that Fleur will lose her land. These feelings of betrayal, hatred, and jealousy seeded by the colonials' manipulative policies have often caused and aggravated the problem of fragmentation of the Native peoples. This, added with the intrusion of white religions and diseases has deprived the tribes of their strength and endurance. Larson aptly comments:

> The fragmentation of Indian tribes can be seen as having been accomplished in a number of ways. The introduction of European diseases weakened the tribes sufficiently to make them vulnerable; after that happened, however, the influence of the English and French fur traders, the application of European religions and political exploitation of mixed-blood people were considerable factors as well (Larson 4).

By confining Native peoples into the reservations, the colonials had already deprived them of their rightful place on earth. By further dividing the reservation in the name of allotment, the colonial forces dismantle the social fabric of the Native world as well.

With their feelings of deep respect of the land as Mother Earth, the loss of land symbolizes the orphanization of the Native communities and the struggle for keeping or getting back the land also signifies protecting or recovering the mother from outsiders. However, when the Native peoples grasp the inevitable realities of losing their land, their resistance, supported by the mythical powers of their culture, becomes violent and explicit. Fleur, the fascinating traditional Chippewa woman in *Tracks* who is endowed with mythical powers and the Pillager smile also fails to keep her land. But her contempt for the colonials' policies and tools such as the map is evident in these lines of Nanapush:

> ... she spoke with contempt for the map, for those who drew it, for the money required, even for the priest. She said the paper had no bearing or sense, as no one would be reckless enough to try collecting for land where the Pillagers were buried (174).

Betrayed by one of her own friends, Fleur is forced to leave the reservation. But that does not deter her from taking a final revenge against the forces of colonization. When the colonizers come to her land with their men and machinery, Fleur sends a wind that destroys the machinery and frightens the men. Peter G. Beirder comments on Fleur's final act:

> The carefully directed wind blows down the trees around Fleur's cabin, smashing equipment but sparing the men. That wind is apparently Fleur's final hurrah, her last revenge before she takes her cart and heads away from the land that the white man has taken from her, rapist like, by force (Beirder 45).

In her final act of revenge, Fleur demonstrates that Native culture cannot be diminished nor has it lost all its power. While the colonizing forces have certainly affected the Native ways of life, Native life and tradition will continue.

Postcolonial literature is concerned, among other things, with the construction of an identity for the periphery, a representation of the unrepresented. As Erdrich defines the definite dimensions of Native culture in *Tracks*, she simultaneously constructs the picture of contemporary Chippewa identity. By her "narrative construction of identity" through the stories of two alternating, starkly different narrators, Erdrich, like her postcolonial, postmodernist peers, demonstrates her   51 "reaction against the master narrative which tells reality according to conventions of linearity, the inevitability of progress, and especially the coherent self" (Farwell 1327 A).

Tracks concentrates on the various aspects of Native culture "to recover an identity" and ensure "the continuity of native culture" (Tanrisal 71). Towards this end, *Tracks* foregrounds a communal sense of identity. A primary concern of Nanapush's narrative is to stop Lulu from marrying a "no-good Morrissey" and thus lose her Chippewa identity. As the young Chippewa like Lulu get away from their roots, the community as well as individual identity of the Native is endangered. Nanapush laments on the various traps the Native youth fall into that results in the loss of a traditional sense of identity. Nanapush tells:

> We lose our children in different ways. They turn their faces to the white towns ... or they become so full of what they see in the mirror there is no reasoning with them anymore (170).

There is no coherent plot structure in *Tracks*. Nor does it follow the linear pattern of the western narrative. This technique of Erdrich's has been seen by many critics as a means for the construction of a textual identity of the Native American that is tribal in spirit. While *Tracks* documents the Native sense of a community identity, it also underlines the dangers the community faces in the contemporary postcolonial world for the construction of such an identity. Strouse reflects:

> That other tragic story- of incomprehensible taxes and allotment fees, government treachery, church collision, liquor, the dollar, the loss of the "old" life and powers and finally the loss of the land- runs all through the tales Pauline and Nanapush tell. And the saddest part isn't in the machinations of some far-off bureaucracy; it's in the way these changes bring on the betrayal of one Indian by another, in shocking abdications of love (Strouse 142).

Pauline, the mixed-blood narrator of *Tracks*, joins the Other side of the Native in search of an identity. Rejecting the Native concept of a relational identity, Pauline, lost to assimilation, seeks an identity that is individual and exclusive. Her denial of her Native blood demonstrates the seeking of a more "victorious" and "upmarket" identity: "'The Indians,' I said now, 'them.' Never *neenawind* or us. And I soon found it was good that I did" (emphasis original) (138). By referring to her own people as "them," Pauline extinguishes the Indian spirit inside herself and ultimately as she acquires a new name, "Pauline" is left behind and dead.

But Native identity continues to define Fleur, Nanapush and Lulu. With Nanapush's "adoption" of Lulu, tribal life continues and the tribal system of kinship survives. As Hughes remarks: "A certain level of integrity, in terms of traditional and relational ties, must be maintained if survival is to be culturally meaningful" (Hughes np). *Tracks*, thus demonstrates the conflict of two cultural codes, a war of discourses. By showcasing two ways of life, two different traditions, Native and Christian, while clearly siding with the Native and without any nostalgic romanticization of either, Erdrich, as a mixed-blood Chippewa, constructs a cultural identity for her text and provides definite contours to the Native culture. The life experiences of the Turtle Mountain Chippewa as well as the frustration of the mixed-breed population, the children of post-contact Native world, both are depicted with first-hand keenness in *Tracks*.

Erdrich's fusion of magic, myth, reality, and fiction also points to a blurring of cultural artifacts as is understood in the western culture. While in the western discourse myth and magic exist and function in a realm separate and distant from that of reality, for the Native Americans, myth, magic and reality cohabit in their cultural world. Keeping with the Chippewa worldview where the mythic and the realistic overlap each other, Erdrich's characters in *Tracks* live simultaneously in the contemporary experience as well as in the mythic plane. All major characters in *Tracks*, like Nanapush, Fleur, and Pauline, are contemporary Native persons who do not blink twice before practicing magic, medicines and songs, the knowledge of which foregrounds a mythic past. Drawing from this mixture of myth and reality, *Tracks* demonstrates Erdrich's ability to emphasize on the clash of cultural codes. Though no synthesis is offered, Erdrich comfortably uses both Native American mythicality and the western realistic discourse to write her fiction.

Erdrich's portrayal of Fleur is enchantingly powerful as she demonstrates in Fleur a living myth. As the traditional "longhair," a young girl believing in and practicing the "old ways," Fleur's mythic stature is heightened in her acts of continuity and resistance. Fleur's departure at the end of the novel is undoubtedly tragic, but her show of strength even in her vulnerability manifests the mythical power of Native culture that will help her survive. Brehm thus comments on Fleur: "As such, she is Erdrich's statement that American Indian culture will survive and thrive- despite capitalism, Christianity, and the U.S government- because the persistence of mythology is an indication of long-term cultural stability" (Brehm 693). Thus, while there is a clash of cultures in *Tracks*, it does not advocate a doomsday scenario for Native cultures. Rather, it seems to emphasize that Native culture will survive, along with the hegemonic cultures, or despite the hegemonic cultures.

Tracks celebrates Native culture in all its complexities. As a postcolonial, postmodern text it achieves this objective by engaging its textual intention in dialogism. Erdrich's   53 writing in *Tracks* textualizes Native ideologies through continuous deconstruction and reconstruction of narratives at all levels- personal, political and historical. In the process, Erdrich succeeds to highlight multiple realities, historical, philosophical, sociological, economic, religious and technological of the contemporary Chippewa world. As history is engaged in dialogue with mythology, Native reality is reemphasized as unique and independent. Stories start and end at the same point, demonstrating the Native pattern of a circle. Erdrich's narrative strategy of simultaneously establishing/demolishing the reliability/unreliability of her characters advocates the postmodern idea of relativity and creates a constant dialogic tension in the text.

In *Tracks*, Nanapush's traditional, non-Christian, Ojibwa voice is in constant dialogue with Pauline's Christianized, assimilationist, English voice. As the truth is shaped and reshaped continuously through these two voices, the postmodern relativity of truth comes to the forefront. The meanings of identity, community, tradition and values of life unmask themselves in multiple avatars through this dialogic. In their oral/textual interaction, Nanapush and Pauline, through their stories, reconstruct truth as a cultural conceptualization and thus manifest different versions of reality. To put it in the words of Delicka:

> The "ethnic" is in a constant dialogue with the "whiteness" in *Tracks*...truth is not born nor of itself found in the head of the Individual person; it is born between people collectively searching for the truth, in the process of their dialogic interaction. As we, the readers, enter the discourse between the two dimensions of reality, we are challenged to stretch out our imagination and to pose questions about our values, ideas and beliefs (Delicka 26).

Further, as both narrators tell their stories in relation to another character, Fleur, and as this other character is shaped through their stories, *Tracks* is also dialogical at another level. This dialogic fluidity of the text emphasizes the postmodern in *Tracks*. Like the Native storyteller whose stories are all interconnected in the hoop of tradition, there are stories within stories and all are connected in a subtle manner. While the two narrators tell their own stories, they also illuminate stories from the tribal past and present and thus the Native experience is recorded in their voices. For Erdrich, it seems that her characters must talk and pass on stories rather than bind themselves in the machinations of plot and structure.

As each narration, each chapter in *Tracks* is complete and "whole" on its own, reading Erdrich is akin to the experience of listening to stories in a Native American community gathering. Stories make things happen in Erdrich's fictional world. In their telling of the stories, both narrators mould the world around them and present stories that are radically different from each other and thus

54

contribute to the understanding of Native culture as a whole. Catherine Rainwater thus comments on the challenge for the reader in Erdrich's writing: "The reader must consider a possibility forcefully posited in all of Erdrich's works... the world takes on the shape of the stories we tell" (Rainwater 422).

With her use of multiple narrators reflecting on multiple realities, Erdrich also imbibes her fiction with a community voice. As varying points of view from varying quarters shape truth, the Native American respect for a community understanding is highlighted. While Erdrich's characters in *Tracks* certainly have a rich multiplicity of voices, the mythical Fleur's voicelessness is intriguing. But by denying Fleur a direct voice in the text, Erdrich negates the possibility of a romanticization of Native culture while simultaneously ensuring to show it in all its strength and variety.

The Nativeness of Erdrich's text is further illustrated in her use of the Ojibwa language in *Tracks*. In the postcolonial world where Native cultures and languages are fast losing ground, Erdrich's conscious use of her Native language signifies tradition and the celebration of Native culture in its varied hues. That the Ojibwa language is tied to the landscape is sampled in the chapter names of *Tracks*. As Erdrich provides the English translations of the Ojibwa phrases used as chapter headings, certain things become evident. Firstly, all the phrases refer to the sun, the earth, a "skeleton winter" and to the natural elements of the Chippewa land such as blueberry, woodlouse, and wild rice, all soaked in the spirit of the land. Secondly, by giving an Ojibwa name to the chapters along with a linear numbering and dating of the chapters, Erdrich emphasizes on the co-existence of two belief systems, two epistemological and teleological codes. Moreover, by giving the chapter names in *Tracks* both English linearity and a tinge of Ojibwa orality, Erdrich seems to empower the readers to "pick and choose" the one code that suits them better. Also, through the use of dual chapter name, drawn from two language systems, one pre-contact and another post-contact, Erdrich emphasizes on the place between the two worlds. Erdrich's use of the Ojibwa phrases for the chapter names in *Tracks* also points to the cyclical time of Native American traditions. As stories come from all times, past, present and future without any linearity attached to them, the Native circle of life is emphasized. Lee comments on Erdrich's fiction:

> Figuratively speaking an 'Indian' pattern runs right through
> her novels, one in which the circle is all and life operates as a
> kind of mysterious or magic revolving wheel (Lee 150).

Erdrich's dualistic chapter names in *Tracks* thus set the ground for the Native American "accreative and achronological narrative" (Owens 172). While Erdrich's stories contemporize   55 history and myth, her use of cyclic time alongside western dates and numbers underlines the dual realities of the postcolonial world. To quote Delicka on Erdrich's chapterization of *Tracks*:

> The temporal and spatial dimensions possess a duality that mirrors two equally important ways of perceiving the world: the one inherent in marginalized cultures and the other ingrained in dominant Western society. If we take up time first, in *Tracks* the titles of the chapters account for both the realistic, logical understanding of time and for the Indian perception of that concept (Delicka 30).

As the events unfold in *Tracks*, one is made aware of the absurdity of believing in a singular passage of time. In *Tracks*, as in the Native American worldview, events occur simultaneously in the zone of time and timelessness, thus creating a sense of orality in the written text.

Erdrich's understanding of her Chippewa tradition is further reflected in her portrayal of the traditional Native women. One such character is that of Fleur. The Native perception of women as powerful and good is foregrounded through Fleur. Although Fleur's story comes through the two contradictory narrative voices of Nanapush and Pauline, she comes up as a woman following the "old ways of life." A member of the feared and powerful Pillager clan, Fleur remains one of the last survivors of her family that had been engulfed by the consumption. There is a certain mythicality to Fleur's character. Both narrators tell stories about Fleur's powers, her connection to the Chippewa spirit bear and the lake monster Missipeshu, and her sexuality, albeit in strikingly different tones. Fleur is initially described by Nanapush as "a filthy wolf, a big, bony girl" (3) "with raw power" (7) and her bodily strength is repeatedly alluded to in the text. Fleur lives alone in the Pillager cabin inside the woods, is a good hunter, better than most men on reservation, practices magic and medicine and has a deadly charm that men cannot resist. In Pauline's stories, Fleur appears as the mistress of Missipeshu and messing with Fleur is to anger Missipeshu and get "death by drowning, the death a Chippewa cannot survive" (11). Much of Fleur's mythicality comes from Pauline's description of her. Pauline tells us about Fleur's powers in the following passage:

> She messed with evil, laughed at the old woman's advice and dressed like a man. She got herself into some half-forgotten medicine, studied ways we shouldn't talk about. Some say she kept the finger of a child in her pocket and powder of unborn rabbits in a leather thong around her neck. She laid the heart of an owl on her tongue so she could see at night, and went out, hunting, not even in her own body. We know for sure because the next

56

morning, in the snow or dust, we followed the tracks of
her bare feet and saw where they changed, where the
claws sprang out, the pad broadened and pressed into
the dirt. By night we heard her chuffing cough, the bear
cough. By day her silence and the wide grin she threw to
bring down our guard made us frightened (12).

Pauline's description portrays Fleur as a near-mythical figure,
but Pauline's unreliability as a narrator also challenges the authenticity
of her description. Pauline has a habit of shifting guilt-there are at least
two instances in the novel to suggest so. It is Pauline who puts the latch
with Fleur's rapists inside the freezer in the butcher shop in Argus and
then spreads the story among the townspeople blaming Fleur for the
deaths. Towards the end of the novel, Fleur is again rumored to have
killed Napoleon Morrissey with the help of Missipeshu while it is actually
Pauline who kills Napoleon in her hallucination mistaking him for the
water monster. However, Fleur's power is also a reality in that she can
command the wind to bring a tornado and destroy the town of Argus after
her rape and again cause the fall of trees to frighten the white intruders
when her land is being taken away. She can also punish Boy Lazzare by
twisting his tongue reverse, for his voyeurism of her and Eli's passionate
sessions of lovemaking. Delicka observes:

Fleur is the medium through which the supernatural
works. The Chippewa believe that Missipeshu, the water
monster inhabiting Matchimanito Lake, enforces his
commands through her. It is thanks to Missipeshu that
Fleur can drown people, cause tornadoes and order the
trees (Delicka 27).

Fleur's clan marker is infused with bear power as it consists of
"four cross hatched bears and a marten" and as a Pillager, Fleur's bear
power is evident in her appearance and skills. Pauline tells us:

Power travels in bloodlines, handed out before birth. It
comes down through the hands, which in the Pillagers are
strong and knotted, big, spidery and rough, with sensitive
fingertips good at dealing cards. It comes through the eyes,
too, belligerent, darkest brown, the eyes of those in the bear
clan, impolite as they gaze directly at a person (31).

Fleur is the true carrier of the Native strength and energy, and more
than that she is the true representative of Native culture. Commenting on
Fleur's bear power Vidmar writes:

> Fleur portrays the traditional 'long hair' or hold-out, for
> the Indian nation. She does not confirm to colonization.
> She is the bear in this story … In the Chippewa myth, the
> bear symbolizes strength and courage (Vidmar np).

While Nanapush gives Eli the charm to court Fleur and help them make love "like animals in their season" (48), he is not sure if the magic has not worked both ways-Fleur might have sewn her private hairs to Eli's shirt button as well and wore a charm doll in between her legs, Nanapush speculates. But Fleur and Eli's love is not merely about magic. It also comes to symbolize the continuance of life imbued with tradition. Fleur and Eli's love, though punctured later by Pauline's destructive use of love medicine, signifies the survival of Native ways of life and a hope for future in terms of their child, Lulu. By means of this love, Fleur continues her community and familial identity.

The feminine is deified in the Native culture, a fact which has been emphasized again and again in Erdrich's *Tracks*. By giving birth to two children and pampering her daughter, Fleur also symbolizes the Native feminine entity. Whereas Pauline, consumed by colonization, abandons her own child and motherhood, Fleur pampers her first-born, even though without any clear hint of who her father is, there is a possibility that Lulu might be a bastard child. Tanrisal observes:

> Two different types of mothers are depicted in *Tracks*.
> They are the mixed-blood Pauline Puyat or Sister
> Leopolda, the "anti-mother," and the full-blood Fleur
> Pillager, the "mythic mother" (Tanrisal 74).

Nanapush's narrative is directed towards Lulu and one prime motif of this storytelling is to explain and justify Fleur's actions to Lulu, to reintegrate Lulu into the community fold and to the lap of the Native mother. Fleur's story comes through Nanapush because Lulu has drifted away from her mother. Lulu does not understand that Fleur has sent her away because as a Native mother she wanted to protect her child from the trauma of loss of land and culture on the reservation. Having lived a hard life in a young age, Fleur has become a fighter like her strong feminine ancestors; but she does not want her pampered child to face the hardships. Even early on in the narrative, Fleur's maternal qualities are hinted at. In spite of her overt sexuality, Fleur, in a strange sort of way, tries to discipline Pauline as only a mother would do. Pauline would say about Fleur:

> She knew the effect she had on men, even the very
> youngest of them. She swayed them, sotted them,
> 58 made them curious about her habits, drew them close
> with careless ease and cast them off with the same

indifference. She was good to Russell, it is true, even fussed abut him like a mother, combed his hair with her fingers, and scolded me for kicking or teasing him (17).

Later in the novel, Fleur again mothers Pauline by cleaning her and giving her a bath. By cleaning Pauline, Fleur metaphorically contributes to the keeping of tradition that is getting lost and replaced by Christianity. Even Pauline's fanaticism temporarily seems to take a backseat as she undergoes a cathartic purgation. Pauline tells about the bath: "It was so terrible, so pleasant, that I abandoned my Lord and all His rules and special requirements" (154). Sexually jealous of and yet attracted to Fleur, Pauline seems to enjoy Fleur's touch on her deprived body. But Fleur does not succeed at bringing back Pauline to the Native fold of life. And as Pauline grows in her power, Fleur, the traditional Anishinabe loses ground. Though Fleur is able to give birth to a healthy child in spite of Pauline's presence during her first labour, she loses her second child to Pauline's death-filled eyes and with the loss of her child, which, this time, could have actually been a powerful child of Missipeshu's, Fleur loses some of her power. When her family is starving, like a traditional Chippewa woman bestowed with the dream vision, Fleur dreams of a venison meal, and Eli hunts a venison that day through Fleur's guidance.

Erdrich dramatizes the armageddon between the forces of the colonizer and the colonized in her novel *Tracks*. Towards the later part in the novel, in spite of having paid the tax for her land for two/three years and having managed with great difficulty the payment for the current year, Fleur loses the land to white trickery and a treacherous act by her own people. Margaret and Nector Kashpaw, Eli's mother and younger brother, keep the Kashpaw land at the cost of the Pillager land. Fleur, like Native culture, has been powerful. But the colonizer's presence and policies are continuously shrinking her powers. With Fleur's loss of power, traditional Chippewa life is endangered and a fragmentation of the land and Native community becomes inevitable. In that sense, Fleur's powers are limited.

Though Fleur regains some of her power with Nanapush's healing ritual for her, Pauline's interruption affects the wholeness of the ritual and Fleur, even with her Pillager smile is no more as powerful. At the end of the novel, Fleur leaves the reservation "without leaving tracks." With Fleur gone, Erdrich depicts the loss of traditions in contemporary Chippewa world and Fleur's tracklessness, as critics have pointed out, signifies a bleak vision for the survival of Native culture. But her tracklessness also manifests the need for a retelling of yet untold stories. To quote Peterson:

> ... Fleur's disappearance and tracklessness at the end
> of the novel function as a present absence-her absence   59
> becomes a haunting presence in the narrative,

signifying the need for a recontextualization of history, for a new historicity that both refers to the past and makes a space for what can never be known of it (Peterson 987).

That Fleur's story is told in other's tongues also points to the lack of her own voice in the text. While this tonguelessness of Fleur might suggest the author's denial of giving a voice to the wholly Native, it can paradoxically symbolize a more powerful presence in the text because of the very tonguelessness. Fleur is no less enchanting or Native for appearing through other voices. In fact, Fleur's Nativeness is enhanced for she is considered significant enough to appear in other people's stories, unlike Pauline who has to tell her own story. Storied in other people's tongues, one friend and another enemy, Fleur's story confirms the Native concept of wholeness. Further, by being told in both positive and negative lights, Fleur's becomes a manifestation of the Sacred Feminine, a Native Manitou, capable of both good and bad, reward and punishment. Ferrari remarks:

> While the metaphor of Fleur's tracklessness can suggest pessimism regarding cultural preservation, the narrative that conveys the (non) image of tracklessness also cancels it. Fleur's alleged ability to move invisibly, grants her the magical power of a Manitou, worthy of being told in story, traced in the tracks of narrative while always existing somewhere beyond it (Ferrari np).

By choosing to live in the traditional way, Fleur does not necessarily romanticize Chippewa life. But in her life story is found an alternative way of life for the Native, a life dignified on its own terms and independent of colonization.

Tracks begins and ends with the voice of Nanapush. Named after the Chippewa trickster Nanabozho, Nanapush's name exudes mythicality and tricksterism. As Nanapush tells us:

> My father said, 'Nanapush. That's what you'll be called.
> Because it's got to do with trickery and living in the bush.
> Because it's got to do with something a girl can't resist.
> The first Nanapush stole fire. You will steal hearts' (33).

As a representative of the Chippewa tradition, Nanapush, the trickster culture hero "loses power" every time his name "is written and stored in a government file" (32). Nevertheless, his tricksterish qualities are evident in the similarities he has with Nanabozho. Like the Native trickster, Nanapush lives on the fringes of society inside the forest. His seductive tongue and sexuality can attract even an elderly woman like Margaret Kashpaw. Like the Native

60

trickster, too, most of the humor in *Tracks* is generated by the words and actions of Nanapush. With his tricksterish qualities, Nanapush survives many near death experiences and lives to tell the stories. Moreover, Nanapush's feats like taking out meat with his bare hands from the depth of a boiling pot, his burying of the Pillagers when no one else would dare to touch them, his act of saving Fleur and Lulu, his having taken three wives, his scatological pranksterism, all these further confirm his trickster status. As the Chippewa culture hero, Nanapush also has the responsibility to maintain the Native tradition. The whole of his narrative is addressed to Lulu, the Chippewa hope for future and continuity, as Nanapush attempts to draw the young girl back into the fold of traditions. As Brhem rightly observes:

> Nanapush, as trickster in *Tracks*, attempts to talk Lulu, Fleur's daughter, back into traditional culture... As a Trickster and world creator, his power is as great as Micipijiu's. As a cultural leader, he respiritualizes Lulu after white schooling (Brhem 694).

In spite of being a traditional Chippewa elder, Nanapush is adept at appropriating the other's language for his own purposes, like he does when he "writes" his own name as Lulu's father or later when he uses the colonizer's language to bring Lulu back home. His blurring of boundaries underlines the contemporary Chippewa experience. Simultaneously powerful and powerless owing to his liminal status, Nanapush, the Native trickster is also at times tricked by others. While he is powerful enough to break Pauline's most "secret practice" of restricting her "low functions" through a scatological water story, his "sweet talk" does not save Margaret from the insult of the shaving of her braids by the Morrissey and Lazzare boys. Further, while he is able to save the lives of Fleur and Lulu at different occasions, Nanapush is himself tricked by the Kashpaws, which results in the loss of his spiritual daughter Fleur's land. Thus, through the portrayal of Nanapush, Erdrich draws attention to the marginality of the Native in his own Nation.

As a medicine man and a maternal caretaker, Nanapush gives new lease of life to many- Fleur Pillager, her cousin Moses Pillager and Lulu being prominent among them. When the Pillager clan succumbs to consumption leaving a 17 year old infected Fleur behind, it is Nanapush's curing and healing songs that bring her back to life and health. Later, when Lulu suffers from frostbite and the white doctor offers to amputate her, Nanapush metaphorically resists the laming of Chippewa future by nursing Lulu back to health through traditional medicine and soothing healing songs. By saving the lives of both Fleur and Lulu, Nanapush, the Native grandfather figure also simultaneously becomes grandmother, the Native creatrix.   61
Tanrisal observes about Nanapush:

> ...by taking on the role of the mother, caring for characters
> like Fleur and her daughter Lulu, he is able to deliver
> them into life and to ease his former loss by restoring the
> natural order...Acting like a mother, he contributes to the
> survival of his people (Tanrisal 71).

As mothers and women in Native societies maintain and continue traditions, so does Nanapush in _Tracks_. Like the grandmother figure of Native mythologies, acting as the keeper of traditions, he embalms the tragedies of his people with humor, healing rituals, stories, and songs. As one with the knowledge of both worlds, Nanapush also blurs the boundaries of gender with his maternal qualities. It's amazing how keenly he understands the feelings of women. As he sings Lulu to the path of recovery, Nanapush reflects:

> Many times in my life, as my children were born, I
> wondered what it was like to be a woman, able to invent
> a human from the extra materials of her own body. In
> the terrible times, the evils I do not speak of, when the
> earth swallowed back all it had given me to love, I gave
> birth in loss. I was like a woman in my suffering, but my
> children were all delivered into death. It was contrary,
> backward, but now I had a chance to put things into a
> proper order (167).

This dualistic understanding of the male and the female likens Nanapush to what Julie Barak describes as the Native American figure of a "berdache," who were "both respected and ridiculed among their people" because "on the one hand, his ritual and ceremonial power was highly regarded and his womanly talents highly praised, but because of his awesome vision and exotic life, the berdache also had a feared and avoided place in social relations" (Barak 185).

Thus, by the portrayal of Nanapush, Erdrich revokes the practices and figures from the Native American tradition and highlights some lesser-known sides of Native culture. Nanapush, as a representative figure of Native traditions, is a storyteller par excellence. He frequently highlights the importance of stories and speech for survival. As a Native storyteller, Nanapush understands the web of stories and the old man's experiences have taught him that stories can defeat death. He would tell of stories:

> They are all attached, and once I start there is no end to
> telling because they're hooked from one sideto the
> other, mouth to tail. During the year of
> sickness, when I was the last one left, I saved

myself by starting a story ... I got well by talking. Death
could not get a word in edgewise, grew discouraged, and
traveled on (146).

Nanapush's stories do not merely guarantee individual survival;
they are also the means for defining a community identity and for the
continuation of Native culture. Nanapush's use of the pronoun 'we' when
he speaks about the tragedies the Chippewas have faced, points to his
communal understanding of life and identity. Suzanne Ferguson points
out that "Erdrich's theory of fiction appears to be based upon a conviction
that people tell stories constantly to make sense of their lives, that 'reality'
itself- the reality of family, of love, of success or defeat-is for humans the
stories that we tell as means to analyze, understand, and control our
history and identity" (Ferguson 553).
Through the voice of Nanapush, Erdrich also refers to the oral
tradition of the Native peoples. Nanapush's stories, even though written
in the text, are addressed primarily to a listening audience, the audience
here being Lulu. Nanapush avoids Euroamerican terminologies like
Chippewa or Ojibwa to refer to his people. He addresses them in the
Native term "Anishinabe." He also refers to small pox as the "spotted
sickness." The Euroamerican treaties are for Nanapush "government
papers." The orality of *Tracks* is marked by Nanapush's address to Lulu
as "My girl," and "granddaughter." His detailing of the past experiences
uses the pronoun "I" which creates an intimacy with the audience. Talk
being "an old man's last vice," Nanapush talks on to empower Lulu with
tradition and a knowledge of the past. His jokes and stories are also quite
often in the "old language." Peterson observes:

> Since traditional written history, based on documents, is
> another kind of violence inflicted on oppressed peoples,
> *Tracks* features oral history. The opening of the novel
> uses oral storytelling markers... The turn to oral history
> in *Tracks* signals the need for indigenous peoples to tell
> their own stories and their own histories (Peterson 985).

Though Nanapush had a "Jesuit education" and can speak
in "good English" (33), he does not get into the "method of leading
others with a pen and piece of paper" (209) till he has to adapt to
the ways of the oppressor to get Lulu, the hope for the continuation
of Chippewa culture, back from the clutches of the "white school."
Not merely Nanapush's stories but his actions also emphasize his
role as a keeper of traditions. While his stories are meant to highlight
the tribal culture and tradition, and a community sense of identity and
integrity, Nanapush's "adoption" of three young Chippewas,
Fleur, Eli and Lulu, albeit under different circumstances   63
and on different occasions, also underscores his attempt to

rejuvenate the tribal kinship system. Nanapush's medicine practices and healing rituals sustain his three adopted children in the lifeblood of Native tradition. As the upholder of tribal traditions, Nanapush resists the loss of land and a subsequent loss of culture because he understands the plight of contemporary Chippewa life. He knows what his tribe has become:

> ...a tribe of file cabinets and triplicates, a tribe of single-space documents, directives, policy. A Tribe of pressed trees. A tribe of chicken-scratch that can be scattered by a wind, diminished to ashes by one struck match (225).

As the witness of the last buffalo hunt, Nanapush tells us that "Starvation makes fools of everyone" and it was at this weak moment in Native history that they had to part with their lands. Although Nanapush too loses his land, his act of resistance serves as an encouragement for survival and continuity of Native traditions. As Whitson remarks "Nanapush's resistance is important; he provides a cultural touchstone that gives encouragement to those who seek to maintain their tribal integrity, and he picks the conscience of those who are willing to abandon the ancient ways out of desperation or the lure of government money" (Whitson 167).

As the voice of tradition, Nanapush debunks Pauline, the assimilationist voice of the text and even "punishes" her in a humorous way. Nanapush manifests the tribal survival instinct by adapting "to a new bureaucratic identity at the end of the novel" which "literally and figuratively ensures the survival of the tribe, a tribe whose future is clearly tied to young Lulu's self and story" (Reid np). Further, by giving Nanapush the first and last chapters for narration, Erdrich emphasizes the survival of the traditional ways of life and storytelling. Erdrich in her interview with Bruchac tells that "one of the strengths of Indian culture" is that one can "pick and choose and keep and discard" (Bruchac 136). Nanapush's narrative foregrounds this quality of the Native culture.

Different dimensions of the Native culture are foregrounded through Erdrich's portrayal of the Native characters. In *Tracks*, it comes through the stories of the Kashpaw family, their experiences, their laughter and tragedies, the friendships and enmities and their fragmentation as a result of colonization. The matrilineality of Native societies is reinforced through the character of Margaret Kashpaw, a widow living with her two youngest sons, Eli and Nector. Erdrich being a woman herself, the women characters in her novels are almost always vivacious and interesting. As Jean Strouse comments: "Ms. Erdrich's women are for the most part fiercer, nastier, more powerful, effective and inexorable than her men" (Strouse 172).

Margaret Kashpaw is one of Erdrich's women. She is strong, bold and determined, fiercely protective of her family and has knowledge of the herbs and roots of the forest, qualities associated with a Native woman. But she is not a stereotype, be it her unconventional sexuality or her sharp tongue. Like Fleur and Nanapush, Margaret too wants to live the life of a traditional Chippewa. As a "headlong, bossy" woman "scared of nobody and full of vinegar," Margaret does not initially approve of her son's relationship with Fleur Pillager. But with the birth of Lulu, things ease out, and Fleur and Margaret become thick friends to such an extent that when Margaret is "raped" by Clarence Morrissey and Boy Lazzare who shave her head as an act of revenge against Eli, Fleur shaves off her own hair and punishes the "rapists" with her medicine. (Peterson 987). Margaret also demonstrates the virtue of Native kindness by hiding Nanapush's shame of not being able to save her from the grievous insult. Further, she also becomes Nanapush's companion in an act of solidarity and understanding. In spite of all the stories surrounding Fleur, Margaret attends Fleur at her first pregnancy and helps her deliver a healthy child. Though Nanapush dismisses Margaret as a woman who would "swell up on the power of giving life" (55), their association lasts long.

But this relationship is damaged and irrevocably changed when with the white officials' imposition of a late fine, Margaret and her son Nector pay off the money they had saved along with Fleur and Nanapush for the Pillager land to keep the Kashpaw land. Fleur and Margaret's friendship also breaks down with this incident. In spite of her remarkable Nativeness and strength, Margaret too, like many contemporary Natives, falls into the trap of fragmentation. Julie Tharp comments:

> The very struggle to keep land often tore families and friends apart. Erdrich dramatizes this in *Tracks* when Margaret and Nector Kashpaw use all the money saved to pay for Fleur Pillagers' land allotment to instead pay off their own. Once close friends, Margaret and Fleur are wedged apart over the struggle for newly limited resources (Tharp 163).

Eli Kashpaw, eldest of Margaret's two younger children, all her older children having moved to their allotment land in Montana, is Margaret's "best chance." Eli "knows the woods" and "wanted to be a hunter." Living in tradition, Eli debunks white education. Nor does he believe in the white man's religion. Trained in hunting and trapping by Nanapush, he lives amidst nature. So much so that Nanapush observes, "At fifteen, he was uncomfortable around humans, especially women" (40). With Nanapush's help he wins over Fleur. In spite of Fleur's dangerous reputation, Eli's winning her over manifests his inherent courage and charm. Eli's simplicity and large-heartedness   65
is evident when he starts living with Fleur and takes good

care of her without bothering about the fact that she might be pregnant with someone else's child. Like a responsible Native man, Eli hunts and gathers food for his family. By taking advice from Nanapush and working upon it, Eli demonstrates the Native virtue of respecting tribal elders. His love for Fleur is not a passing fascination. Though he is witched by Pauline to enter into a fling with Sophie Morrissey, he is repentant as soon as the sorcery wears off and comes back to Fleur ashamed and seeking forgiveness. In fact, one of the most enduring facets of *Tracks* is Erdrich's portrayal of Eli and Fleur's love. Like a traditional Chippewa, Eli respects his beloved's dream visions as is evident when he goes hunting following Fleur's directions. Also, as a Chippewa youth, he follows the guidance and directions of old Nanapush in hunting and courtship. Towards the end of the novel, however, Eli can neither live in the traditional way nor keep his beloved. Ashamed and guilt-ridden by his mother and brother's treacherous act, Eli promises to buy back the Pillager land and to keep his promise he goes off the reservation to work in a log-house in the town and gather money for the land. In the postcolonial era, Eli is a Native person who in spite of his respect for and willingness to live in tradition, has to leave his land and search for survival elsewhere.

Nector Kashpaw is Margaret's youngest son and with his white education he is not exactly a Chippewa in spirit. Even Margaret would not trust him much because his "love of town ways seemed to head him so clearly for the off-reservation schools" (57). Even at the tender age of nine, unlike Eli who follows the traditional ways of hunting and providing for the family, Nector wants to know "how land was parceled out, what sorts of fees were required" (121). Having betrayed Fleur by paying for the Kashpaw land at the cost of the Pillager land, Nector, white-like, shows no sign of guilt or remorse. He rather seems to bask in the glory of his treacherous act. Nanapush, however, blames himself for Nector's act. Comparing the two brothers Nanapush further adds: "As he grew older, he resembled Eli more in face and less in spirit. Whereas the elder brother never lost his tie to the past, the younger already looked ahead" (209).

Invisibility stands as a great mountain before the identity of the Natives. Erdrich deals with the question of invisibility in *Tracks* in a symbolic manner. Lulu, Fleur's daughter, is the designated audience for Nanapush's stories and thus is present all over the text in spite of her absence. Lulu, as Nanapush tells, is "the child of the invisible" (1). By constructing Lulu inside and still away from the text, Erdrich portrays the precarious condition of the contemporary Native who, even though present in the consciousness of the hegemonic discourse, is never "seen," never "realized." Ferrari thus comments on Lulu's invisibility:

> Nanapush's narration which is an effort to get Lulu to understand her family and tribal past and thus affect the present, will counteract the invisibility

66

> wreaked by cultural imperialism...Nanapush's calling
> Lulu a child of the "invisible ones" simultaneously
> invokes her inheritance of cultural oppression and of
> cultural/spiritual empowerment (Ferrari np).

Nanapush names Lulu after one of his dead daughters, gives her his official paternity, and ensures the continuity of his clan and, as such, the tribal trickster lives through Lulu. Through this act of his, Nanapush also binds Lulu to tradition. Community kinship being as good as biological relations in the tribal vision, Nanapush's lending of his name to Lulu also bestows her with the power of his name. Pauline, blinded by her assimilationist dreams and Christian devilry, does not understand the significance of kinship. Raged with jealousy, she comments on Lulu's family: "They formed a kind of clan, the new made up of bits of the old, some religious in the old way and some in the new" (70). It is more than possible that Lulu, with Fleur's rape in Argus, could be a bastard child. But by accepting Lulu to the community fold, Nanapush as well as Margaret demonstrate the Chippewa spirit of understanding and accommodation. Further, the dynamism of Native culture is underlined in its acceptance of change. Commenting on Chippewa group norms Margaret J. Downes writes:

> It is not good, for example, if a child is born a bastard;
> yet that child is incorporated into the tribe, and the
> paradigms of acceptability, old and thick as they are,
> shift a bit as a result (Downes 55).

Again, by giving her a Chippewa name, Nanapush, as a keeper of traditions, ensures a tribal identity for Lulu. Unlike Pauline who seeks an alteration of her identity by a change of name, Lulu will always be known as a Nanapush and thus a Chippewa. Moreover, by listening to the stories of her tribal childhood from a Chippewa elder, her official father and spiritual grandfather Nanapush, Lulu is reconnected to her tribal identity and community self.

By throwing into fire Lulu's "red shoes" that "melt and stink," Margaret as a Native grandmother burns away the stinking influence of white culture on her granddaughter. And by absorbing the cold from Lulu's frostbitten feet, Nanapush recirculates the warmth of Native tradition into Lulu's spirit. Though agitated and angry with her mother for sending her to a boarding school, Lulu, with Nanapush's trickery, comes backs home. Lulu's return symbolizes a hope for continuance and survival of the Native traditions.

Nanapush's story begins at a point when the colonizing forces have brought "exile" for the Anishinabeg "in a storm of government papers" (1). Having witnessed the passing of history, the loss of land, livelihood, and culture that occurred as a result of the colonizer's self-serving policies, Nanapush is pained at the devastation his peoples have gone through, reduced to "figures and numbers" in the records of the hegemonic discourse. The Native peoples' plight is a consequence of the bureaucrats' play with pen and paper, Nanapush would tell: "...once the bureaucrats sink their barbed pens into the lives of Indians, the paper starts flying, a blizzard of legal forms, a waste of ink by the gallon, a correspondence to which there is no end or reason" (225). Having been "taught by the Jesuits," Nanapush understands the treacherous acts of the government better than his brethren, many of whom are troubled by the mystery of the written word. Nanapush tells the Father: "I know about law. I know that 'trust' means they can't 'tax' our parcels" (174). However, unlike Fleur whose complete distrust in the written word forces her to leave her land and even send her child away from herself, Nanapush's tricksterish understanding and twisting of the power of written word enables him to facilitate the homecoming of Fleur's child Lulu. By putting his name on the white record alongside Lulu's name that is both a truth and lie, Nanapush tricks the hegemonic discourse and brings in Lulu, the continuer of Native life.

While there are two narrators in *Tracks*, Nanapush, the first narrator being the voice of tribal integrity and tradition, Pauline, the second narrator of *Tracks*, speaks from a space in between two worlds. Her voice is marked by internalized oppression. As one continually in struggle with her "Nativeness" and with an intense desire and effort to become the Other, Pauline is the *marginal mimic* woman (emphasis mine).

Pauline's narrative is addressed to none in particular, thus stressing her alignment with the colonial weapon of the written word rather than the Native oral tradition. Like the colonizer, Pauline indulges in the "improvisation of truth" but at the same time, like the Chippewa, she believes in the power of Missipeshu and Fleur Pillager. At pains to become "white" while all the people who matter in her life are Native, Pauline is Erdrich's portrayal of the devastating possibility of a conflict of cultural codes. In her fanatical rejection of self, Pauline takes pride in the fact that the Chippewa talk to her in English rather than the Native tongue and in her conscious unlearning of skills integral to the Native life like the quillwork or tanning of hides, her family being "skinners in the clan for which the name was lost" (14). For Pauline, survival translates into denial of one's own tradition and roots. She would tell:

> I wanted to be like my mother, who showed her half-white. I wanted to be like my grandfather, pure Canadian. That was because even as a child I saw that to hang back was to perish. I saw through the eyes of the world outside of us. I would not speak our language (14).

Pauline's "White," Christian dreams lead her on a path of insane disintegration and self-abnegation. Her distorted sexuality, her lack of comfort with the positive forces of birth and creation and a half-baked sense of identity that is "invisible" even to her own self contribute to her practice of fanatical Catholicism. As the internally oppressed Native self, Pauline seeks refuge in an alien religion that has actually nothing to comfort her. Pauline's denial of her own race and religion doubly uproots her. Like the stories she tells, Pauline's self-suffers from a number of cold deaths. As Nanapush would tell about Pauline: "Good at easing souls into death but bad at breathing them into life, afraid of life in fact" (57).

Pauline's power, which like her narrative, stinks of lie and treachery, is the power of an antagonist within. During Fleur's first pregnancy, when Fleur is swelling with labour pain, a bear enters the house and seeing the bear Fleur raises up with fear and gives birth to Lulu. In a way, the bear that leaves without tracks, thus suggesting that it might have been a Chippewa spirit bear, facilitates the childbirth. But Pauline shoots the bear on its heart. This, according to Shawn Vidmar, establishes Pauline as an oppressed and colonized Native. Vidmar argues:

> Knowing her tribe's belief in the bear spirit, it is odd that Pauline attempted to kill such a powerful dodem with the modern tool, a gun. She is a good example of the colonized Indian (Vidmar np).

As the confused and pained mixed-blood narrator, "Pauline's narrative erupts from the war inside her, from her loudness, cowardice and desire. Her story is told to whoever will listen," suggests Patricia Vidgerman in a review of *Tracks* (Vidgerman 171).

It is interesting to note that while Nanapush, being a Chippewa male, respects the feminine and, also, himself exhibits certain maternal qualities, paradoxically, Pauline distances herself from all powers of creation in her job as the keeper of the dead and even denies motherhood for herself. In her adoption of the male-dominated religion of Christianity that "demands a sacrifice of the semiotic maternal body in order to identify with the symbolic holy mother" (Sanders np), Pauline negates her own femininity. Thus, Pauline not only denies her race and religion but also her gender. In an attempt to become whatever she is not, Pauline loses whatever she has been. In an exhibition of utter self-hatred, Pauline even violates her own body by attempting to kill her unborn child inside the womb. Tanrisal rightly observes:

> By turning against motherhood, she turns against life. Christianity makes her anti-mother and anti-Indian. She serves as a counter to traditional ways (Tanrisal 74).

69

Pauline's rejection of her own self, a consequence of cultural alienation that starts with her rejection of her own child, distorts further in her fanatical practices of self-abnegation for the sake of a Catholic salvation. In her literally stinking logic of saintly acts and in her growing devilry, Pauline sought "devotion's air" (153). Her pervert sexuality also seems to be resulting from a confused juggling between worlds. From her sexual experience with Napoleon Morrissey to her bearing his child and ultimately her murder of Napoleon, Pauline's story is an oppressed Native's "tragic parody" (Whitson 189). In her erasure of her own Native past and thus Native history as such, Pauline functions as an agent of the hegemonic whitewashing of facts. At the end of the novel, Pauline's negation is complete with her rejection of the name given by her family and the taking up of a new name, Leopolda. This act symbolizes Pauline's ultimate disconnection with her own past. Peterson remarks:

> Pauline's assimilation into the dominant culture results in a voice that echoes hegemonic history. Moreover, by forgetting the past and radically rewriting her own identity and experience, Pauline signifies history as pure fiction with no referential value whatsoever-a position that Erdrich's work ultimately rejects (Peterson 990).

Pauline knows that while she "hardly rinsed through the white girls' thoughts" (115), she is also the "crow of the reservation" who lived off the scraps of the Chippewa people. Further, Pauline's bestiality also seems to have grown out of her jealousy of Fleur's beauty and power. Throughout her narrative, one constant motif of Pauline is to abnegate Fleur's charm. Possessed by her sexual jealousy, Pauline seems to have derived the pleasure of a voyeur in witnessing Fleur's rape and later in her act of tricking Eli, Fleur's lover, into a bewitched act of lovemaking with Sophie, the young and dull-witted Morrissey. While she attempts unsuccessfully to kill Fleur's bear power during her first pregnancy, Pauline succeeds in complicating Fleur's second pregnancy and thus killing her child, resulting in Fleur's losing of some of her Pillager power. Pauline, destructively powerful on her own, also spreads much of the stories regarding Fleur being the mistress of Missipeshu, the Chippewa water monster. But death seems to be at Pauline's command, and her magic unlike Nanapush's, results in destruction. She also refers to her own birdlike qualities more than once in the text. In her first job as a keeper of the dead, Pauline is found "in the tree later that morning," while "everyone was shot with fear at the way I [Pauline] hung, precarious, above the ground" (68) and in her first sexual experience she says that she did not like the sight of her having been "naked, skinned, plucked."

70 Brehm points out: "Pauline appears to belong to the bird clan, the creature of the air who challenge Micipiju's power, but Pauline is more Windigo than Thunderbird" (Brehm

695). Pauline's hallucinatory world is filled with acts of destruction. More importantly, she is quick to shift her own guilty acts to others, especially Fleur. While she spreads the story of Fleur's rape, her probable pregnancy and Fleur's revenge of killing her rapists, the reader later comes to know from Pauline's narrative itself that it was Pauline and not Fleur who locked Fleur's rapists to their cold deaths.

If Nanapush's narrative voice ensures the representation of Native culture and orality, Pauline's self-representation is bound in the written word. In her search for an identity, Pauline, however, loses her "self" and her "name" in her redefinition/rechristening in the hegemonic discourse:

> I asked for the grace to accept, to leave Pauline behind,
> to remember that my name, any name, was no more than
> a crumbling skin. Leopolda. I tried out the unfamiliar
> syllables. They fit, they cracked in my ears like a fist
> through ice (205).

Pauline's narrative ends at a point when she is sure that "the land will be sold and divided" and "Fleur's cabin will tumble into the ground and be covered by leaves." Further, she also becomes a teacher at a convent school in Argus where she can contribute to the oppressor's mission of "blinding" and "deafening" the Native child. She justifies her decision thus: "I have vowed to use my influence to guide them, to purify their minds, to mold them in my own image" (205). Peterson remarks:

> Pauline recognizes that indoctrination into white culture
> is a kind of mutilation- her students will be "blinded"
> and "deafened" as she herself has been- but she sees this
> development as inevitable. The White Christian capitalists
> will win the cultural-epistemological war, in Pauline's
> view, and she will side with the victor (Peterson 980).

But by denying her the first and last chance of narration in the text and by frequently emphasizing on her lies, Erdrich denies Pauline authority and continuity. Pauline, Erdrich seems to suggest, is a possibility in the contemporary Chippewa experience, but she is definitely not the first and last word on Native cultural continuity.

Erdrich's technique to use multiple narrators in her novels is deeply influenced by the Chippewa storytelling traditions. For the reader, it also makes the reading a postmodern process of discovering and understanding shifting points of view. As Native storytellers often use the techniques of repetition, parallelism, re-telling and personal improvisation, truth becomes relational in such stories. This also takes the reader close to the experience of listening to 71 stories in a community gathering where the storytellers interpret the same story from varying perspectives. In doing so, Erdrich's narrative technique thus criticizes the idea of a master narrative and adheres to the postmodern concept of relativity.

Erdrich's use of multiple narrators in *Tracks* also hints at the postmodern possibility of the existence and experience of multiple realities. In their narration of the stories of the land, the people and religion, Nanapush and Pauline thus let the reader comprehend their own truths and this narrative technique thus adds to the imaginative freshness of both stories. Also, this strategy of using multiple narrators helps the author tell the stories without taking sides, without falling into the binary thought patterns of good/bad, right/wrong or moral/immoral. Erdrich lets the story speak for itself. To quote Rita Ferrari in this context:

> Erdrich does not install a new monolithic viewpoint, moving the margins to the centre; instead she causes the margins to proliferate. Writing about characters who are displaced by definition, Erdrich uses aesthetic displacement to critique any master narrative or totalizing viewpoint (Ferrari np).

The shifting points of view and multivocality of *Tracks* emphasizes a community perspective. As Native societies culturally define truth and identity in terms of the community, an individual voice like those in Western texts would not suffice to mark the "wholeness" of the story. In the Native culture, it is "the storyteller's responsibility to retell stories to remind them of their past and of their identities" (Tanrisal 71). Erdrich's narrators, especially Nanapush, tell stories that ensure survival and continuity. Pauline's stories, too, tell of a past time, the past of Fleur Pillager and stories from her own past. Rainwater thus comments on the two narrators of *Tracks*: "Events narrated by both narrators take on meaning within a framework of American Indian beliefs about life, death and mystical experiences" (Rainwater 408).

Set in early twentieth century, the plot of *Tracks* portrays the contemporary experiences of the Chippewa people, the conflict between tradition and assimilation, and in the two narrators of *Tracks*, Erdrich is able to give a picture of the contemporary Chippewa life. As Christopher Vescey notes in his 1998 review of *Tracks*:

> *Tracks* brings the reader back to the early years of this century, 1912-1924, and it ties a knot of narrative around the previous novels ...The narrative technique reveals the structure of the plot that in itself means to set forward the oppositional strands of twentieth-century Chippewa (Vescey 139).

Stories are shaped in the Native pattern of a circle in *Tracks*. In the telling of stories through different narrators in *Tracks*, Erdrich enables the shifting of moulds so as to relate to experiences from the past and present. With little respect for the conventions of coherence and linearity, Erdrich deconstructs the western mould of narration and reconstructs it with a Native tradition of storytelling. As the two narrators of *Tracks* narrate their stories from different perspectives of time, place and gender, at the same time dismissing each other on grounds of reliability and authenticity, the author is also able to create what Ferrari terms as "gaps in the stories" (Ferrari np). Quoting Alice Jarnine's poststructuralist concept of the "hole in the text," Ferrari notes that:

> While these gaps are sometime "filled" by other characters and are sometimes "filled" by the reader's interpretation, they still assert a textual silence or hole... This linguistic subtlety has an obvious correlative in how *Tracks* and *Love Medicine* focus on Native Americans who historically have been unrepresented or represented in manipulative ways in the service of a dominant group's ideology (Ferrari np).

The web of stories for the Native is not merely a tool of amusement or entertainment. As they narrate stories, the narration revises history, both personal and political, ensures continuity and survival of the individual, the community, the culture and of storytelling itself. As Nanapush tells us:

> There is a story to it the way there is a story to all, never visible while it is happening. Only after, when an old man sits dreaming and talking in his chair, the design springs clear (24).

By representing the unrepresented in terms of history, politics and culture, Erdrich's narrative functions with the motif of giving shape to the definite dimensions of Native culture. In between the two narrators of *Tracks* lies an oral/written divide. While Nanapush's orality brings an ultimate success for him in the homecoming of Lulu, Pauline's belief in the supremacy of the written word "erases" her from the Chippewa land and "rewrites" her in the hegemonic discourse as "Leopolda." Through her use of orality as the preferred mode for Native communication, Erdrich ultimately emphasizes the importance of Native culture. Her fiction is English in language, but Native in spirit. While as a postmodern work of fiction Erdrich's novels "resist any interpretative urge which is founded on epistemological or theological certainty" (Rainwater 413), as literary productions from the   73

American Indian tradition, Erdrich's writings and *Tracks* in particular recreate orality and ensure survival of the definite dimensions of Native culture.

Chapter III:
The Storytelling Tradition:
Leslie Marmon Silko's *Ceremony*

Postcolonialism has brought back the emphasis on indigenous traditions of storytelling. Unlike what the western canonical discourse assumes, "stories" in ancient cultures and communities are not regarded as mere tools of entertainment. Stories are, in fact, revered and accorded definite functions. In Native societies, stories contribute to the construction of sociocultural practices and norms, as bridges between people and their communities-material and spiritual, past and present, cause and effect and so on. Stories thus inform, evolve, instruct and interpret the immediate world and its trappings for the peoples and in doing so, these shape and reshape communities, their ways of life and their cultures. This chapter shall deal with Leslie Marmon Silko's majestic recreation of the ancient Laguna storytelling tradition in *Ceremony*. This chapter shall focus exclusively on the "stories" *Ceremony* has, the "telling" of these stories in the novel, and the effect of these on the development and culmination of the novel. This chapter shall also focus on the importance and power accorded to stories in the Laguna culture and how Silko's employment of Laguna mythologies and clan stories serve to establish *Ceremony* as a representative text of the postcolonial Native American world. It seeks to explore how Tayo, the mixed-breed protagonist of *Ceremony*, rediscovers his own identity in the postcolonial world through an understanding of the stories. This chapter also looks into the likes of Emo whose faith in the wrong stories erases them from the Native landscape.

I

Storytelling being integral to the oral cultures of the Native Americans, the postcolonial literary productions by Native writers often draw from this ancient tradition. In the process, Native authors become storytellers with a responsibility towards their own communities as well as towards the upkeep of the stories. One such Native American storyteller is Leslie Marmon Silko. Born in Albuquerque, New Mexico on 5 March 1948, Silko is of mixed Laguna Pueblo, Mexican 75 and Anglo-American descent. In spite of the Marmon family's brush with community responsibility and position, Silko's family lived in the margins of the community, both literally and otherwise. However, there was no dearth of grandmothers and aunts in her family who would tell stories to a young Sliko – an experience that sensitized Sliko to the importance of "stories" and their role in the forming of identities early in life.

Silko wrote her first short story "The Man to Send Rain Clouds" when she was still in school that showcased her early genius. In 1974, Silko's collection of poems and stories appeared as *Laguna Woman: Poems* that drew heavily from the Laguna culture and reflected on the images of land, colour, weather, animals and stories etc. which were to appear time and again in her future writing.

Silko's semi-autobiographical novel *Storyteller* was published in 1981 and it largely deals with family, landscape, love, Native American mythology and identity issues, themes which recur in *Ceremony* as well. Silko's style of interlinking prose and poems is nicely manifested in *Storyteller* and she carries on this lyrical quality to *Ceremony* too.

Silko's *Almanac of the Dead*, a massive 763 page novel, has been well-received for its lucid, flowing prose. Though the novel has a very violent, dark undertone, Silko's employment of her signature style to repeat phrases, events, actions, thoughts and images makes it an interesting read. Like she does in *Ceremony*, Silko embroils one story onto the next in *Almanac of the Dead* as well. The likeness of the two novels is further established in Silko's portrayal of the whites as a selfish, brutal and self-destructive force. The witchery story in *Ceremony* too lays emphasis on the self-destructive tinge of the hegemonic forces. The stories Silko tells in *Almanac of the Dead* are not merely stories but they have their own lessons too. Further, as a Native writer, Sliko focuses on the importance accorded to Mother earth in the Laguna society and the mainstream culture's contemptuous view of it, a theme that resonates in *Ceremony* where the war-torn Tayo comes back to health and identity only after regaining his connection with the land.

Drawing from the Laguna Pueblo mythology such figures as Thought Woman, Corn Mother, Spider Woman, Sun Father, Kau'pa'ta the Gambler, Reed Woman and such like, Silko weaves even her contemporary stories in a mythical fashion. As is true for Native peoples all over, things start happening when stories are told. In Silko, thus, stories blur boundaries. The mythical and the real appear on the same plane, with similar intentions. This results in an overlap of stories. Layers and layers of stories are formed, meanings created and in fact "stories are valued for their overlap, for the way they lead to new stories in turn" (Dasenbrock 313). Thus, stories shape the Native worldview as they are shaped by it. It is through stories that all things begin, are manifested and sustained and it is through the living tradition that stories become reality. As one occupied with continuous innovation and renovation of the Laguna stories, Sliko employs the postmodernist tools of multiplicity in her fictional writing. The following section seeks to highlight such indigenous storytelling tradition as it manifests itself in *Ceremony*.

II

Postcolonial fiction has essentially emerged from the telling of stories, by people whose 'stories' till recently were untold in the globe in their right perspective. The Native Americans being one such people, whose 'stories' are coming to the forefront only recently, repose a lot of faith in stories and their definitive functions. For such communities, which practice orality in the absence of a written tradition, stories continue the tradition and pass on the knowledge of the ancestors. Story and history in such a context become one and the same because what is told was what has happened. Thus the marginals of the world adopt the medium of stories to reinforce their identities in a postcolonial world. To quote Edith Swan:

> For a people without writing, history is stories. Stories encode the knowledge of generations about how the world and human beings came to be as they are. Stories teach what one must know in order to belong, to have health and prosperity, to survive crisis and rear one's children. (Swan 42).

Stories being integral to the very continuance of life in these communities, it became natural for the storyteller to be placed highly in the communities' scheme of things. The storyteller thus was a powerful persona in the oral cultures, not "powerful" in the Foucouldian sense of the term, but in a rather different communal sense. The storyteller was powerful in drawing out the past and present of the communities s/he belonged to, in readying the peoples for survival, in bringing laughter and hope in the same breath that s/he foretold events or warned about an unforeseen calamity.

Storytelling in oral cultures ought to be communal in nature. This is owing to the fact that the telling" of stories being "performances," audience was always present for the events and in indigenous communities storytelling was participatory and involving in nature. In such circumstances, everyone enjoyed the privilege of both listening to and telling stories. Lincoln thus comments on the importance of storytelling in community settings:

> Storytelling personally brings people together; it engages them collectively in giving and receiving the events of their lives. In such storytelling times, people occupy space with focused attention; they enter their common world more fully (Lincoln 223).

Central to the formation of "cultural ideas" and the achievement of "cultural goals," storytelling thus served as a community process that enhanced and enriched the said community's ways of life, rituals, ceremonies, histories and so on. As a conscious attempt towards cultural and communal survival, storytelling was practiced among the young and the old alike. To quote from Leslie Marmon Silko's beautiful essay in this context:

> Traditionally everyone, from the youngest child to the oldest person, was expected to listen to and be able to recall or tell a portion, if only a small detail, from a narrative account or story. Thus the remembering and retelling were a communal process. Even if a key figure, an elder who knew much more than others, were to die unexpectedly, the system would remain intact. Through the efforts of a great many people, the community was able to piece together valuable accounts and crucial information that might otherwise have died with an individual (Silko 502).

This being so, for the Native peoples of the United States and Canada whose cultures were primarily and essentially community cultures, storytelling was as integral to Native life as hunting, fishing or food gathering. Stories shaped their identities, their ancestry and origins, their ways of life, religious practices, social and familial relationships, kinships and rivalries, history and contemporary practices and so on. Lincoln observes:

78

Indian storytelling, old and new, is drawn from living history. Its angle of truth derives from a belief in families telling their lives directly. Its sense of art turns on tribal integrity (Lincoln 222).

Keeping with the Native worldview of the universe as living and whole where all the "peoples" were intertwined in reciprocal relationships, tribal stories were often circular in nature. Space being spherical and time cyclical in the Native Universe, all stories connected to some other story and thus created what Silko has termed as "the long story of the people."

Using the tradition of orality and storytelling, Silko has produced her classic novel *Ceremony*. Hailed as one of its kind, *Ceremony* has lapped up appreciation almost unprecedented by any other Native American novel. *Ceremony* can be considered as a representative text of the postcolonial Native American world though this does not amount to a glorification of the "temporal, ontological, epistemological other" (Sequoya-Magdaleno 100).

Ceremony is the story of Tayo, a half-white, half-Laguna World War II veteran who has come back from the war to the Laguna reservation all shattered and confused with a hazy mind and fragmented memories. Apparently, devastated from his witnessing of the horrific scenes of WW II, he is suffering from post-traumatic stress disorder. But if that is the case, the white medicines fail to cure him. Wrapping one story unto the next, repeating phrases, thoughts and actions time and again, Silko unweaves Tayo's mindscape. Torn between the white and the Native world, Tayo must come out of his nightmares to live a life of belonging. And his cure lies, as family and friends suggest, not in the white walls of the Army hospital, but in the healing ceremonies of the community. However, *Ceremony* does not look at a bygone era with starry eyes; rather it, as is characteristic of postmodernity, questions the age-old ceremonies practiced by the communities as well as the contemporary annihilation of the earlier ways of life. From the Native point of view, the story shapes and controls one as much as one controls and shapes a story. The choice lies within, whether to settle on a wrong story and die out or to understand the most important story of it all, understand the significance it has to one's life and act accordingly. Linguistically always in the present and temporally simultaneously present in past, present and future, Silko's stories represent the Native cosmology and contemporary conflicts in the same breath.   79

Silko's sense of transition and boundarylessness helps her characters move from the mythical to the real plane and vice-versa with uninhibited ease. For example, as Tayo learns the story of SunMan's rescuing the storm clouds from the clutches of Kau'pa'ta, the Gambler, he, in a sense, also become Sun Man in his attempt to bring in rain to the drought-ridden parched Laguna land. Or for that matter, T'seh, who, it is evident, is a spirit being, also has a physical address somewhere in Mount Taylor. Even Laura, Tayo's dead mother, treads in between mythicality and mortality.

Bringing a communion between the mythical and the mortal, between a bygone time and the present existence, between white and Native American, the very hybridity of Silko's stories tell us a tale that has a spirit both local and global. Contextualizing the stories of the land and its people, Silko creates a harmonious whole of a story. Using vital elements of oral tradition such as prayers, songs, rituals, narratives and storytelling, Silko foregrounds a story that would bring the pride back to the tribes and also further their survival. To quote Simon Ortiz: "But because of the insistence to keep telling and creating stories, Indian life continues" (Ortiz 68).

Search for the identity of self and the community is one of the functions of storytelling. At the centre of *Ceremony* is Tayo's story. Living in between cultures, and searching for an identity that has been long lost, Tayo has to seek answers from the community and for the community. Suffering from a guilt consciousness, Tayo holds himself responsible for the death of his cousin Rocky in the war, and for the draught at Laguna Pueblo which he believes is a consequence of his praying the rain away during his stint at Philippines. Tayo prefers darkness to light to escape from the hallucinatory images that trouble him. Light makes him vomit. He does not feel nor does he understand the cyclical nature of Laguna time. Allen tells us that "Tayo's illness is a result of separation from the ancient unity of person, ceremony and land" (Allen 128). It is a matter of a story gone wrong (emphasis mine). Tayo is sick because he does not 'know' the story. His sickness is physical as well as spiritual and psychological, as it is both personal and communal.

Since they are marginals, marginal perspectives are invariably tied down to the telling of the stories. Along with and parallel to Tayo's story, Silko intercepts a Laguna creation story. Tayo, like Silko, attempts to interpret the story from a margin. He must realize his role in the story. As Elaine Jahner observes, "He can shape the story because he understands something about the real boundaries

80

that relate and separate actions and persons" (Jahner 244). His sickness is partly because of his inability to negotiate his varied experiences. Memories entangle and Japanese, Keresan, and other voices overlap in his mind. Having become "White Smoke" (14) with "no consciousness of itself"(14), Tayo has lost his voice and when he feels his tongue, "it was dry and dead, the carcass of a tiny rodent" (15).The unlearning that happened in the Indian School Tayo attended has also contributed to his sickness. In earlier days, he knew that "it depended on whether you knew the story" (19). And it is vital that he regains this faith in stories for his own as well as the community's recovery.

The Half-breed storytellers, by the very nature of their genealogical history, have their own advantages. They are at once insider and outsider, enjoying the advantages of both the cultures. Like Silko, the protagonist of *Ceremony*, Tayo is also a mixed-blood, which as Velie has pointed out, "meant being different from, and not fully accepted by either the full-bloods or the whites" (Velie 106). Tayo, thus, doesn't belong. Paradoxically, he belongs to both places/cultures. Ashamed of his hybrid descent, Tayo is fast losing hope. Taunted by Emo and others, he has never been made to forget his "Mexican Eyes." Twice abandoned, the first time by his mother and again by his auntie, Tayo has lost the thread with the feminine. This also adds to his woes, as he does not understand which culture to follow and which to reject. This inbetweenness causes his alienation from both the worlds. To put it in the words of Karen Wallace:

> Tayo had never been perceived as a contributing member of either the household or the community, having inherited the alienation his mother had both suffered and caused. Presented as a consequence of his mixed blood, Tayo's alienation is compounded by his inability to master either American or Laguna codes of behaviour (Wallace 98).

The hero in these Halfbreed stories enjoys the company of a medicine man who always carries with him the wisdom of both the cultures. The hero who walks between two cultures- one old, another new, is buttressed by the medicine man having rich experiences in both the cultures. Tayo does not understand his own story until he meets Betonie, the breed medicine man. He has to become aware of the fact that this very inbetweenness that makes him so   81 powerless has made Betonie powerful. In direct contrast to the Anglo-American discourse's disregard for cultural hybridity, for Tayo, as for Silko, "this hybridity become the primary determinant of personal identity" (Patell 6). Doing so, Silko, through Tayo, questions the concept of "purity of cultures" in the postcolonial, postmodern climate where all cultures are post-contact and hence not "pure" in the traditional sense of the term. Tayo's biculturalism manifests itself in his sickness; but in his recovery too, this biculturalism will have a role to play.

Ku'oosh, the mere carrier of the tradition, is the first person of the Laguna to have come to Tayo's help. He is also the one who rekindles Tayo's faith in the stories. Initially, Tayo, the half-breed that he is, does not understand Ku'oosh's words nor is he able to communicate with the old medicine man without taking refuge in English words and this surely shames him. Ku'oosh talks to him about the fragility of this world. Ku'oosh also tells him about the power of words and the responsibility that come with being human:

> ... no word exists alone, and the reason for choosing each word had to be explained with a story about why it must be said this certain way. That was the responsibility that went with being human, old Ku'oosh said, the story behind each word must be told so there could be no mistake in the meaning of what had been said; and this demanded great patience and love" (35-36).

Ku'oosh fails to cure Tayo because his experiences, his language, and his ceremonies do not go beyond Laguna. What Tayo needs is a broader view, a more global perspective.

When Kuoo'sh fails, Betonie succeeds, since Betonie is exposed to a great extent to the cultural nuances of both the worlds, that of the Indian as well as the white. It is through Betonie's vision and guidance that Tayo undertakes the ritual journey. Betonie will make him understand that his identity can be "found in the telling and receiving of stories" (Reck np). Betonie's Hogan confuses him because being in the colonized, oppressed, oppositional frame of mind, Tayo cannot see the bridge; the bridge that he can be to the peoples, Laguna and white. Josiah's cattle that he searches for are also mixed breed like him and he along with the cattle can represent both hope and despair. Betonie sensitizes him to this part of the story. Kevin Concannon observes in this context: "... the clutter of Betonie's Hogan is meant to create for Tayo a new way of seeing the world and his place within it, even as colonial

82

narratives that attempt to define or understand the Pueblos only in terms of otherness counter this mixture" (Concannon 191-192). Four being the sacred number of Laguna, Tayo's ceremonial journey is envisioned by Betonie in four parts. As Tayo starts his journey, "Betonie's vision of stars, cattle, a woman, and a mountain had seemed remote" (186). He learns about the witchery story from Betonie. His nightmares and hallucinations are gradually fading but he has not yet regained the vision to read the story, the story of his life and his people's destiny. He has witnessed the constellation of stars in the north sky (178) and he has met "her" (186). But he is not sure yet. That is until he has reached the ranch where "suddenly Betonie's vision was a story he could feel happening from the stars and the woman, the mountain and the cattle would come" (186).

As soon as this acknowledgement happens, Tayo starts feeling happy and excited. He hopes of taking "the cattle home again, and they would follow the plans Josiah had made and raise a new breed of cattle that could live in spite of drought and hard weather" (187). The cattle's hybridity, like Tayo's, is to be considered in terms of the changes happening in and around Laguna. Tayo, like the cattle, can be the bringer of hope as well as keeper of traditions, albeit changing and alive.

The celestial laughter Silko calls forth by her celebration of the Native oral tradition demonstrates that the Native Indian civilization and its traditions are living in characters and they possess the ability to totally transform the Anglo culture. In that sense, Silko's is a representative voice and *Ceremony*, a representative text.

Stories in the Laguna tradition are not always told for their own sake. They have their own functions to perform. In *Ceremony*, for example, the purpose of the storytelling is to set Tayo into order. Having been helped by Betonie's Wisdom, Ts'eh's love and the Mountain Lion's footprints, Tayo comes from hollowness to wholeness. As he sprinkles yellow pollen on the mountain Lion's footprints, he makes a choice of life over death, of sobriety over drunkenness, of love over violence, of hope over despair, and finally of Laguna over his father's white culture. In doing so, he is not falling into the trap of binaries; rather he thinks whole and global and his choices reflect stories that would result in good. He almost empathizes with the dominant culture and its people because his newly acquired knowledge of the witchery story tells him that the whites have been a creation of the Native witchery. And whatever they do, they do because the witchery wants them to. They are mere tools of the witchery. From his earlier state of being speechless, formless "white smoke," Tayo comes back to the scheme of the Laguna   83 world. From Josiah's dead body in the rain-drenched Philippines to the visualization of A'moo'ooh, the pregnant she-Elk, the most sacred symbol of the Laguna, Tayo in fact comes a long way. As he recovers, he is no more afraid of death nor does he seek it; because he now knows that:

> "... nothing was lost; all was retained between the sky and the earth, and within himself. He had lost nothing" (219).

Now, on his path to recovery:

> He cried the relief he felt at finally seeing the pattern, the way all stories fit together- the old stories, the war stories, their stories- to become the story that was still being told. He was not crazy; he had never been crazy. He had only seen and heard the world as it always was: no boundaries, only transitions through all distances and time (246).

Tayo has found the cattle and led them home safe and he has also gathered the plants and seeds Ts'eh has urged him to. He has become aware of the delicate and graceful balance that must be maintained in the universe. He has recognized Thought Woman's patterns. He has found his own place in the spider's web. He is, at last, at peace with himself and with his surroundings. He knows now that the shiwana (rain clouds) will be coming soon.

Tayo is also aware of the final ceremonial sandpainting of the witchery. Silko, in an excellent manifestation of her globality has juxtaposed the Indian witchery story with uranium mining in Laguna land and the explosive monsterity of the atom bomb. Standing in the mine shaft, Tayo gathers that it was at Trinity site, three hundred miles southeast from where he is standing now, that the bomb was created in the secret laboratories set in the Jemez Mountains. And this was witchery's work. Tempted as he is to kill Emo, the witch whose "monstrous design" is taking away Harley's life, Tayo must reject violence. Because Ts'eh has already warned him and made him ready to face it, to foil the plans of the witchery. Tayo has to see the witchery's ritual and not act violent. Tayo expands his love for Ts'eh by denying to participate in the witchery's final ceremony, observes William Oandson (Oandson 242).

Tayo's very inaction at the last stage of the ceremony foils the witchery's plans. Emo is sent off the reservation, possibly forever. Tayo has come back home. Had he succumbed to the temptation of killing or being killed by Emo at the uranium mine shaft, the witchery's "deadly ritual for the autumn solstice would have been completed by him. He would have been another victim..." (253). But he has acted wise. He can "see the stars" (254) and understand the "convergence of patterns" (254). He has come home; he has come to health. He is planning to gather the seeds and wait for the plants to "grow there like the story" (254). He has developed "the ear for the story and the eye for the pattern" (255).

Having finished the ceremony successfully and understood the story, Tayo is now ready to take responsibility of his family and his community, the Laguna. Tayo has learnt the stories and as Ortiz predicts, he will "live on, wealthy with story and tradition, because he realizes the use and value of the ritual of story-making which is his own and his people's lives in the making" (Ortiz 68). That Tayo is no more ashamed of his appearance is proving the fact that his is not an identity that is oppositional or bound by binaries. He is at peace with his mixed-blood now and he chooses to lead the Laguna way of life.

In the web of stories Silko weaves in *Ceremony*, intricately woven with Tayo's story is Ts'eh's story. Tayo's ritual journey from illness to health, from ignorance to knowledge, from storylessness to storied, has materialized because of Ts'eh. In the book she tells her name to Tayo for the first time after they had already and intimately met twice. Upon Tayo's asking her name, she says: "I'm a Montaño ...You can call me Ts'eh..." (223).

The boundless energy of consciousness which Ts'eh represents is characterized by a sense of eternity. The temporal is thwarted by timelessness. At their first meeting near the mesa, standing under an apricot tree Ts'eh asks Tayo, "What are you doing here?" With a ring of familiarity in the question, the reader is bound to doubt, if Tayo and this feminine entity have met before. That she wore her hair "like the old woman did" is perhaps Silko's strategy to hint at the timelessness of this entity. Her hand-woven blanket had designs woven across it "in four colors: patterns of storm clouds in white and grey; black lightning scattered through brown wind"(177). When Tayo follows her to the door, "The smell of clay and mountain sage stirred *old memories*" (emphasis mine) (178). Ts'eh, the hints suggest, is not an ordinary human being. As the story unfolds, the reader along with Tayo comes to the knowledge of her various manifestations. Ts'eh represents all that is beautiful and living and growing in the universe. She is the manifestation of the Native American "oceanic consciousness" Allen talks about (Allen 63).

85

The Indian tradition of storytelling does not depend upon a definite plot or a set of characters. A woman creatrix spins the stories spontaneously from her womb. Hence, it is all the more different from the western definition of telling stories. When Ts'eh gives us her name, she also lets us know it is a kind of nickname she has taken because her "Indian name is so long"(223). In choosing to be known in a nickname rather than her long "Indian name," Ts'eh is appropriating the postcolonial practice of naming things. But she is also giving us a hint of her longer name, by calling herself Ts'eh; She is, in all probability, the one who has named things; she is Tsi'its'tsi'nako, Thought-Woman:

> Thought-Woman, the spider,
> named things and
> as she named them
> they appeared (1).

Through Ts'eh, or Tsi'its'tsi'nako, as she is in her first avatar, Silko also foregrounds the fundamental feminine principle of the Native American universe - that story and reality are one and the same and all the stories come from the woman who thinks and the woman who spins. To quote Edith Swan:

> Thought Woman is the source of names, language, and knowledge ... Variously, She is Mother, Sister, Grandmother- the syncretic woman who is the "naming" and "knowledgeable" creatrix birthing the universe of stories spun from her abdomen; She is the "master-mind" teaching, nourishing, determining how things will be, and deciding what must be done (Swan 317).

In the Native Indian set-up, the sacred and the secular are blended together. An intimate relationship is between the two, so much so that it is difficult to put them asunder. Ts'eh is a mythical character owing to which a certain sacredness prevails when she is around. She has an aura and a vitality that represents the Native worldview of a living universe. All this is more or less true for Night Swan as well, Josiah's Mexican Cantina dancer girlfriend, a mythical and mysterious figure living on her own. By initiating Tayo to man-woman love, the central balancing principle of the earth through the exchange of sexual energy, Night Swan prepares him for the and ceremony that has not started yet and for the love Ts'eh would bring for him. She soothes his soul and tells him to be ready:

> "You don't have to understand what is happening. But remember this day. You will recognize it later. You are part of it now" (100).

Night Swan is also the first one to tell Tayo about people's fear for change and to pursue him not to be ashamed because he is different. Night Swan's room is filled with blue: blue armchair, blue sheets on the bed, blue pottery nearby the window. All this also hint at Night Swan as the blue Mount Taylor, known as Ts'epina in Laguna, meaning Woman Veiled in Clouds. And Tayo could feel this:

> He could feel something back there, something of her life which he could not explain. The room pulsed with feeling, the feeling flowing with the music and the breeze from the curtains, feeling coloured by the blue flowers painted in a border around the walls. He could feel it everywhere, even in the blue sheets that were stretched tightly across the bed (98).

Magic realism is a part of the Native Indian storytelling tradition. An arc of wonder shrouds the events that happen to the characters. There is a feeling of oneness amongst things present there. Ts'eh has this timelessness about her. In her various manifestations, she inculcates in Tayo a sense of place and time and of the interconnectedness of all things. Lisa Orr observes that Ts'eh "as a woman of the oldways who understands the natural world around her and practices the rituals that enable her to maintain her connection with the earth" is the major agent of Tayo's healing (Orr 147). It is through Ts'eh's love that Tayo regains vitality as well as a willingness to live. It is by making love to her that Tayo is guided to the universal connectedness. Guided by the mountain lion, the hunter's helper and Ts'eh's companion, Tayo is able to locate his cattle. Soon after the lovemaking Tayo sees the cattle in a dream that was "continuous" and "not interrupted."

The Indian storytelling tradition has it that the stories are not confined to the limited life of the earth. Characters often border on the supernatural whose dimensions are staggering

87

enough to measure by the terrestrial standards. In her act of collecting seeds and plant of various hues and colours, Ts'eh becomes Yellow woman, the Laguna all women. "Through Ts'eh, Tayo grows to a unity with the land and its creatures that is neither grasping nor selfish" (Copeland 186). Ts'eh is life force personified. Everywhere around her is the earth with all its life and fertility, growth and beauty. Ts'eh wears a blue shawl that has a pattern of storm clouds on it. One can very well think of her as the harbinger of rain and recognize the special connection she shares with Betonie's Mexican grandmother as well as Night Swan and hence Tayo by means of the color of her eyes. It is Ts'eh who reintroduces Tayo to the land. Observing the intimate connection between Ts'eh, Betonie and Tayo, Wiget observes:

> She may in fact be a mountain spirit and he a Mountain Lion Man. Her blue shawl links her with both Descheeney's wife three generations earlier and Night Swan, with her blue sheets and dress, women who are themselves related to Tayo and Betonie by their hazel eyes and Mexican ancestry. All three are associated with rain and a vital sexuality (Wiget 88).

The tradition of storytelling has its own dynamics in the Native Indian culture. The stories themselves do not have a fixed source as is the case with the mainstream white culture. The Natives believe that stories could be created from anything and everything. There is no definite source to it. Hence, Betonie is found equipped with more than one cultural matrix. He carries all sorts of things with him to create a recipe of stories then and there. The intimacy Tayo develops with Ts'eh restores him from "flesh to memory and memory to land" (Garcia 39). As he regains his memory, Tayo understands the story. Ts'eh warns him about the ending of the witchery's story and through her love helps him defeat the witchery and withdraw from violence. By being her lover and thus a part of herself, Tayo becomes involved with the creative forces of life and thus rejects the destroyers' ending of the story. Having understood the boundarylessness of the universe through Ts'eh's various manifestations, Tayo comes, as Ellen L Arnold suggests, "to a new way of being and knowing in which he can both participate fully in and consciously conceptualize the interrelatedness of all of life" (Arnold 76).

88   The man who guides Tayo to Ts'eh is Betonie, a half-breed Navajo medicine man. Ku'oosh's inability to cure Tayo

leads him to Betonie living on the margins of Gallup, a town that plays to the stereotype of alcohol, prostitution and Indian to the hilt. Betonie's appearance is more or less akin to the traditional full-blood medicine man of Laguna, complete with "his hair tied back neatly with red yarn in a congo knot, like the oldtimers wore" (117). Some things Tayo notices first about Betonie are his Hogan, his good English and the colour of his eyes that matched Tayo's, hazel. Betonie is unconventional in every sense of the term. Tayo observes that Betonie does not talk or behave "like a medicine man at all" (118). His Hogan confuses Tayo further. It has the usual paraphernalia of a traditional medicine man such as "Hard shrunken skin pouches and black leather purses trimmed with hammered silver buttons ... laid beside the painted gourd rattles and deer-hoof clackers of the ceremony" (120). But it also had "bundle of newspapers, their edges curled stiff and brown, barricading piles of telephone books with the years scattered among cities- St. Louis, Seattle, New York, Oakland" and "Coke bottles" (120). It also had "layers of old calendars, the sequences of years confused and lost" (120) along with Santa. Fe Railroad Calendars that were common in Reservation premise. Tayo is unable to make out anything from it. He is not aware till Betonie tells him that "All these things have stories alive in them" (121).

Like Tayo, Betonie too is a half-breed and like his patient, the medicine man also has been doubly excluded in his life. But unlike Tayo who is ashamed of his in between condition and hence has lost a willingness to live and heal, Betonie draws his power from his own liminality. Being the insider outsider that he is, Betonie understands how to benefit from the margin. Shamoon Zamir depicts Betonie as "the embodiment of a process of cultural transformation and innovation that sustains creative survival rather than the more familiar narratives of psychological and social disintegration of Native American cultures in the face of Western colonization" (Zamir 396). As a product of two cultures, Betonie rejects exclusivist paradigms. In a sense, Betonie is the new and improved postcolonial storyteller who can speak for both sides because as a negotiator of the margins of cultures, he "knows" the stories (emphasis mine). He is ready to take from both worlds and contemporize, localize and contextualize it. To extend it further, Silko's story is Betonie's story as well. Betonie's hybridity is manifested in the novel *Ceremony* itself.

What Betonie advocates and represents is change because change signifies survival; Ethnic purity being a thing of the past in the contemporary postcolonial climate, Betonie in fact takes   89 a certain pride in his hybridity. And behaving like a true postmodernist, he questions the unchanging of traditional ceremonies (emphasis mine). Betonie represents change, adaptation, acceptance and survival; by debunking the Native Laguna traditions, he doesn't necessarily discard it altogether as useless. Rather he becomes the keeper of traditions changing. Giving the story of his grandmother's origin, Descheeny's Mexican wife, Betonie lets us know that the change in ceremonies have started much earlier. He tells: "She was doing it before I was born, and he was working before she came" (120).

Betonie inverts the very problematic of hybridity by showing a willingness to change and thus survive. Change being the only permanence Betonie readily understands that "things which don't shift and grow are dead things" (126). Empowered with his grandmother's wisdom, he can declare that without change "We won't survive" (126). As Dennis Cutchins rightly points out, "If Ku'oosh represents the idea that Pueblo culture should be preserved, then Betonie embodies the attempt, not to preserve, but to *revitalize* Native American culture (emphasis original) (Cutchins 83). To survive is to change. To stick to the old ways is to perish. This is the bottom-line of Betonie's teaching. As a half-breed, he knows better because he has survived.

Despite the fact that the Native stories stress on the broad perspectives, large-heartedness, and inter-relatedness, they do not squash the existence of the white cultures. It is held that layers of cultures could live together without erasing any one of them. Betonie heals Tayo by making him understand that the criteria for trust need not always depend on the color of one's skin. Tayo's earlier learning from Josiah about the relativity of all things, i.e. "Nothing was all good or all bad either; it all depended" (11) is strengthened by Betonie's teaching of the layers that make the universe. Foregrounding the complexity of it all Betonie warns, "you don't write off all the white people, just like you don't trust all the Indians" (128). This is because, as Betonie's witchery story tells us, it was the Natives at the first place who "invented the whites" (132) and "white people are only tools that the witchery manipulates" (132). As David L. Moore suggests, "By Betonie's description and prescription, which deny autonomous cultures and autonomous individuals, identities of individuals and communities survive by their very interaction" (Moore 376).

By making the witchery the villain of the plot, Silko, through Betonie, not only subverts the white account of things and white view of the universe, but also foregrounds humanity above race and thus expands the scope of *Ceremony* from merely Native American to a global spectrum:

90

```
...      ...      ...
```
Some had slanty eyes
others had black skin.
```
...      ...      ...
```
witches from all the Pueblos
and all the tribes (emphasis mine) (133).

The lines emphasized point towards the global nature of Silko's thought process. Whereas "slanty eyes" and "black skin" might be referring to Mongolian and African peoples respectively, Silko also adds witches "from all the Pueblos and all the tribes" in the story. By allowing the witchery the devilry, Betonie evades "both oppressive and destructive conventions" and thus "is able to establish new rituals that will refresh the ceremonies essential to the survival of Indian Culture," as is observed by Michael Hobbs (Hobbs 307).

Betonie's vision gives Tayo the story of life, growth and cyclical continuity. And Betonie's witchery story warns Tayo that these are exactly what the witches are set out to destroy. By telling Tayo the stories, Betonie makes him a part of it and thus Tayo has to take the responsibility of defending the right stories. Betonie's creative, positive, life-giving vision for Tayo's ceremony along with his story of the evil witchery, together weave the story of Tayo into a Laguna story and in doing so, Betonie becomes one in the best storyteller tradition because he, thus, "helps to make the story, not just record it or comment on it," observes Dasenbrock (Dasenbrock 316). Betonie's stories guide and heal Tayo by making him aware of the fact that there are no boundaries, only transitions.

Unlike the western tradition of storytelling that takes pride in making the stories counter-earthy, the Laguna storytelling tradition moves on a larger canvass and goes beyond mundane boundaries. The storyteller assumes God-like proportions and indulges in making greater exposures to the characters, so that the characters become Buddha-like. As soon as the novel begins, Josiah, Tayo's maternal uncle, is dead or dying in Tayo's nightmares in Philippines and as Tayo experiences the merging of Japanese voices with Laguna voices "he could hear Uncle Josiah calling to him, Josiah bringing him the fever medicine when he had been sick a long time ago. But before Josiah could come, the fever voices would drift and whirl and emerge again" (6).

Rocky makes a futile attempt to convince Tayo that their uncle couldn't be there in the jungles of Philippines;   91
But Tayo is seeing Josiah " *still* lying there ... Tayo started

screaming because it wasn't a Jap, it was Josiah, eyes shrinking back in the skull and all their shining black light glazed over by death" (emphasis original) (8). Much later, Tayo comes to understand these pictures. He comes to know about the boundarylessness of the universe and of all things; He comes to understand the cyclicality of it all. He comes to understand the transitions. But right then in Philippines, in the weather all around, in his surrounding, he could have a continuous feeling about Josiah. Jeff Karem Observes:

> Both during and after the war Tayo is haunted by the face of his uncle Josiah that he saw on a Japanese corpse. While this idea is dismissed as a 'hallucination' by his superiors, and indeed by some scholars as well, Tayo is recognizing a commonality in life and death, across the lines of friend and foe (Karem 25).

Josiah is the one who initiates Tayo to life's varied hues. Tayo's understanding of stories, the land, the community, the power of the feminine and his own hybridity are all initiated by Josiah. Tayo's rejection of a binary vision of the world is largely due to Josiah's early teachings on life and stories. Josiah, in a sense has been Tayo's first spiritual guru, the first one to tell him about the interconnectedness of the land and the peoples. Sitting by the eternally flowing spring of the pueblo Josiah tells Tayo *the story of the people's origin* (emphasis mine); He gives Tayo the wisdom only community elders can possess:

> 'You see' ... 'there are some things worth more than money'. He pointed his chin at the springs and around at the narrow canyon. 'This is where we come from, see. This sand, this stone, these trees, the vines, all the wildflowers. This earth keeps us going.' ... 'These dry years you hear some people complaining the wind and the dust, they are part of life too, like the sun and the sky. You don't swear at them. It's people, see. They're the ones. The old people used to say that droughts happen when people forget, when people misbehave' (45-46).

92

In the Laguna society, Josiah performs his traditional role, observes Edith Swan:

> To his sister's children, mother's brother is the primary teacher, guardian and disciplinarian ... the closeness of this relationship is marked at Laguna, and indicated in kinship nomenclature with the reciprocal term *"anawe"* - the form of address exchanged between mother's brother (Josiah) and sister's son (Tayo, son of Sis, and Rocky, son of Auntie) (41) (emphasis original).

And as the primary teacher of his nephew, Josiah introduces Tayo to the rituals of the community too. Even when Tayo is abandoned by his mother forever, it's in Josiah's arms that the young Tayo buries his face and cries the loss. Later on, when Tayo loses the only picture he had of his mother, it is Josiah who comes to comfort him though Tayo "loved Josiah too much to admit the shame" (71). Through the deer ritual and his teachings about the cattle they bought from the Mexican Ulibarri, Josiah arouses in Tayo a love for all beings, including animals. Even after Josiah's death, Tayo is guided by his teachings regarding the capture of the cattle: who went off the reservation land. In the postcolonial, poststructural fashion, Josiah even hints at creating a Native discourse while discussing the rearing of the cattle. He tells:

> We'll have to do things our own way. May be we'll even *write our own book* (emphasis mine), *Cattle Raising on Indian Land* (emphasis original) or how to raise cattle that don't eat grass or drink water (75).

It was difficult for Tayo to reckon "Josiah's theories" (80) about the cattle; but Josiah was sure of his half-breed cattle. He was sure that "they would grow up heavy and covered with meat like Herefords, but tough too, like the Mexican cows, able to withstand hard winters and many dry years" (80). Later in the story, as Tayo heals and finds his cattle he understands that Josiah was true, that he has succeeded in creating a breed that would survive in the Laguna. Josiah also reconnects Tayo to the feminine through Night Swan. It's when Tayo goes to deliver a message Josiah has sent for his Mexican girlfriend, Night Swan, that he coincidentally experiences man-woman love   93
by making love to Night Swan. *Josiah makes Tayo aware of*

the stories (emphasis mine). Once when Josiah finds Tayo killing flies, he tells him the story of the green bottlefly. In the story, the green bottlefly asks for forgiveness for the people from the mother of the people for their misbehavior and thus helps bring back rain. Josiah tells Tayo, *"Next time, just remember the story"* (102) (emphasis mine). As he progresses in his ceremony, Tayo's dreams about Josiah change. His guilt gives way to a feeling of love. He once more finds Josiah:

> Josiah and Rocky were not far away. They were close; they had always been close. And he loved them then as he had always loved them, the feeling pulsing over him as strong as it had ever been. They loved him that way; he could still feel the love they had for him (220).

The Native Indian stories do not function in a vacuum, nor do they revel in the description of the mere mundane surroundings. There is always a morale embedded in it. The stories are often loaded with a strong sense of ethics, moral principles. If the alienated, broken-hearted Tayo comes round, it is because of the strong moral oeuvre which is created by Josiah's stories. Josiah is already dead when the novel starts. But it is in his absent presence that Tayo is cured. It is in remembering Josiah's stories that Tayo's problems are solved and his sickness healed. It's in Josiah's teachings that Tayo learns the traditions and rituals of the land, respect for community and all beings of the universe and responsibility for stories. Josiah shows Tayo what it takes to be a Laguna man, living with tradition, respecting the feminine, seeing the cyclicality of the universe, understanding the whole and believing in stories. Even though physically dead, Josiah is very much alive in Tayo's "blood memory" and in his recollection of the stories. Josiah, like the stories, lives on because he "understood the importance of the conjunction between the right place and the right time," observes Elaine Jahner (Jahner 243). Tayo lives on with "Josiah's smell" (32) and with the satisfaction of having been loved "with all the love there was" (32).

The witchery story told to Tayo by Betonie also contributes to Tayo's gaining of an insight to the contemporary problem of the Native peoples through an understanding of a past story. Contrary to the usual Native perception of the whites as the destroyers of the Native worlds, Betonie creates a parallel discourse by suggesting that "That is the trickery of the witchcraft" (132). He starts talking about an earlier, mythical time when the white people were not yet born and there was a world conference of witches where the witches were contesting with each other over their witchery. Writing in the folklorist tradition of a prose-poem, Silko tells us:

> They all got together for a contest
> the way people have baseball tournament nowadays
> except this was a contest
> in dark things (133).

As the witches continue with the demonstration of their deadly charms and ugly rituals, there is this one witch who "stood in the shadows beyond the fire" (134) and "no one ever knew where this witch came from" (134). No one knew the tribe or gender of that witch. And this mysterious witch had a story:

> This one just told them to listen:
> "What I have is a story" (135).

Unconvinced, the other witches started laughing. Upon this the witch with the story warned:

> *Okay*
> *go ahead*
> *laugh if you want to*
> *but as I tell the story*
> *it will begin to happen* (135) (emphasis mine).

And the worst part is that as it is being told, it starts happening and there is no calling back.

The traditional Scalp ceremony doesn't cure Tayo because these ceremonies haven't changed from time immemorial. But the witches have changed their ceremonies and rituals and hence are growing in their wickedness. As Copeland points out:

> When denying Ku'oosh's power...Tayo is right —old
> time witches did not kill like that, but the Ku'oosh of
> Tayo's mind is also right: witches vital and alive, whose
> ceremonies have changed and adapted as Ku'oosh's have
> not, do kill like that." (Copeland 160).

95

If Tayo wants to cure himself and the drought stricken Laguna land, he must fight the witchery and turn it upon itself. It's the witchery that killed the Japanese. It's the witchery that kills the Indians. As these new witches have changed their ceremonies and rituals, they have also mutated their tools that would serve their witchery. Serving as the "tools of witchery" as both Betonie and Ts'eh tell Tayo, the whites are afraid of the world around and of themselves too. As the machinery of the witchery *"They destroy what they fear"* (emphasis original) (135). This results in the destruction of the world as well as of themselves. As they spread over the world they kill with objects "which can shoot death/faster than the eye can see" (136), thus bringing in corpses and blood for the witchery. They poison the water and spoil it away as a consequence of which drought and starvation engulf the land. The current drought that Tayo's land is going through, thus is a direct consequence of the witchery's story. As they have stolen the land and rivers and mountains, the witches have messed with the power and energy inherent in the rocks "with veins of green and yellow and black." Silko's allusion to the creation of the atomic bomb in Trinity Site of the Pueblos mountains is clear in the following lines: *"They will lay the final pattern with these rocks/they will lay it across the world/ and explode everything"* (emphasis original) (137).

At the end of this story of the witchery, Silko achieves two objectives. The first, by alluding to the "invention" of whites as a result of Indian witchery, she, in true postcolonial fashion, subverts the master narrative to create a counter narrative, simultaneously creating a new center, a Native American centre. By describing the whites as mere tools of witchery she further decentralizes the dominant discourse. The second objective Silko achieves at the end of the story is that by bringing in the concept of the atomic bomb that will "explode everything" (137), Silko moves from being concerned merely about the Native Americas to the globe as a whole. This, more than anything else, establishes the universality of *Ceremony.*

The witchery story, paradoxically, enlightens Tayo in a sense that he now understands the world and its "fragility" in a fuller perspective. He understands that his sickness has a link with it, that he is a victim; but he also knows that the Japanese and even the whites are victims of the witchery. He is ready to combat the witchery because he knows that it is the wrong story, "The lie" (191). And it was the witchery at work that with its lies "devoured the white hearts," because "If the white people never looked beyond the lie, to see that theirs was a nation built on stolen land, then they would never be able to

96

understand how they had been used by the witchery" (191). The witchery
story helps Tayo look beyond the binaries and understand this as a trick
the witchery plays against people, "the starving against the fat, the colored
against the white" (191), lies that would do nothing less than "destroy the
world" (192). Barbara Blair opines that the whites, alienated and fearful as
they were, became destroyers and thus served the cause of witchery rather
than harmony (Blair 60).

Silko warns us against a dichotomous, divisive worldview and
emphasizes the common destiny of all peoples which is threatened by the
destructive forces of the witchery such as the atom bomb and machine
guns. These tools of witchery do not discriminate when they are in a
killing spree nor do they bother about the skin color of their victims. As
Jeff Karem rightly points out:

> The fact that both whites and Natives are manipulated
> by witchery gives them *a common fate*, which obligates
> them to step outside their traditional cultural boundaries
> to fight the witchery together. In particular, Tayo
> recognizes that the global threat of nuclear destruction
> demands the cooperation of a common humanity
> (Karem 29) (emphasis original).

As Tayo develops "an eye for the story" and "an ear for the pattern"
(255), he understands that he, both personally as well as communally, has
the responsibility "to keep the story out of the reach of the destroyers"
(247). He knows that Betonie's wisdom and Ts'eh's love are guiding
him. He knows that the witchery is failing when "The snow was covering
everything, burying the Mountain lion's tracks and obliterating his scent"
(205) to protect "the mountain lion's tracks and all signs of the cattle
too" (205). He knows that his "protection was there in the sky," in the
position of the sun, in the pattern of stars" (247). He knows that he is
being cured because the "only cure is a good ceremony" (3). By refusing
to use violence, Tayo foils the witchery's plans, because "to combat evil
through violence is to succumb to it and be lost" (Benediktsson 129). Tayo,
empowered with the story, knows that he has to make the right choice if
his own life and his community's as well as the world are to continue. Lee
Schweninger comments thus: "Tayo's cure depends on his ability to learn
not to hate the destroyer, for in hating the destroyer, he too

97

becomes a destroyer" (Schweninger 55). As Emo, the witch leader, is killing Harley, Tayo has to choose life over death and continuity over destruction. To quote Karem:

> The decisive moment is Tayo's choice of *how* (emphasis original) to react to the death and whether to join in the violence himself, to accede to the cycle of destruction he has been observing around him throughout the novel. His refusal to kill Emo stands as a rejection of all resolutions rooted in violence, sacrificial or otherwise; he opts instead for a restorative path, returning the native cattle to the mountains and planting Ts'eh's seeds. Tayo's *inaction brings an end to the cycle of violence planned by the destroyers* (emphasis mine) (Karem 30).

But Silko doesn't want the readers to be so sure. She warns in the end of the book that the witchery is only dead for now" (261). By repeating the line four times in the manner of a chant, she emphasizes that the witchery *can and will return* (emphasis mine) (261).

The Native Indian storytelling tradition dismisses such premises from its stories which could create what Franz fanon calls as "Manechian delirium." The Native Indian cultural tradition itself is up against such thought. Emo's story which has been woven into the witchery story clearly focuses on this aspect. Emo too, like Tayo, is a World War II veteran who has come back to the reservation. Early on in the novel, it becomes evident that there has been a certain undercurrent of tension between him and Tayo since schooldays. But this is not the story of a school bully gone wrong. There is definitely something terribly wrong with Emo because in spite of being a Native himself, he does not mind insulting the Indian's Mother Earth as an "Old dried-up thing" (25). There's no ambiguity in the fact that Emo hates Tayo and his hatred is a manifestation of his dichotomous thinking. He hates Tayo and "the only reason for this hate was that Tayo was part white" (57). Silko, in a clever maneuver, takes Emo, the "drunk Indian" stereotype of the colonial mindset and presents him as the representative of the witchery. David Moore thus comments on Emo: "Silko sets the social construction of his [Tayo's] optional role as 'a drunk Indian war veteran' within a mythic construction of witchery, personified by Emo, which feeds on antinomies of colonial dynamics, of Indian hating white hating Indian" (Moore 386).

98

Emo is the *bete noire* of Tayo. He represents all that is opposite of creativity, growth, life and the feminine. Tayo seeks to restore kinship bonds. Emo kills two of his buddies. Tayo seeks to reject violence and plant Ts'eh's seeds. Emo's laughter comes out of violence and bloodshed. Tayo takes refuge in the Laguna spirituality. Emo seeks happiness through alcohol. Tayo heals through Ts'eh's love. Emo boasts of loveless gratification. Tayo, even though mixed blood, seeks unity and harmony for the land. Emo, even though full blood, fails to find his place in the community. In all this, Emo represents a loss of balance of the world "when the people of Laguna...neglected the mother corn altar" and began to participate in "C'koyo magic" (48), "in their acceptance of white values, in their hatred of whites, in the internal splits—within families, between mixed blood and full blood, tradition and assimilation—that divided them, in the mining of Uranium, and participation in a world war," observes Arnold (Arnold 78).

As opposed to Tayo's stories which are life giving and full of élan vital, Emo's stories are not only violent but also represent loss, betrayal, killing and destruction. By narrating his sexual escapades with white women during the war, he is in fact telling the witchery's story. And by using the mythical form of telling the story, he elevates it to the witchery's prayer. By twisting the tale, and attempting to change through the tale the beliefs and values of his community, Emo becomes one of the destroyers. The theme of his Gallup bar song is one of control and conquest, the much sought-after values among colonialists.

Like Tayo, Emo goes through his own ritual journey. But while Tayo's ceremony is determined and empowered by the creative forces of growth and regeneration such as the stars, wind, sun, moon and earth, Emo's journey is marked by dead bodies and corpses, war, mutilation, the atom bomb and such like. Whereas Tayo "learns to move across dualities, choosing to merge or withdraw, to defend or to dissolve boundaries" (Arnold 81), Emo's witchery depends on creating boundaries, dividing feelings and replacing "the *content* of the stories" (emphasis original) (Cutchins 85). Emo and the likes of Emo thrive on violence and destruction. They derive all their power from it.

As the master of the witchery's ceremonies, Emo tells the stories; he also performs the witchery's rituals. His one point programme is spreading hatred, as fast and wide as possible. But he does not stop there. He must *convert* others to this witchery too (emphasis mine). And in order to do that he showcases the rituals of the witchery.   99
Unlike the Indian medicine men whose paraphernalia for

the traditional ceremonies included, apart from other things, plants and herbs and sand paintings, Emo's paraphernalia for the witchery's rituals are ghastly. The witchery's ritual kicks off with the tossing off of human teeth collected from dead enemies like dice. The witchery's final ritual, as prophesized by the mysterious witch (137) lies with a "final pattern" (137) in which they would lay the "beautiful rocks" in a "monstrous design" (246) to "explode everything" (137).

Right on the centre of the mine shaft, the witchery's final ceremony takes place. Tayo, now armed with stories can hear "the sound of witchery" (250). He witnesses Emo, the master witch and Leroy and Pinkie, the converts, killing Harley. Tayo's ceremonial healing has brought him new knowledge and he knows through the stories that Emo turned upon the witchery on Harley because Harley failed to procure Tayo for the ritual. But the destroyers won't accept defeat so easily. Tayo comprehends "either way they had a victim and a corpse" (251). As Pinkie holds Harley's legs and Leroy cuts the whorl from the bottom of his big toe, a part of the witchery's ritual is observed:

Whorls of skin
Cut from fingertips (C134).

Bennani and Bennani look at this as a "castration ritual":

Emo...has not only shown an abusive attitude towards women, but has also given himself a new identity as a witch. Part of the final witching ceremony which was intended for Tayo and then turned on Harley who had been designated to lure Tayo to the witches' snare is a castration ritual. Before the "destroyers", as the witches are called, take their corpse, they remove whorls of flesh from significant parts of the body that provide identity. Including on their list is, of course, fingertips and genitals (Bennani and Bennani 254).

But for the story to continue, for life to continue, Tayo, as the Laguna culture hero, must avoid violence, the weapon of the witches. Emo is the manifestation of the evil witchery. Though in a sense Emo is a victim of the mechanized culture of contemporary America, he is already

possessed by the witchery and hence must be abandoned.

Tayo's ultimate redemption depends on the rich moral ground in which he has been continually nurtured and nourished. If he is cured, it is because he gathers the seeds from which "plants would grow there like the story" (254). Emo is thrown off the reservation with a warning to *never come back* (emphasis mine), as the witchery "has returned upon it" (261). The witchery "has returned to its belly" and "stiffened." But Silko carefully avoids the word "destroy." The witchery has not been destroyed. It has only been kept close. But the witchery's weapon, Emo, by having been sent off the reservation, has been *let loose* (emphasis mine). The witchery is temporarily dead, as long as Tayo and others don't forget, as long as they tell the right stories and act accordingly, as long as they live with love and reject hatred.

An integral element of Tayo's story is his cousin Rocky. Rocky is Auntie's son and in the matrilineal Laguna tradition, Tayo's brother, though he has been denied that bond by Auntie. Tayo returns guilt-stricken from the war because in spite of his best efforts, Rocky has died in the war and Tayo has failed in his promise to Auntie of bringing Rocky back home safe. In Tayo's stories, Rocky was a hero, "the best football player Albuquerque Indian School ever had" (44). Rocky's death shatters Tayo, because he had never planned "to go any farther than Rocky went" (44). Tayo is convinced Rocky's death was an accident of time and space. He was not supposed to die. Moreover Rocky lived in the stories that surrounded him-the best footballs star, the much wanted son of the family, the full blood dream; Tayo felt that it was he who was actually dead because he never featured in the stories. It was with a hope to save Rocky from the clutches of death that Tayo prays the rain away in the jungles of Philippines, as a consequence of which, he believes, the Laguna Land is facing its worst drought ever. If Rocky did not survive in the story, it is because he never believed in the rich storytelling tradition of the Laguna. He was halfhearted about the efficiency of his own tradition. In the dominant discourse, Rocky had all that was required to make a success (emphasis mine) of him:

> "He was an A-student and all-state in football and track.
> He had to win; *he said he was always going to win*
> (emphasis mine) (51).

But Rocky died because in spite of being a full-blood Native, he rejected the tradition he came from. He attempted to imbibe the values and ways of an alien culture that didn't have provisions   101
for the Native understanding of the world. He died because

in running after white ideals of success and happiness, in dreaming of getting assimilated into the white world, he lost the fuller worldview and belonged to neither. In that sense Rocky was the real half-breed, struck in no man's land. The witchery that works to make people feel ashamed of themselves and their kin people makes Rocky discard the old ways of life, rituals and ceremonies included. Rocky fails and dies because he becomes a victim of this witchery. Rocky, Concannon observes, "both before and during the war-moves away from Native American ritual, while working to reason out the differences between 'us' and 'them'" (Concannon 186).

Rocky's ultimate failure lies in the fact that he did not believe in the grain of the storytelling tradition of the Natives. Rocky wanted to be like a white man; He wanted to be the voice of reason. Even when Tayo, due to his inherent understanding of the blurring of boundaries, would see the face of Josiah in the Japanese soldier, Rocky wanted to reason it out. Contrary to Tayo's faith in Josiah's stories, Rocky adamantly refuses Josiah's teaching and unlearns the Laguna stories. This is proven in Rocky's being ashamed of the deer ritual and later again in his rejection of Josiah's vision for a hybrid cattle; while Tayo and Robert laugh with Josiah at his suggestion that they should go with their "own way" (emphasis mine) (75) of cattle raising, Rocky keeps quiet and puts an argument in favor of the knowledge of the dominant discourse, irrespective of however inappropriate it might have been from a Native perspective. It is through the stories of Old Grandma that Tayo learns many a lessons of life. But Rocky disregards Grandma's stories too. Rocky fails to make his own stories because he believes too much in the Other's stories and in doing so, violates and rejects the stories of his own land and people.

There is, however, no sibling rivalry between Tayo and Rocky owing to their different value and belief systems. In fact, Tayo is proud of Rocky. There is one example of this when Emo taunts Tayo about Rocky's achievements in school:

> "'You think you're hot shit, like your cousin. Big football star. Big hero.' ... Tayo thought of Rocky then, and he was proud that Emo was so envious" (60).

By withdrawing from his own people "naturally, like a rabbit leaping away from a shadow suddenly above him" (67), Rocky gets lost. By evading his own tradition and trying to adapt to a new one, 102 Rocky falters his story. By taking his learning from the Indian school too seriously, Rocky unlearns his family's and his community's stories from both past and present. By being excited "about the war and joining the army" (91) even before he gets drafted, Rocky crosses the ultimate line- he starts believing in the violent stories of the witchery and hence is consumed by it. Drawing a contrast between Tayo and Rocky, Kenneth Lincoln observes:

> In *Ceremony* the blood "cousin-brother," Rocky, killed in the war, and the returning mixed-breed, Tayo, reenact a contemporary variant of old twin myths, reasserting the need for idiosyncratic pairing: a full-blood who imitates and dies for whites, a half-breed who gaps the two, accepted in neither, surviving (Lincoln 236).

At this stage, the juxtaposition of Tayo and Rocky will throw light on the truth of the Native Indian storytelling tradition. Tayo cures as he wakes up to the stories, the stories of ritual regeneration. Rocky dies because he sides with the stories of violence and destruction. But Tayo has never hated Rocky. He could not afford to– because he had to reject the binary view of the world Rocky had succumbed to and rejoice in the living and changing tradition. It is with Rocky's calling him "brother" (65) that Tayo's problems start and it is with Rocky's calling him "my brother" (254) that Tayo is ultimately cured. Rocky, in spite of his full-blood lineage is not able to survive; And Tayo in spite of, or perhaps because of his hybrid identity, is able to make his own story and survive. As Barbara Blair rightly observes, "Thus, it may be in the people with mixed blood the hope for survival of Indian cultural identity lies, since they are often in the forefront of change, and it is through change that tradition survives" (Blair 61-62).

But Rocky's mother, Aunt Thelma had been proud of her son because of her belief in the white man's religion and its ways. Auntie, like Rocky, lives in denial of the old ways of the land. She, like many Native peoples colonized in their mindscapes, is ashamed of her family and even more of her half-breed nephew. In fact, Tayo's own sense of shame and guilt at his hybridity largely stems from Auntie's dealings with him. In spite of him being her sister's son, Tayo is never accepted in Auntie's scheme of things. When Tayo comes back from the war alone, with Rocky dead in the jungles of Philippines, Auntie stiffens up even more and makes him re-live the shame. Cutchins points out:

103

> Although Tayo is allowed to return to Laguna, fitting in a
> matrilineal society, he is never allowed to forget his status
> as an outsider...

Not only does Auntie not "conceal" the details of Tayo's birth, she makes sure, at every opportunity, to use this knowledge to perpetuate Tayo's status as an outsider. He is well aware that as far as his aunt is concerned, he will never be genuine Indian. (Cutchins 79)

When Rocky starts showing the first signs of colonization by avoiding "the old-time ways" (51), Auntie is the only one to support him. In that sense, she too becomes a believer in the witchery's stories. By helping Rocky in rejecting his Native tradition, she contributes to his ultimate destruction. It is her dream of becoming like the white people that costs Auntie her son; by living up to the stereotype, Auntie plays to the tunes of the witchery. Auntie is not at peace with herself because of her faith in the wrong stories, in the stories of divisiveness and separation, in the stories of what she understands to be shame, in believing in the binary vision of the world propagated by the witchery, by keeping a distance between two brothers, by remembering and recalling the wrong story:

> 'They're not brothers,' 'she'd say, 'that's Laura's boy. You
> know the one'. She had a way of saying it, a tone of voice
> which bitterly told the story, and the disgrace she and the
> family had suffered (65).

Alienated from her own tradition, she seeks to attain a status and identity in her new community, the church, and thus perpetuates hatred for her own kin, which, at close examination, reveals itself as self-hatred. To manifest her self-avowed Christianity, it becomes essential to manifest her burdens (emphasis mine). She makes a deliberate attempt to show that Tayo is a burden: "She needed a new struggle, another opportunity to show those who might gossip that she had still another unfortunate burden which proved that, above all else, she was a Christian woman" (30). In the Laguna universe, the corn mother "loved and cared for them as her children, as her family" (68). On the contrary, Auntie's Christianity "separated the people from themselves; it tried to crush the single clan name, encouraging each person to stand alone, because Jesus Christ would save only the individual soul" (68). Thus Auntie's Christianity is "More corrosive than the war" (Wiget 86).

Being on the side of destroyers, Auntie fails to understand the manifestation of Thought Woman in Night Swan, Josiah's Mexican girlfriend. Under the spell of the witchery, she remembers the wrong story, a story of violence and death as she discusses Josiah's affair with Night Swan. She is not convinced about the cattle Night Swan advocated either. By recalling the wrong stories, Auntie fails to recognize the importance of Night Swan in Josiah's and Tayo's stories and hence her significance in the larger family story.

In spite of it all, Auntie lives on in the novel because she shows signs of change. As Tayo comes towards the end of his personal ceremony, Auntie attempts to accept him as one of their own. And it's Auntie's acceptance of him as a family member at last that completes Tayo's ceremony. He is back to health and family when Auntie starts speaking to him without reserve: "Auntie talked to him the way she had talked to Robert and Old Grandma all those years, with an edge of accusation about to surface between her words" (259). Even though she still nourishes the binary vision of the world, as is evident from her happiness at Pinkie's death, she now seems more ready to accept the mixed-blood Tayo's experiences in the family and community sphere.

In the Laguna world, Grandmothers enjoy a status of respect and reverence. Silko herself has many a time acknowledged her great-grandmother's influence on her childhood and her storytelling abilities. Like Silko's, Tayo's grandmother too is a storyteller, and a keeper of traditions. Edith Swan points out:

> In *Ceremony* Grandma is traditional, bearing her Laguna heritage with pride. She exemplifies a generation that adheres to native teachings, respects the wisdom and status of the elders, and honors the way it has always been. She is convinced of the dignity and effacious nature of tribal methods of curing and sanity-precepts undergirding her insistence that medicine men (Ku'oosh and Betonie) treat her grandson Tayo.... Grandma embodies the traditional Laguna ethos in counterpoint to the bicultural entrapment in which Auntie struggles (Swan 313).

Pained by Tayo's suffering, Grandma insists on a healing ceremony for Tayo because with her wisdom she knows that white medicine is toxic for Tayo. Fiercely protective of her family and the well being of her family members, Grandma, unlike Auntie, dismisses people's opinion about her family. When Auntie tries to reject the idea of a ceremony for Tayo, thus almost pushing him to a slow death, Grandma persists on it; she says: "He's my grandson. If I send for old Ku'oosh, he'll come. Let them talk if they want to. Why do you care what they say?" (33-34).

Moreover, as Grandmother and the matrilineal head of the family, she teaches the importance of up keeping of rituals and ceremonies to her grandsons. She performs the ritual of the deer in the family so that her descendants would imbibe and maintain the practice. When Rocky starts rejecting the traditions of the Laguna, Grandma shows her concern by disapproving his alien ways. Old Grandma shows her contempt for Christianity in her disapproval of Auntie's church visits. Like the people of her generation, she too, believes in the power of stories. For her, all that matters is the story. Stories can serve as weapons, according to Grandma:

> Grandma didn't care what anyone said. She liked to sit by her stove and gossip about the people who were talking about their family ... The story was all that counted. If she had a better one about them, then it didn't matter what they said (89).

It's only in one of Grandmother's stories, an experience narrated to him, that Tayo comes to understand the pattern, the story of the witchery. It is in her narration that Tayo finds a clue to the making of his own story. She relates her witnessing a false sunrise, the witchery's sunrise, which helps Tayo come to the end of his ceremony and get the whole picture. It's in seeking an answer to this question of Grandma's that Tayo comes to understand the connection between the Japanese and the Laguna, the atom bomb, the weapons of the witchery and it is in defeating this witchery that Tayo is eventually cured. The stories to the people of Laguna are not something abstract but something very concrete, having the power to heal the suffering.

Keeping with the importance of Grandmothers in the Laguna tradition, *Ceremony* closes with grandma's comment on the stories. She claims that the goings-on around Laguna don't excite her anymore: "It seems like I already heard these stories before ... only thing, is, the names sound different" (260). Old Grandma thus is representative of the traditional wisdom of the Native elders on one hand and a fading away of this very wisdom and a resistance, albeit feeble,

106

to change according to the needs of time. In comparing her to the old and blind gray mule (27), Silko metaphorically refers to the two planes on which Grandma exists. As he dreams of Grandma, (254) Tayo comes home.

Like the mythical spider woman, Silko thus very efficiently builds up webs of stories and layers of meaning. A juxtaposition of the Native American orality and western narrative practices define the style of Silko's *Ceremony*. To quote Arnold Krupat: "...to begin with visions, dreams, prophecy, and the granting of special powers seems consistent with what we know of Native American narrative modes" (Krupat 153).

In *Ceremony* we come across visions (of Betonie, Tayo, Ts'eh, Grandmother), dreams (Tayo's), prophecy (the witchery's as well as Betonie's grandmother's), granting of special powers (to Sun-Man, Tayo, Betonie's grandparents) and even more (clan stories, Laguna myths to quote a few). But Silko's gift lies in expanding these modes of the Native American narrative techniques in order to interfuse these with the western form of novel writing in a realistic manner. Continually emphasizing the boundarylessness of all things in the universe, Silko cleverly blurs the boundaries between Native traditions and western literary practices. By negotiating the gaps between two essentially powerful discourses, Silko succeeds in creating a novel that is mixed breed like herself in its physicality and truly Native in spirit, thus constructing a work of postcolonial, postmodern relativity. As David Moore rightly points out:

> To elude the dialectical subjection of colonial subjectivity, which would merely mirror the oppression, postcolonial agents must find what I will call a relational rather than oppositional concept of identity. 'Relational' suggest a multiplicity rather than a duality of directions for subjectivity. A postcolonial task of native discourse becomes then a redefining of the multiple possibilities of the subject to elude subjection to dualistic, self-other ideas of subjectivity (Moore 373).

Writing thus from a postcolonial space, Silko defies conventions and dismisses the cry for authenticity. As one can see, her stories, even the mythical stories are not unadulterated Laguna myths; rather they are appropriated to the contemporary postcolonial perspective as and when required. Silko is not to fool herself with the traditionalists who advocate that Native cultures can be maintained by   107 disassociating themselves from the changes brought forth in the postcolonial era. In that sense, Silko's stories are actually authentic and contextual.

This is suggestive of the fact that while Silko makes ample use of her Laguna sources, she does not limit her stories to the Native idea of cosmology. And the clan stories that she uses like that of the Reed woman and corn woman, the arrow boy, the Bear-child, the Kau'pa'ta gambler etc. add to the mythicality of the novel. These stories while occurring in mythical space and time, simultaneously affect the realist story of Tayo's in the novel. It's when Tayo's story merges into the Laguna story that the wholeness of the novel is achieved. Benediksson observes:

> The stories inscribe and circumscribe Tayo's own story, until the ceremonies by which he is healed serve a kind of hermeneutic: he can read his own life as a Pueblo story. Just as the limited claims of realism have become subsumed into the much greater claims of Pueblo storytelling tradition, Silko's role as novelist has been subsumed into the role of the Pueblo storyteller —naming the world, defending the people, helping fight off illness and death. In the process, the linear flow of meaning that dominates mimetic representation has been supplanted by a kind of 'Spider web' of meaning in which the interrelationships among the stories revise time and space, just as Thought Woman tells her stories in a timeless realm (Benediktsson 125).

Silko contrasts these mythical stories of life, fertility and sunrise, pollen and water with what Wiget calls the "antimyth" of the witchery story (Wiget 85), symbolized by death, destruction, sub-human sexuality, uranium and alcohol. Interestingly, Silko uses similar patterns of mythical telling for presenting both stories. By describing the "good" and "bad" stories in the same pattern, Silko again demonstrates the liminality of her very telling of the stories. By "structurally reflecting the mythic dimensions of even quotidian events in the narrative as equally part of the mythic song," Silko, David Moore observes, breaks the "boundaries of sacred and profane" (Moore 377). Moreover, by using a prose-poetry interface in the text, Silko fuses myth and reality to a point where they acquire a quality like that of human memory. To achieve this objective, instead of using a singular, authoritative narrative

108

voice, Silko uses a multiplicity of voices to tell her stories. Thus, she is able to represent multiple points of view and a plurality of voices adds to the authenticity of the text. In true postmodernist tradition, Silko sublimes a singular authority in favor of a pluralistic, multivocal discourse.

While Silko unhesitatingly uses Native lore and myths to tell the story of her land, she does not see it as inappropriate to use the colonizer's language for appropriating Native stories. Silko, like Tayo, thus sees the interconnectedness of all things and truly believes in the wholeness of the universe. To quote Konrad Gross: "Instead of falling into the trap of separation, she invites her white readers to follow her into the world of native consciousness and to encounter the other culture from within" (Gross 580). In the Laguna, as in the Native America, stories construct and reconstruct identities, bridge the gap between past and present, establish rituals and ceremonies and thus function as the lifeblood of the Native peoples. Silko, in *Ceremony*, uses the stories for reconstructing Tayo's personal and communal identity, for building connections between the mythical and the real, for helping Tayo as well as Betonie create and practice new ceremonies. In that sense, *Ceremony* is a truly Native Tale.

Time, in Silko's *Ceremony*, like the story itself, does not progress in a linear fashion; This is so because in the Laguna universe, as in Native American worldview elsewhere, all times are simultaneously present and things happen concurrently in different planes and different times. Traditional storytellers in the Laguna often move from past to present and vice versa without creating any definite boundaries. Silko again blurs the dual notions of time, as it occurs in Native American and western practices and uses these according to the advantage her storytelling. Allen thus comments on Silko's use of time:

> She makes several references to industrial notions of time, notably in the collection of calendars amassed by the maverick healer Betonie. One time referent she takes is galactic: the placement of stars is the basis of what time it is. The other ceremonial: it is time for the witchery to be undone. The role of the protagonist Tayo is to behave in proper ritual manner, and to this end he loses his mechanical time sense in the void, his mechanical space sense in the Philippines, and his sense of his identity as isolated in his movement within the mountain and within the ceremony he must exact (Allen 152).

109

Silko, thus, like a truly Native storyteller, believes in the power of stories. She represents the idea that stories can heal, instruct and help create an identity to survive. By rejecting oppositional mindsets and a binary vision of the world, Silko also becomes global in her stories. By advocating change in ceremonies and in the telling of stories, she foregrounds the essential strategies for survival in a postcolonial era. By emphasizing on the communal, Silko underlines the importance of a social identity for a healthy personal story. By blurring the boundaries of time, space and stories, Silko thus emerges as a truly postcolonial writer who can "speak for both sides."

Chapter IV:
Confronting the Tradition:
Thomas King's *Green Grass, Running Water*

The postcolonial paradigm has justifiably created a voice for the hitherto voiceless and the cultural productions originating from these new voices have often taken up the postmodernist stance of questioning established moulds and thus raised doubts about the apparently valid and 'legitimate' versions of history and tradition. The cannibalization of the Natives of the world has resulted in the production of a canon the authenticity of which is being questioned in the current postmodern atmosphere. Writing with a purpose to right the wrongs of the past, Native writers have worked towards creating a space wherefrom they can define and represent their own identities and communities. Towards that cause, it has become increasingly essential for them to dismantle the so-called canon and rewrite the rules of representation. In keeping with the postmodern nuance of questioning stereotypes and marked givens, Native writers of Canada have deconstructed and reconstructed the mainstream perceptions. This chapter shall deal with Thomas King's second novel *Green Grass, Running Water* from a postcolonial, poststructural, postmodernist point of view in order to find out the authorial confrontation with the canonical tradition and to underscore what Sylvia Söderlind has termed as the "discourse of marginality" (Söderlind 3). This chapter shall examine how King's novel as a postmodern text opens the field for contextual narratives that depict multiple realities and multiple histories and thus subverts the singular orientations of the earlier constructed discourses. It shall look into King's use of subversion and comic imagination at a textual level that changes the dynamics of the dominant discourse and thus assures identity and representation of a Native discourse. It will also highlight the various postmodernist devices inside a Native text for confronting held notions and traditions.

I

The Native writers of Canada, writing from a postcolonial, poststructural, postmodern perception of the world have taken up the issues of identity, history, and representation   111 through a revision of the hegemonic discourses. Rejecting the monolithic and homogenizing representations of the past has been a practice of the postcolonial literary productions and in that sense, the Native writers have confronted the traditions of the past. Canonical texts have narrativized points of view that have completely eroded, wiped out, and negated Native worldviews, experiences, and even histories. As Julie Cruickshank rightly points out:

> The writing of history has always involved collecting, analyzing, and retelling stories about the past, yet the very act of collection means that some stories are enshrined in books while others remain marginalized (Cruickshank 4).

Thomas King's fiction seeks to bring forth these stories from the margin to the forefront. Counted as one of the most vibrant and prominent Native authors of the contemporary era, King was born in 1943 in Sacramento, California to a Cherokee Indian father and a German American mother. Presently working as a Professor in the Department of Creative Writing at University of Guelph (New 577), King's first novel *Medicine River* appeared in 1989. This novel deals with Will, a Blackfoot photographer from Toronto and his journey towards his own identity. Thematically and stylistically *Medicine River* falls into the category of postmodernist fiction as is evident from King's use of subversive humor, parody, and a distinct dialogic writing in the text. As W.H. New rightly remarks: "King's deadpan HUMOUR, his portrayal of his character's daily life, and his deft handling of dialogue become hallmarks of his distinctive style" (New 578).

King's brilliant short story "A Coyote Columbus Story" (1992) deals with the tricksterish persona of Coyote and subverts the myth of the "discovery" of Americas by Christopher Columbus. This story was nominated for the Governor General's Award in 1992. King's other works include *All My Relations: An Anthology of Short Fiction* by Native Writers in Canada, a series of comic 1990's Radio Script called The Dead Dog Café, an anecdotal novel entitled *Truth and Bright Water* (1990) and *Dreadful Water Shows Up* (2002). *Green Grass, Running Water* appeared in 1993 and won King a nomination for the Governor General's Award.

King's fiction is often driven by an intelligent mixture of Native narrative style, orality, a foregrounding of tribal traditions with the postmodernist craft of parody, subversion, intertextuality, self-reflexivity and such like. As in his other textual productions,

112

in *Green Grass, Running Water* too, there is a fusion of Native traditions with the postmodern tools of fiction. As Robin Riley Fast rightly points out:

> *GGRW* challenges readers in numerous, related ways: shifts in narrative voice, perspective, and setting; parodies of sacred Western texts, historical narratives, and ideologies; unexplained intersections of story worlds; a relentless barrage of proper names... (Fast 42).

The section that follows will vividly look into the aforementioned perspectives of *Green Grass, Running Water* and attempt to study the significance of such practices for the cause of confronting the canonical traditions.

II

Speaking from a space that raises hopes for assertion of identities, recognition of marginalities, and a re-making of a Nation through cultural differences, Native writers of Canada, like those of the United States, have confronted the dominant "traditions" in order to rewrite their own narratives and reclaim their rightful place in the scheme of the "Nation." Rejecting the Western hegemonic and homogenizing notions of history and tradition, and redefining held notions of texts, images and forms, the Native writings of Canada have twisted the previous constructs and thus influenced the postcolonial world where the earlier perceptions of the world stand nullified and startled, driving readers and critics to modify their understanding of the present as well as the past. As Darias-Beautell aptly points out:

> Due to the postcolonial we feel the presence of the Other, no longer Out There, but Here, at Home. Suddenly we are forced to rethink old categories of identity, culture, and nation (Darias-Beautell 119).

The western imperial authority has in the past invented, innovated, circumscribed, doctored, and as a whole constructed the image of the other as per its own convenience and requirement, so as to exercise power through the construction of knowledge. As has been pointed out by critics ranging from Aimé Césaire to Homi Bhaba,   113 the western practice of "Othering" has often been a direct offshoot of their own imperial agenda that demanded justification of the colonization of an-other people by inferiorizing and demonizing them. In such a scenario, visual and textual representations of the Natives have been as far-flung and away from "truth" as they could have been. Hence Bhaba rightly observes that the so-called "necessary fictions" created under the aegis of the hegemonic writers "tragically believed too much in their necessity and too little in their own fictionality" (Bhaba 97).

To effectuate an accurate representation of their peoples, their traditions, their histories and their worldview, Native writers of the United States and Canada have drawn largely from the postmodernist tools of parody, irony, metafiction, self-reflexivity, subversion and mimicry to name a few. By problematizing the hegemonic discourse and reappropriating their own multiple discourses, Native writers have opened, as Thomas King would tell us, "a whole can of worms... a pretty nasty can of worms" (Lutz 108). Retelling of the stories of the past as well as present and rewriting of history of the Native world has given rise to a re-presentation of the aboriginal peoples of the land. Writing from a site of resistance and political and cultural appropriation, contemporary Native writers of Canada have come up with the production of an alternative discourse. Addressing the issue of "postcolonial" in Canada, Linda Hutcheon thus rightly argues that "when Canadian culture is called post-colonial today, the reference is very rarely (at least explicitly) to the native culture, which might be the more accurate historical use of the term" (Vautier 7).

In this chapter, the focus shall be on Thomas King's use of contextual narration, inter-textuality, trickster discourse, subversive humor, rewriting of identity, religion and history, the debunking of stereotypes, characterizations, narrative styles and forms in order to establish that King's *Green Grass, Running Water* (henceforth *GGRW*) is a writing that confronts and thus dares to challenge held notions and traditions.

GGRW decenters the master narratives and foregrounds the Othered discourse. In the context of Canada, the Other has been constructed in the negated presence of the indigene. The indigene comes to stand for all that the white Canadian "cannot be." Continually constructed and fabricated by an-Other discourse, the Natives of Canada have been simultaneously represented and also categorically discarded in the dominant discourse. The Native writers consciously use the indigenous tradition in order to show its difference from the white tradition. At the same time, they subvert the white tradition. Hence, Percy Walton aptly observes "...for s/he (the Native)

114

functions only as Other ... Native presence is an absence which highlights the white cultural norm because it is different. The Native is both a part of the signifying system, and forever excluded from it" (Walton 78).

Altering this binary discourse is the major agenda of *GGRW*. King's parody of the canonical literature, literary theory, popular culture and his subsequent retelling of the Native history and traditions create the space for an ardently dialogical discourse which discards the apparent superiority of the hegemonic discourse over the alter/Native discourse. *GGRW* gives us an opportunity to understand the possibility of the presence of multiple histories, multiple truths and hence multiple discourses. Juxtaposing two different discourses, the white and the Native, one dominant and the other marginalized, King's *GGRW* manipulates language, narrative and representation so as to generate a tension and confrontation between two warring discourses. King's game starts with the very title of the book. As King alludes to the title inside the text, we come to know that the title stands for the abnegations the Natives have been historically subjected to through the so-called treaties and oft-broken promises of the colonizers and something that continues till date. One character in *GGRW* tells us:

> As long as the grass is green and the waters run. It was a nice phrase, all right. But it didn't mean anything. It was a metaphor ... Every Indian on the reserve knew that Treaties were hardly sacred documents. They were contracts, and no one signed a contract for eternity (257).

GGRW is replete with language games and King's abundant references to texts, historical figures, literary figures, popular culture, images from the past and present, media and such like foreground the postmodernist intertextual quality of the book. Derived from the Bakhtinian concept of dialogism that refers to the fusion and intersection of two voices in a discourse, intertextuality has been termed by Julia Kristeva as "the result of the intersection of a number of voices, [and] of a number of textual interventions" (Rohrbacher np). King's use of intertextuality in *GGRW* is meant to poke fun at the 'fictionality' of all 'truths' and vice versa. In *GGRW*, everyone from Pauline Johnson to John Wayne to Salman Rushdie show up, but not merely to add to the theatricality of the text. Contrary to Ihab Hassan's differentiation of modernism/postmodernism in the binarisms of purpose/

play (Hassan 91-92), King's intertextuality is not only playful and self-reflexive but also purposeful. As King himself puts it in an interview with Jeffrey Canton:

> I picked those characters quite carefully- Jeannette MacDonald and Nelson Eddy, E. Pauline Johnson. And in addition to their power as entities within history, within film and literature, they also blur the line between reality and fiction and between what we think of as history and just gossip- between Indian and non-Indian. I love doing that-putting the reader on the skids. Especially if I can get them to go along with it (Canton 100).

Thais Morgan in his essay "The Space of Intertextuality" observes that "an intertextual citation is never innocent or direct, but always transformed, distorted, displaced, condensed, or edited in some way in order to suit the speaking subject's value system" (Morgan 280). *GGRW* having been written by King, a mixed-blood Cherokee, hence speaks from the Native point of view. As a result of this, we find Tom and Gerry, literally cartoon characters appear as two security guards in the text (63) and the two policemen accompanying Lionel to jail are Chip and Dale, cartoon characters again. Such instances are abundant in the text. By appropriating the dominant discourse through parodic intertextuality, King's *GGRW* resists the hegemonic force through a retelling of stories, from both discourses and thus creates, as Donaldson puts it, a "contestatory intertextuality," which brings in "a subversive reordering of relations in the dominant fields of imperialist, capitalist and masculinist power" (Donaldson 40).

Rejecting the notion of an all powerful theory or an all powerful discourse, King thus goes on to produce meaning and knowledge through a rethinking of the tradition and all that is assorted to it. Oral storytelling, literature, reality, movies-all interfuse and thus create a zigzag narrative that conforms to none and unsettles all, in the process transforming the text and all that is beyond the text, adequately satisfying Kristeva's notion of intertextuality that says "... any text is constructed as a mosaic of quotations; any text is the absorption and transformation of another" (Darias-Beautell 86). King's namedropping in *GGRW* does not merely complicate the challenge for the reader but within each name is enscored a narrative, a telling, and a story.

Three texts that resonate in the narrative of *GGRW* are Herman Melville's novella *Benito Cereno* and his epic *Moby-Dick* and Timothy Findley's 1985 novel *Not Wanted on the Voyage*. There are allusions to other texts too like Susanna Moodie's *Roughing it in the Bush* (1852), James Fenimore Cooper's *Leather Stocking Saga* (1826-1841), Daniel Defoe's *Robinson Crusoe* (1719) to name a few. However, King's treatment of Melville and Findley's texts explicitly influences the narrative both directly and indirectly and in King's radical retelling of these stories he furthers his confrontation with tradition. King's deliberate tampering of the stories of the now canonical Melville undermines held notions of the written word as everlasting and unchangeable. Almost as soon as the narrative unfolds, we come to know about the disappearance of four 'old' Indians from the asylum of Dr. Joseph Hovaugh (Jehovah) and we come across one Sergeant Cereno investigating the case. He has, along with him, his patrolman Jimmy Delano. Allusion to Melville's novella *Benito Cereno* is complete with the presence of Babo Jones, the African-American cleaning woman in Hovaugh's institution whose "great-great grandfather was a barber on a ship" (92). Melville's *Benito Cereno* is set in 1799 and narrates the story of a successful slave revolt led by Babo, the barber slave, his overpowering of Benito Cereno, the captain of the ship and a subsequent crushing of the rebellion by Amansa Delano, a Massachusetts sea captain who takes control of the ship and kills Babo, thus establishing white supremacy. Babo's rejection of the "slave" identity imposed upon them by the dominant discourse is in direct confrontation with the authoritative power:

> "Your ancestors were slaves, were they not?" said Dr. Hovaugh.
> "Nope," said Babo. "But some of my folks were enslaved."
> "Ah," said Dr. Hovaugh.
> "There's a difference," said Babo.
> "Of course," said Dr.Hovaugh (314).

Subverting this story within its own narrative, *GGRW* portrays a comical Cereno and an inconsequential Delano along with a knowledgeable Babo. As Robin Ridington points out:

King's Babo recalls the role played by Melville's Babo, but with a coyote twist. Melville's Babo was a black slave who overthrew his master; King's Babo is a black woman who knows more than her master, the godlike Dr. J. Hovaugh" (Ridington 351).

King's allusion to Melville's *Moby Dick* is evidently manifested in his narration of the magical, mythical narrative of Changing Woman. Changing Woman is there in an island and not much later she is swimming to a ship named Pequod, the captain of which is Ahab. Melville's famous opening line is alluded to when the captain of the ship tells "Call me Ishmael" (195). "Ishmael" tells Changing Woman that theirs is a "whaling ship" and their job is to "catch the whales" and "kill them" (195). In a postmodernist play of intertextuality, King debunks Melville's legendary story of *Moby-Dick*, the great male white whale and subverts it with the creation of a new legend that of *Moby-Jane*, a female black whale (emphasis mine). The retelling of the story becomes further complicitous by King's decentering of the Eurocentric idea of compulsory heterosexuality. The first allusion to the blackness and the homosexuality of the whale gets submerged in the big shout of Ahab's men. But soon the reader is thrown off the seat with the dual appropriation of Melville's story:

> blackwhaleblackwhalesbianblackwhalesbianblackwhale, they all shout.
> Black whale? Yells Ahab. You mean white whale, don't you? Moby-Dick, the great male white whale?
> That's not a white whale, says Changing Woman, that's a female whale and she's black.
> Nonsense, says Ahab. It's Moby-Dick, the great white whale.
> You're mistaken, says Changing Woman, I believe that is Moby-Jane, the Great Black Whale (196).

Working on multiple levels, King's intertextual take on *Moby-Dick* also undermines the authority of the book and hence the written word, and hints at the possibility of the presence of alternative versions of history, tradition, and storytelling:

118

"She means Moby-Dick," says Coyote. "*I read the book.* It's Moby-Dick, the great white whale who destroys the *Pequod.*"
"You haven't been reading *your history,*" I tells Coyote.
"It's English colonists who destroy the Pequots."
"But there isn't any Moby-Jane."
"Sure there is," I says. "*Just look out over there.* What do you see?"
"Well ... I'll be," says Coyote (Emphasis in 1st, 3rd, 6th line mine) (196).

King's Ahab, in true colonial fashion, does not entertain differences of opinion and "throws overboard" whoever asks him to see the truth, i.e., Moby-Jane, the female black whale and not Moby-Dick whom Ahab chooses to see. Further, King's Moby-Jane "talks" to Changing Woman as they swim "back and forth" amidst the waves, thus foregrounding the tradition of storytelling in Indian communities where everyone, including animals, can have a voice and are free to speak. This is again in confrontation with the colonial discourse where let alone animals, even people of a different skin colour are denied voice and presence in the discourse. King's intertextuality thus works at various levels to decenter the Melvillian text and retell the story from a subaltern's point of view. King's play on the homosexuality of the 'female,' 'black' whale serves towards this purpose. Priscila Walton puts forth:

By offering an alternative version of Melville's *Moby Dick*, *Green Grass, Running Water* highlights the homoerotic subtext of Melville's novel as he shifts the gender of the characters from male to female (Walton 79).

In the narrative of *GGRW*, before encountering a host of characters from Melville's *Moby Dick*, Changing Woman falls into a 'big,' 'white' canoe "full of animals" (105). King ironically refers to the commoditization of woman in the patriarchal religion of Christianity that is addressed to in this conversation between Changing Woman and Noah:

I fell out of the sky, says Changing Woman...
The sky! shouts the little man, Hallelujah! A gift from heaven. My name's Noah and you must be my new wife.
I doubt that, says Changing Woman.

119

> Lemme see your breasts, says Noah, I like woman with
> big breasts. I hope God remembered that. (145)

King's Noah pursues Changing Woman without success and goes on to declare that:

> This is a Christian ship, he shouts. I am a Christian man.
> This is a Christian journey. And if you can't follow our
> Christian rules, then you're *not wanted on the voyage*
> (emphasis mine) (148).

King's allusion to Findley's novel *Not Wanted on the Voyage* can be taken as the author's recognition of Findley's Text as an essential predecessor to his own in that both the texts subvert the mainstream discourse by dismantling the conventions of gender issues and rejecting the gender binaries as the primary markers of identity, and in their production of counter-narratives of the dominant discourse, expose the arbitrariness of patriarchal systems of thought.

While categories are questioned and reappropriated in *GGRW*, the novel also works towards reclaiming the Native worldview and to achieve this, King makes use of the archetypal figures from his own tradition. "Tricksterism" thus becomes central to the narration as well as progression of the story in the text. As King's playing with names, texts, representations from the dominant discourse continues, the novel simultaneously also becomes a "trickster discourse." To start with, there are seven archetypal figures in the text- Old Coyote, the clownish Coyote, four Native Women spirits and "I," King's ambivalent narrator.

As the creator of mess and beauty, as one residing in the in-between space, as a powerful figure making mockery of all givens, the Trickster is full of possibilities and King, like other contemporary Native authors such as Vizenor cleverly manipulates the trickster into *GGRW* and thus speculates, regulates and administers an anti-discourse that becomes as powerful and full of possibilities as the trickster himself. While Old Coyote's appearance is limited in the text, Coyote is there throughout the text, laughing and making us laugh, subverted and subverting, creating and destroying, fixing the world, fixing the stories, fixing the lives of people and retaining his trademark unapologetic self, exposing the possibilities of the sinister and the good, even self-reflexively mocking at his own self, taking the reader along with him to the "edge of the world," dancing and singing, bringing in floods and earthquakes and creating new life, continually constructing, deconstructing, reconstructing and co-constructing the narrative itself, creating a space for dialogue and simultaneously failing to shut up his motor-mouth, fusing the mythical and the real and de-marking boundaries. Coyote's unpredictability not only adds to the postmodern destabilizing quality of the text but also equips the author to speak from a Native space. As Janne Korkka aptly comments:

> The most lasting image inspired by Thomas King's fiction is, perhaps, a coyote footprint behind a barn somewhere in the vast Albertan prairies. Its symbolic functions are diverse: it reflects the ancient beliefs of the Native peoples and the artificial nature of societal structures we take for granted but which are so easily subverted by a mere juxtaposition of different stories. Also, it reminds the audiences about the fact that despite any single culture trying to obtain dominant position, there will always be deviant voices (Korkka 152).

Coyote trickery underlines *GGRW*. It's a "backward dog dream" of Coyote that creates a ballistic 'little god' who later becomes the Christian "God"; Coyote claims responsibility for Alberta's "immaculate conception," Alberta who wants a child without the bother of a husband (allusion to Mary's conception of Jesus is but obvious) and in the same vein dismisses it as just being a little helpful, his 'hee-hee's and 'sorry's flowing with insincerity. At the very outset of the narrative we get to know Coyote's capabilities: "When that Coyote dreams, anything can happen" (1). Coyote is the one who "turns on the light" (230), loves "stories with happy endings" (225) and declares that he "can be very helpful" (229). But unlike the hierarchical religion of Christianity, Coyote is not omnipotent and omniscient. There are limits to his power; he is as capable of making mistakes as anyone else and doesn't know the ending of all the stories. Apart from Coyote, there are five more Transcendental tricksterish figures in the text, the narrator "I" and the four old Indians who flee from the mental asylum they were incarcerated in since 1891.

Adding to the carnivalesque unfolding of the story in *GGRW* is the presence of the narrative "I" as the "alter ego of Coyote" (Linton 218), "I" could be the author as narrator though King's use of the third person tense form for "I" makes that a dim possibility. "I" could   121 more convincingly be the voice of the subaltern speaking. As is noticed many a time in the text, it is "I" who emphasizes the importance of "getting the story right" lest earlier falsifications of the Native might concretize or new fabrications may take place by the telling of the "wrong" story. Often asking Coyote to "concentrate" and "pay attention," "I" could also be an authorial strategy to remind and reprimand the reader about the etiquette of listening to stories. "I" also diminishes the authority of the book and hence the written word, thus re-establishing the oral/aural culture of the Native peoples. When Coyote is apparently duped by the written word, the book, and insists on the supremacy of the book in the whale episode, "I" asks him to reread history, "your history" (196), creates the language game of Pequod/ Pequot (146) and thus insists on a revision of history as well. Coyote's perception of history is challenged once again by "I" when Coyote sings the Canadian National Anthem as "Hosanna-da, in-in the highest, hosanna forever...Oh Canada, our home and native land" and "I" dismisses it as the wrong song and rephrases the Canadian National Anthem as "Hosanna-da, our home on Native's land" (270). Wendy Rohrbarcher aptly states:

> In this rewriting of the Canadian National Anthem ... 'I' attacks the cultural perception that the European settlers were 'native' to Canada. It is 'I' who (re)shapes Coyote's perceptions of history and ostensibly, the reader's as well (Rohrbarcher np).

"I" perhaps points out towards a regeneration of the Native communities, their traditions and cultures and ways of life and "I" also sizes up Coyote's arrogance by emphasizing on the supremacy and uniqueness of the feminine spirit in Native lore and beyond:

"But here is only one Thought Woman," says Coyote.
"That's right," I says.
"And there is only one Coyote," says Coyote.
"No," I says. "This World is full of Coyotes" (272).

Apart from Coyote and "I," there are four other tricksterish characters in *GGRW*. These four old Indian trickster-transformer figures escape from a mental hospital to "fix the world." These ageless Natives move back and forth from the mythical to the real plane and, on their way, encounter characters from the canonical

122

history, literature, media and so on. They are apparently male, with their names alluding to popular images from the canon-Lone Ranger, Ishmael, Robinson Crusoe and Hawkeye. But they are actually four ancient female spirits from Native lore-First Woman, Changing Woman, Thought Woman and Old Woman. The comic/cosmic worldview recontextualized by these four female spirits changes the reader's perception of the canon and highlights the other side of the story. They transform themselves to perhaps sustain as well as to move around in the world without too many prying eyes. King has this to tell us about the four old Indians:

In actual fact, these are four archetypal Indian Women who come right out of oral creation stories ... but they've just been forced to assume their guises– by history, by literature, by just the general run of the world- and so that's what they call themselves now (emphasis original) (Gzowski 67).

Whereas these four Native spirits go about their business of fixing history and in the process alter many a history and realities, unlike the Christian patriarchal God, they do not claim omnipotence and omniscience. They are aware and humble enough to admit that their earlier attempts to "fix the world" have also brought in their own share of catastrophes and even though they can see the "edges of the world in all directions" (29) from their vision, they are also afraid of getting lost and making mistakes. As the reader moves back and forth in time and space with the trickster and "listens" to the retelling of stories, contradictions appear to be less cumbersome and more plausible. In their rewriting of key texts, histories and events from the canon, these transcendental figures establish *GGRW* as a trickster story. By subverting the grid of master narrative, these tricksters alter the binaries of racism, sexism and other centrisms.

As language and interpretation confront the previous modes of knowledge, humor becomes a handy strategy to configure new stories and appropriate the already existing ones, often serving the cause of resistance and reaction. As the subaltern starts poking fun at the master narratives, their well-demarcated, isolated subject positions lose quick ground and the binaries of centre and periphery ought to get revised and even redefined. The margin's procurement of a voice then happens, in a subversion of earlier practices, at the cost of the centre. And this 'cost' involves serious retextualization of the earlier discourse as it gets reappropriated by a *parodic gaze* of the margin at the centre (emphasis mine). The earlier ideological constructs are taken over by the comic and ironic reinterpretation of these constructs in the hands of the   123
"constructed." This double play of discourse and counter-

discourse thus result in a farcical, comical tone in the postmodernist text. *GGRW* is one such text. Speaking from the postcolonial space, Thomas King, like his contemporary Native authors, frequently plunges into the recourse of humor, parody and irony, often subversive in nature and always unfailingly witty and funny in representation.

King's *GGRW* thus ridicules, pokes fun at the dominant discourse and enjoys the resultant laughter. In having Henry Dawes, Mary Rowaldson, and Elaine Goodale as inattentive students in a Native history classroom, in Coyote's prank phone calls from "First Nations Pizza," in the serving of exotic "dog-meat" at Latisha's hilariously named "Dead Dog Café," in Ahdamn's naming practices, in giving the reader a peek into the John Wayne Westerns, and in numerous other instances in *GGRW*, King's subversive humor is at work. Margaret Atwood in her article "A Double-Bladed Knife: Subversive laughter in Two Stories by Thomas King" remarks:

> Humour can be aggressive and oppressive, as in keep-
> `em-in-their-place sexist and racist jokes. But it can also
> be a subversive weapon, as it has often been for people
> who find themselves in fairly tight spot without other,
> more physical, weapon (Atwood 76).

In his playing around with all previous norms of religion, society, sex, politics, literature, art, media and more, King obviously seeks to put things on a Native perspective and to look at these from a Native mirror. And most amusingly, the genius of *GGRW* lies in the fact that even with all his practices of subversion, King makes us laugh with the jokes and not at the colonizing principles/practices per se. One episode that stands out in King's parodic discourse is his comically named and intellectually challenged Ahdamn's naming practices. Created in the image of the "grouchy" Christian God who doesn't know how to "mind his relations," Ahdamn is occupied with "naming everything":

> You are a microwave oven, Ahdamn tells the Elk.
> Nope, says that Elk. Try again.
> You are a garage sale, Ahdamn tells the Bear.
> We got to get you some glasses, says the Bear.
> You are a telephone book, Ahdamn tells the Cedar Tree.
> You're getting closer, says the Cedar Tree.

You're a cheeseburger, Ahdamn tells Old Coyote.
It must be time for lunch, says Old Coyote (41).

Florence Stratton remarks on this episode of the text:

> In this hilarious parody of colonial (mis) naming practices, King highlights, as he does repeatedly in the novel, the values of imperial culture ... a belief in hierarchy, technology, exploitation, mastery over nature, progress, private property (Stratton 92).

Challenging the authoritarian ideology of the dominant discourse, King thus reclaims the world from a Native perspective and comedy serves as a strategy towards that end. Hence, comedy in *GGRW* is not merely to create "innocent fun" but is informed in the postmodernist tradition of confronting the authority and rebelling known mould, and thus achieves carnivalesque proportions. King's humor is never caustic, even when it makes a part of the reader/audience slap their faces with a sense of remorse and perhaps even guilt; it has that moral quality to it. Rather, *GGRW* is a benign attempt to show the mirror to the dominant society and mark the wrongs done by their ancestors. As Scheick rightly points out about humor in *GGRW*:

> Humour is gentle resistance; it is also tolerant hope. Just wait and remember, he implies, and the present rendering of reality will eventually burst its imaginary bounds (Scheick 156).

While the tone of humor in the text is almost farcical, its take on the appropriation of the cosmologies of the Native traditions vis-à-vis the dominant, patriarchal, Christian one is of particular interest. In *GGRW*, King is telling the Native story from a Native point of view by subverting the Judeo-Christian worldview and confronting the dominant cosmologies. As soon as the narrative begins in *GGRW*, Coyote, the tribal culture hero/trickster figure is seen enjoying a dream and not much later Coyote's dream declares itself to be "in charge of the world" and demands to be an upper-case, arrogant GOD:

125

I am God, says that Dog Dream.
"Isn't that cute," says Coyote. That Dog Dream is a
contrary, that Dog Dream has everything backward."
But why am I a little god? shouts that god.
"Not so loud," says Coyote. "You're hurting my ears."
I don't want to be a little god, says that god. I want to be
a big god!
"What a noise," says Coyote. "This dog has no manners."
Big one!
"Okay, okay," says Coyote. Just stop shouting."
There, says that GOD. That's better (emphasis original) (2).

By playing up the dog-god contrary and rewriting the stories of
the origin of the Christian God as a mere figment of Coyote's imagination,
King playfully subverts the very origin of Christianity. In continuation
of turning the colonial practice of trivializing the Native on its head,
King gives the reader a hint about the beginning of the world and thus
superscribes the Native 'story' over and above the 'Christian story':

"In the beginning, God created the heaven and the earth.
And the earth was without form, and void; and darkness
was upon the face of the deep_____."
"wait a minute," said Robinson Crusoe.
"Yes?"
"That's the wrong story," said Ishmael. "That story comes
later" (14).

These lines suggest that the obviously Christian story of the God
as creator "comes later" as the Euroamerican hegemonic discourse comes
later; that the Natives know better because they came here first. In this
context, Linda Lamont-Stewart points out:

Thus the text asserts the precedence of native creation
mythology over the biblical account...Clearly we are
being presented with a counter-narrative, a corrective
to the Judeo-Christian and Eurocentric narratives that
have shaped Western history, including the encounter
between Europeans and the aboriginal peoples of
North America (Lamont-Stewart 123).

In his comical re-production of the Genesis story, King cleverly subverts the colonizer's religion. Working with the Native creation myth of the earth-diver, King in *GGRW* retells the story from the point of view of four Native female spirits, each belonging to a different tribe and thus underlines a pan-Indian consciousness. It's important to note here that the Native world has been created by a woman with the help of animals unlike the Christian world where all power of creation lies with a superior omnipotent male god. Again, the garden, as and when it is created is created by First Woman, one of the feminine Native spirits and not the backward Christian GOD.

Later in the story, First Woman leaves the garden along with Ahdamn because she is disgusted with the greedy Christian God who does not know how to "mind his relations." In a mockery of the colonial idea of hoarding and private property, King draws the picture of a grouchy GOD who "Stands in the garden with his hand on his hips, so everybody can see he is angry" (69). While in distributing the food among all, First Woman is reemphasizing the 'sharing' habit of the Native communities, the Christian God, in getting angry over losing 'his stuff' is exhibiting the 'hoarding' habit of colonials. This brings a contrast between the 'community' worldview of the Natives and the Christian, colonial, 'individualistic' worldview. The Native gods, it seems, are thus reclaiming their lost status and dignity. As noted Native Playwright Tomson Highway puts it:

> One mythology almost destroyed the other, took away the dignity of the other mythology. One god took away the dignity of another god. Now what has to happen is that the god who lost their dignity has to take it back. Just a simple act of taking it back... (Seiler 53).

Through the retelling of the Noah story, King subverts the individualistic, hierarchical notion of Christianity. As Changing Woman leans from the sky to have a better look of herself in the Water World down, she falls from the sky and lands in a canoe full of animals and falls straight on Old Coyote. She also finds a little man with a filthy beard who introduces himself as Noah in the canoe and who seems to be too occupied with himself and his set of rules. Commenting on this Christian insistence on rules, Linton views:

One of the issues that emerges from the conflict among
myths in alternative origin stories is the western insistence
on rules, specifically rules promulgated to establish and
maintain social hierarchies (Linton 225).

The colonial force's claim of being a superior people is subverted
through the mockery of so called Christian practices. We learn more about
Christianity when Changing Woman questions Ahab, the captain of the
ship Pequod, about the mindless killing of whales and Ahab answers:

> *This is a Christian world, you know. We only
> kill things that are useful or things we don't like*
> (emphasis mine) (196).

That connotes the colonial practice of killing everything--people,
Nature and stories too. King's hilarious version of the founding stories
of Christianity thus turns the table in favor of the Native. As Margaret
Atwood points out, "Tit for tat ... we are forced to experience first hand
how it must feel to have your own religious stories retold in a version that
neither 'understands' nor particularly reverences them" (Atwood 78).

In the third telling of the story, Thought Woman encounters A.A.
Gabriel aka 'Archangel Gabriel' (Flick 159) whose nonsensical questions
irritate her. In a parodic mockery of the Canadian Security and Intelligence
Services, King's story also subverts the Christian idea of looking at women
as always submissive and willing to "procreate":

> Virgin Verification form, says A. A. Gabriel. Here's a
> map of the city.
> We're here, and this is where you'll have the baby [...]
> I'm not pregnant, says Thought Woman.
> [...] Let's have you lie down here, and we'll get on with
> procreating. Ready? Hail Mary/Full of grace...
> [...]No, says thought Woman, Absolutely not.
> [...] So, says A.A. Gabriel, you really mean yes, right?
> No, says Thought Woman (All ellipses mine barring line
> 5) (270-271).

In the last of the mythical tellings, Old Woman sees Young Man
Walking on Water trying to stop a boat from drowning. Young
Man Walking on Water talks about rules too. In an ultimate

subversion of the Christian sense of superiority, King displays how as Young Man Walking on Water fails to control the boat, Old Woman, the mythical helper to the Native culture hero, comes to the rescue of Young Man Walking on Water alias Christ, the Christian culture hero.

By subverting the stories of the dominant religion, King succeeds in setting the record straight. The postmodern practice of counter-appropriation turns the biblical stories into comic/cosmic farce. King's playful wit and crisp storytelling thus challenges the notions of the patriarchal, omnipotent, omniscient, authoritarian god and displaces him by altering it with a matriarchal view of religion. Speaking from a Native point of view, King thus demonstrates in the text the alienation that must have been felt by Natives when their cultures and religious practices were appropriated in the dominant discourse. By countering, revisioning and reapppropriating the Christian stories, King also demonstrates the postcolonial practice of indigenizing the dominant discourse, religion included. King's subversive retelling thus renames Jesus as Young Man Walking on Water.

A conscious dismantling of and deconstruction of earlier historical, political, social, geographical, anthropological paradigms and ideologies has taken place in the writings of Native authors who speak from a postcolonial space. By his continuous allusion to the past and a simultaneous subversion of it, King, in *GGRW*, as in other fictions of his, attempts to emphasize the reinvention of the 'recorded' history and a subsequent replacement of it by the Native perception of history. As King's tricksters pop out with canonical names in the text, Judeo-Christian founding myths, western literature, as well as history and popular culture are reappropriated and the revival of Native culture and history is constructed. Simultaneously emphasizing resistance and preservation, the Native history classroom scene foregrounds alternate realities. Again, by ending each telling of the four sections of the novel at the point of the incarceration of one transcendent character in Fort Marion, King's text "emphasizes the centrality of this incident" to the plot (Goldman 23). While King's allusion to the Fort Marion incident rewrites previous constructs of history, his revisionist writing also negotiates contemporary histories and representations of the Natives in popular media as well. One of these is the fixing up of Hollywood movies from a Native perspective.

In his comic interlude of the four mythical Indians' fixing up a John Wayne Western on Lionel's birthday, King reappropriates Hollywood history by creating a victory for the Native peoples 129 in a Western. As the four old Indians begin to chant their coded mantra in the form of "Happy Birthday," the popular culture and the image of the Native is reshaped in a symbolic fixing of the Western and thus is created a reversal of the dominant discourse. The subversion of the Hollywood Western thus undermines the Eurocentric construction of history and retextualizes, or rather in this case, revisualizes history in favor of the subaltern discourse. To quote Goldman in this context: While ... reversing the linear Hollywood script offer[s] instantaneous comic relief ... [T]he text implicitly suggests that readers must not simply revise the content of racist scripts, but challenge their fundamental conventions, specifically the linear, monologist, narrative structure itself (Goldman 29).

King is also aware of the need to revise the spatial paradigms of the dominant narrative in order to relocate the Native with the land. One of the recurrent images of the text towards this purpose is that of the *map*, thus bringing in the issue of the cartographic discourse which served the means of colonization (emphasis mine). As a text and a tool of discourse that presumes unknown territory as its own and binds the same within its lop-sided understanding of specificity, the map underlines the abrogatory principles of colonization. Maps are persistently present in *GGRW*-in the realist plot, Native characters like Alberta and Charlie's constant travels, in Eli's keeping hold of his mother's cabin in the midst of a dam project, in A. A. Gabriel's "town map" shown to Thought Woman, in journeys gone awry and so on. But the most obvious reference to a colonialist's use of the map as a tool of "power and control" (128) is perhaps found in the white colonialist showroom owner Bursum's "The Map":

> The Map. Bursum loved the sound of it. There was a majesty to the name. He stepped back from the screens and looked at *his creation*. It was stupendous. It was more powerful than he had thought. It was like having the universe there on the wall, being able to see everything, being in control (emphasis original) (128).

The map as a tool of territorial appropriation has thus resulted in giving "power and control" to the colonialist of whom Bursum is an offspring and thus dispossessed the Natives off their land and their livelihood. By fixing up the Western right on Bursum's Map, the Native elders send a message of cultural reppropriation and survival. By erasing the colonial version of history and superimposing it with a Native view of history and reality, the text thus achieves the objective of confronting earlier appropriations. By using the

130

map as a writing device, King reappropriates the imperialistic tools to rewrite the history of the land. Further, as an alternative to this colonial tool, King provides certain indigenous practices and observances; one such alternative is found in the Sun Dance.

It's by remembering the Sun Dance that, Eli, one of the central characters in *GGRW*, comes back home and performs his Native duty to resist the dam project on Native land, thus protesting a further tampering with the map of his land. Again, it's by getting his face painted and attending the Sun Dance that Lionel, Eli's nephew and a directionless Native youth finds a direction for his life. By simultaneously entering into and staying away from perceived histories, the four Native spirits fix the map of history, literature and culture. Rejecting the linear, boundaried construct of the Western map and foregrounding the effectivity of the circular pattern even in its narrative structure, the text thus simultaneously displays the importance of Native tradition and confronts the colonial tradition of territorialization. Goldman points out:

> Throughout the novel, the circle and the Sun Dance, in particular, are offered as alternatives to the map. The importance accorded to the Sun Dance makes sense only when readers understand that its goal lies in furnishing participants with a map of the universe in which their location is clearly demarcated (Goldman 34).

However, keeping with the Native perception of a community identity and thus the authorial responsibility to keep certain stories untold, King's allusion to the Sun Dance stops short of giving any intricate details regarding the ceremony to the outside world which may neither aptly understand nor particularly respect the goings on of a Native ceremonial practice. In that sense, King mocks at the early anthropologists' practices of taping Native stories for circulation among non-Natives.

Allusion to past and present histories, subversion of the created images of Natives in the popular culture, revision of colonial tools such as the map, and more such counter-appropriations result in the undermining of the authority of history as it has been known till date and the singularity of "truth" is confronted in *GGRW*. In that sense, King's writing becomes what Hutcheon has put forth as "historiographic metafiction," fiction that is "overtly and resolutely historical ... in an ironic and problematic way that acknowledges that history is not the   131 transparent record of any sure 'truth'" (Hutcheon 129). In his comic rewriting of canonical history, King emphasizes the point that "history can be revisited, endings can be rewritten, the letter does not have to be the law" (Linton 228).

But King's writing does not stop at fixing history. King's Tricksters also fix contemporary problems, lives, and even technology. The realist plot in the text concerns itself with the building of a dam and its repercussions on the adjacent Blackfoot Reserve. King's text emphasizes on the dam as a symbol of inequality in the twentieth century. Thousands of poor, powerless people get displaced from their land and are robbed off their livelihoods for every dam constructed. Their ways of life, their traditions, cultures and practices get lost in the process. *GGRW* focuses on this aspect of Native life and thus also addresses an even greater issue of the conservation of environment. The colonizer's absurd desire of controlling and authoritating nature is questioned in the text. The dam thus metaphorically stands for the Whiteman's futile urge to conquer nature, as becomes evident in the climax when the dam bursts and also for the historically oppressive imperialistic practice of destroying First Nations cultures, livelihoods and lands.

The name of the dam in *GGRW* is "Grand Baleen Dam," an allusion to the Grand Baleine or Great Whale River Project (Flick 150). King hints at the economic and spiritual colonization of the Native peoples because of the great icon of progress in twentieth century, the dam. Again, King's parody of the dam conflict also questions the utility of pursuing the available legal, political, and populist channels for resisting ecologically and community-damaging development (Lousley 28). As Latisha comments that fishing, a source of livelihood for many Natives, is "Probably very good" in Parliament Lake, "But you can't fish. Court order" (326). Similarly, if there are no floods in the river there would be "no cottonwoods" and "... if the cottonwoods die, where are we going to get the Sundance tree" (376). Eli Stands Alone, the person who literally stands alone in the mid of the dam and even stops construction of the dam through court injunctions, knows that "he had won very little" and "that they would find a way to maneuver around him" (260). But, as the dam breaks up, we understand that the mythical beings have exercised their powers in the real world to "fix" a part of it. Coyote's dance brings in an earthquake that destroys the dam, changes the geography of the land and "the water rolled on as it had for eternity" (415). Eli is killed in the process, but even in death he has "come home." Bursum's "property" too is fixed in the process.

132

The four tricksters along with Coyote take help of technology in their "fixing" of the world, their "weapons" being "cars," another symbol of twentieth century progress. King's choice of the names of the cars also resonates with Columbus's three ships: The Nissan, Pinto and Karman-Ghia that are tricked to the dam allude to the three ships of Columbus- Nina, Pinta and Santa-Maria. That the cars, representative of the contemporary automobile culture can be so easily used up by Native tricksters shows that subversion of technology is very much possible for Native tricksters. By using the cars as the weapons for devastating the dam, the tricksters on one hand appropriate technology; on the other hand, they have pitted one imperialistic sign of progress against another, thus creating an intra-discourse confrontation. And the fact that each car is found in a puddle of water before it gets lost points towards the primacy of the water world, and thus the Native worldview over the colonial one. As Brian Johnson notes:

> By transforming the cars into parodies of the ships that brought disease and conquest to the "New World," the tricksters concentrate a genealogy of Gutenberg technology- from the modern car, back to print media which inform Western imperial exploration – in a single image ... Thus, at the end of the novel ... inaugurating a new Creation story, King suggestively links the renewal of Native community with a parodic technological apocalypse (Johnson 34).

As the cars appear, disappear and reappear "as battering rams to destroy the dam" (Goldman 32), Coyote trickery appears even more powerful than the magnificent imperialist icons of progress. King also thus emphasizes the inherent element of violence that technology brings in.

Along with these rewriting of communal and political histories, the tricksters take up the task of rewriting or rather reshaping some personal histories. Alberta, the Blackfoot girl, gets pregnant, as she wished, with some help from Coyote. Lionel's childhood fantasy of becoming John Wayne is partially fulfilled when he gets John Wayne's Jacket as a gift on his birthday from the tricksters. But the Jacket doesn't fit Lionel which reaffirms the authorial point of view that assimilation is not a wise choice for Native peoples and that the assertion of difference and continuance of the indigenous tradition only   133 can ensure survival in the contemporary world. Moreover, whilst the Native tricksters' fixing up of the world brings in a catastrophic end to Eli Stands Alone, one of the most powerful symbols of resistance and decolonization in the text, it nevertheless reasserts a fluidity and continuity of Native life.

One of the methods King takes recourse in to rewrite and appropriate the master narrative is Orality/Native storytelling. *GGRW* is a Native story written in the colonizer's language, and storytelling is central to the narrative pattern of the text. Orality is a pattern, a technique, as well as a theme in the text. Confronting the canonical literary tradition, King writes *GGRW* with a clear-cut emphasis on orality. In his attempt and ability to appropriate techniques of storytelling in the text- repetition of key phrases, ceremonial opening and closing lines of indigenous storytelling, language games, all point towards a construction of meaning through oral and aural means. While King's parodic subversion of canonical history, literature and theology fall in the tradition of postmodern metadiscursivity, his use of Native trickster tales, magic realism, cyclical time, and plurality of stories draw from the rich oral tradition of Native peoples.

In the text, the four mythical spirits tell stories and in their telling, history, literature, religion and representation of the Native in all these are appropriated. They take "turns" to tell the story and Lone Ranger's "turn" comes first. This mythical being attempts many canonical starting lines to start the story but fails. The Lone Ranger's false starts suggest that "traditional European storytelling conventions clearly are not appropriate, nor...is a European stereotype of native speech" (Lamont-Stewart 123). The story begins only when the storyteller begins with a Native starting line:

> "Gha!" said the Lone Ranger. "Higayv:ligé:i."
> "That's better," said Hawkeye. "Tsane:hlanv':hi."
> "Listen," said Robinson Crusoe. "Hade:lohǿ:sgi."
> "It is beginning," said Ishmael. "Dagvyá:dhu:dv:hńi"
> "It is begun well," said the Lone Ranger.
> Tsada:hnǿ:nedíniga:vduyughodv:o:sdv."
> "Okay?"
> "Okay" (15).

Previously, before the story started, the storyteller is reminded that "you can't tell it all by yourself" (14) underlining the 134 fact that the Native tradition of storytelling is *communal* (emphasis mine). Emphasizing on the communal and the non-hierarchical, King's stories stand in stark contrast to the glorification of the individual and the hierarchical in the canonical discourse, and thus foreground an aboriginal perspective of the world. In the Native context, when "Everybody makes mistakes" including the mythically powerful old Indians and Coyote, it is "Best not to make them with stories" (14) because "There are no truths," but "Only stories" (391). Thus in King's narrative, "stories create reality; words have the power to affect the world in ways that go beyond 'pleasure, beauty and interest'" (Chester 53). And hence, as in oral stories, the canonical stories can be altered in the Foucouldian sense of 'who' is speaking and for 'whom.' Moreover, this leads to the debunking of the canonical practice of producing a conclusive, ideological narrative/perception of the world.

King deploys numerous strategies in *GGRW* for the textual production of orality. Whilst the postmodern techniques of pun, allegory, parallelisms and subversions abound in the text, equally evident is the presence of language games, use of Native language and an authorial intention to undermine "textual orthodoxy" (Fast 1). One such strategy is King's use of Cherokee syllabics for the chapter divisions. While these syllabics automatically 'speak' to the Native readers of *GGRW*, these simultaneously exclude the 'outside' readers from a complete understanding of the meaning produced. Goldman views the use of Cherokee syllabics for the chapter names thus:

> ... at the beginning of each section is a word in Cherokee. Rather than signify a linear progression, such as chapter one, two, and so on, each word announces one of the four directions and the sacred colour associated with it. The narrative begins with east and red, then proceeds to south and white, west and black, and north and blue, in that order (Goldman 37).

Thus, it can be argued that the use of Cherokee for chapter divisions which at first hand might appear absurd and out of place is actually adding to the ceremonial storytelling tradition of the Natives on one hand and enhancing the "Nativeness" of the novel on the other. Simultaneously, it is also confronting the "knowledge" of the mainstream and mocking at the myth of the "ignorant savage."

The language games embedded in the text also add to the oral-aural quality of the text. Without reading aloud,   135 one would surely miss the joke inherent in the naming of the director of the mental asylum from which the four Native spirits have escaped, Dr. J. Hovaugh alias the biblical Jehovah. Likewise, King's play on the name of the fierce Métis leader Louis Riel will not be apparent if one does not read the three names given to three characters, Louis, Ray and Al simultaneously. King's play on the names of the three ships of Columbus has already been discussed.

This kind of emphasis on orality also underlines the Native contempt for the written word. With their land, culture, tradition, livelihood all appropriated in the colonizer's language games, King's text declares that the time has now come for the demonstration of some Native word-play, both to subvert the master discourses and to confront the written word. Dismissing the authoritarian language of the written tradition and its representative, book, King emphasizes on forgetting the book and listening to stories instead; Even Coyote is reprimanded when he attaches too much importance to the book:

> "I read a book," says Coyote.
> "Forget the book," I says. "We've got a story to tell. And here's how it goes." (349).

King's confrontation with the written tradition stems from the fact that it was by means of *writing and signing* that the "treaties" were created which became instruments for colonial exploitation of the Native land (emphasis mine). It is the "written" bill with which Milford's truck is claimed by the white authority, complete with a forged signature. It is with an article in *Alberta Now* that the "slick" public relations firm hired by Duplesis International's attempts to "whitewash" facts and figures regarding the dam. The treaties paved the way for "reservation" in the first instance. The truck has to be burnt down as a march of protest in the second. And the article in Alberta Now is laughed at in a Native council meeting with a suggestion to rename the dam as "the Grand Goose" because "that's about all Indians ever got from the government, a goose" (117). This approximate change in the Native reaction to the written word over time also underscores the point that the written word is continually losing its status against the oral.

King's intertwining of the postmodern traditions and devices, the western canon and Native orality thus confront and transform the dominant discourse and "also remind readers that books by

136   Native authors ... constitute a complex polyphonic discourse located at the interface between two radically distinct cultures"

(Goldman 25). Using stories as a means of cultural resistance, King thus affirms the political nature of storytelling and in a parody of the master stories we find that Coyote does not get a turn in telling the story:

> "Wait, wait," says Coyote. "When's my turn?"
> "Coyotes don't get a turn," I says.
> "In a democracy, everyone gets a turn," says Coyote.
> "Nonsense," I says. "In a democracy, only people who can afford it get a turn" (327).

Commenting on the politics of storytelling in *GGRW*, Priscilla Walton remarks that "...the stories in this text suggest that the very act of telling stories is by its nature political, and carries with it attendant responsibilities" (Walton 84).

In *GGRW*, stereotypes are produced only to be debunked and appropriated within the textual space. In a subversion of the Eurocentric ways of thinking, King's Native characters are portrayed as a part of the contemporary world and not some noble/barbaric savage located in a safely distant past. King's strategy is to portray some Native characters beyond all stereotyping and some other satisfying the expectations of the dominant cultures, only to turn the table by demonstrating how myopic these images are. The text resists the usual depiction of the Native as a victim or even as one juggling and struggling between two worlds. King mocks at the "common" portrayal of the Native in literature and popular culture in the following passage:

> It was a common enough theme in novels and movies. Indian leaves the traditional world of the reserve, goes to the city, and is destroyed. Indian leaves the traditional world of reserve, is exposed to white culture, and becomes trapped between two worlds. Indian leaves the traditional world of the reserve, gets an education, and is shunned by his tribe (286).

Self-conscious as a postmodern writer ought to be, King avoids these common themes in *GGRW*. In fact, going a step further, King's Native characters, as is evident in the portrayal of Portland and Latisha, take up the stereotypical garb so as to fool the oppressor with

137

their innovative reconstruction of the constructed image, thus manipulating the stereotyping to their own advantage. Marta Dvorak aptly comments in this context:

> King's Native characters exploit in a creative way the stereotyped images of the other that have been projected onto them, thereby demonstrating an acquired mastery of the domains of technology, commercialization, marketing and packaging that are commonly associated with White civilization (Dvorak 221-222).

The most prominent symbol of Native politico-legal resistance in *GGRW* is Eli Stands Alone. Eli's name has been described as an amalgamation of two names, Elijah Harper, the one who said "No" to the 1990 Meech Lake project and snatched victory for his people and Pete Standing Alone, a Native Elder who was featured in several National Film Board documentaries (Lousley 29, 41). Eli has been a University Professor in English at Toronto and has come back to the reserve after retirement to resist the demolition of his dead mother's cabin that stands in the mid of the Great baleen Dam project. Using white law against their own, Eli has been able to stall the project by court injunctions. Having stayed away for long from the reserve and his own people, he has definitely suffered erosion of his place in the community and does not enjoy a status that his sister Norma is accorded to. However, it is in his resistance to the dam project and his untimely death that Eli's journey back home is complete. Using the very mechanisms of colonial power, law and the colonizer's language, Eli contributes to the reppropriation of the geography of the land resulting in the survival of his own peoples. As far as Eli is concerned, the dam, the grand colonial icon of progress, reminds him "of a toilet" (136). Eli's death perhaps underscores the point that an amount of sacrifice and loss is involved in the process of resistance but that should not become a deterrent for resistance.

When Clifton, the dam engineer discards Eli's Indianness because he is a university professor, Eli confronts it by saying that "Being Indian isn't a profession" (143). He also appropriates the colonizer's idea of superiority by taking pride in his Native Blackfoot language. Also, we witness Eli as the protector of the sanctity of Native customs and rituals in his second time successful attempt to stop the photographing of the Sun Dance, the first being when as a child he was duped with a blank film.

138

Lionel Red Dog is Eli's nephew and a thirty-something T.V. Salesman whose portrayal borders on the suggestion of a hopeless life for the contemporary Native youth. However, as the story rounds up, there seems to be more hope for Lionel. Lionel also hopes of getting married to Alberta and to have babies. There's also a certain tragicomicality to the gold jacket that Lionel's boss Bill Bursum makes him wear in the showroom. Being found at the wrong place and the wrong time seems to be second nature to Lionel. In the self-reflexivity of postmodern writing, King demonstrates the contemptuous view of one's own self, the Other's desire to become a part of the centre through Lionel's illusion of an identity:

> By the time Lionel was six, he knew what he wanted to be. John Wayne. Not the actor, but the character. Not the man, but the hero. The John Wayne who cleaned up cattle towns and made them safe for decent folk. The John Wayne who shot guns out of the hands of outlaws. The John Wayne who saved stagecoaches and wagon trains from Indian attacks (241).

Stratton thus remarks on Lionel:

> ...Lionel "desires not merely to be in the place of the white man but compulsively seeks to look back and down on himself from that position. Indeed what Lionel compulsively seeks to do from that position is to shoot himself. Induced into a state of paralysis by his ambivalent identification, Lionel is unable to do anything about the dismal state of his personal and professional life (Stratton 91).

In the novel, Lionel is gifted a leather jacket by the four Native tricksters, part of their agenda being to "fix" his life. The jacket, in a magic realist manner is the Jacket John Wayne wore in one of his movies and it feels "soft and warm" to Lionel only for him to realize later that its "tight" and "suffocated" him, thus helping him reject an imposed idea of identity and thus regain his place in the community. His uncle's final act of defiance/ resistance also helps Lionel understand his own

139

place in the community. Walton comments thus, "By the end of the novel Lionel rejects the jacket and begins to accept the culture he has been taught to repudiate" (Walton 89).

King debunks the stereotypes also in his portrayal of Amos Frank, Alberta's father. The reader first meets Amos in a condition where he perfectly suits the bill of the stereotypical Native. Drunk, screaming and covered in shit, Amos seems to be King's representation of the defeated Native and the dominant discourse seems to have vindicated itself. Some more pages into the text and one's perception of Amos undergoes a radical change, owing to not one but two incidents. In both incidents, the reader also witnesses the highhandedness of white authorities over the Native. In the first incident, Amos and his family's dancing outfits are disrespected and confiscated without any provocation. Later, when the outfits are recovered by an insincere Canadian government, they are found to be "badly tattered" with "the pattern of dirt on the sleek feathers where someone with boots had walked on them" (283). Further undermining of the stereotype takes place when it is learnt that Amos is not a mere good-for nothing drunken Native but one who is a responsible member of the community. Working for the tribal police, Amos's job is to track down missing cars from the reserve and get them back to their owners. When Amos's repeated efforts to recover his friend Milford's truck from the white authorities fail, Amos sets it afire and even though Coyote is hinted to be responsible for this, the reader gets a gut feeling that it might well could have been Amos.

King's comic portrayal of the Hollywood Indian in Portland Looking Bear exposes the dual purpose of demonstrating the stereotype and subverting it simultaneously. While Hollywood would not, obviously, portray him in a lead role, Portland has to change his name to a more "authentic" sounding "Iron Eyes Screeching Eagle" to gain prominence in Hollywood. King mocks at the Hollywoodish stereotyping of the Indian by showing the absurdities in the representation of the Native in Hollywood. That the dominant culture reduces the Other to the status of clowns becomes evident when Portland is asked to wear a rubber nose to look more "Indian" and "the only professionals he knew who wore rubber noses were clowns" (152). Portland's tragic transformation of his own appearance signifies the hegemonic practice of oppressive mythification. And both Portland's "voice" and appearance undergo a change and dissolve his own identity.

140

In his second stint at Hollywood, roles do not come to Portland and he has to strip and act as a painted savage in a steakhouse. His son Charlie too hesitantly takes up the "Indian" job of parking cars at a joint. Portland, smarter this time with the knowledge of manipulating the stereotype asks his son to "grunt" because "the idiots love it, and you get better tips" (209). Though in keeping up with the "act" Portland succeeds to debunk the stereotype, as a by-product of the "act," a significant aspect of his own identity also gets erased.

Then there is Charlie looking Bear, Portland's son, who even though debunks the stereotype in being a corporate lawyer, is definitely an opportunist assimilationist. He is, as Alberta describes, "sleazy," though he does not agree to the compliment. Charlie knows that it's a white game to have hired a Blackfoot lawyer against Eli Stands Alone; he understands the purpose behind it and still does not mind being a part of it. A firm believer of the materialistic culture of the hegemonic authority, Charlie would rather leave aside his Native identity and earn money, which he sees as the only escape route from the reservation life. Charlie too, like Lionel, is in love with Alberta and thinks of himself as a better option for Alberta, though Alberta is equally noncommittal to both of them. Charlie however, unlike Lionel, does not seem to share any special bonding with his immediate and extended family. Even while working at Remington's, a steak house in Hollywood, Charlie felt that the "Cowboy outfits weren't bad" and he "hoped he'd get one with a blue shirt and a Red bandanna" (209). At one point in the text Charlie even contemplates buying a house inside West Edmonton Mall, the supreme manifestation of colonial progress. However, at the end of the novel, when the dam bursts in the Coyote-created earthquake, the "use and throw" policy of the colonial authority is foregrounded as Charlie loses his job.

The women in *GGRW*, especially Native women, further King's cause of subverting the stereotype and appropriating it to establish a Native discourse. Othered by race and gender as they are, King's women, however, confront victimization and assert their individual dignity. At the same time, they also serve their roles in the community and continue tradition.

Confronting the Euroamerican portrayal of women as submissive and foolish, King draws his Blackfoot women with much more blood and lived experience. The four mythical, powerful tricksters in the text are female archetypes though they take up the guise of canonical male characters. Likewise, the "real" women in King's novel   141
too know how to "fix" their lives on their own. As King himself

states, "The Women in my books don't take things for granted. They work pretty hard to get what they want and have to make specific decisions to "make their lives come together "(Canton 99).

That Alberta Frank, one of the most prominent Blackfoot women in *GGRW* is a University Professor and a woman of today is not a coincidence. Alberta is not the stereotypical, all-suffering, submissive, wife material that the dominant discourse so often glorifies. Rather, she is unconventional in her approach to life and relationships. She dates two men, is willing to marry none and still plans for a baby, all her own. Her almost passionate struggle to have a baby is repeatedly depicted in the novel. Finally, Coyote trickery comes to her rescue and she becomes pregnant without the violation of any of her terms. "Holding to principles is also a theme that resurfaces in Alberta Frank's story," comments Walton (Walton 83). For Alberta, the freedom of being a woman and not merely a wife matters most. She also knows how to assert herself in the face of racial biases. At one point in the text Alberta checks in to "Blossom Lodge" and asks for a university discount:

> "And does the lady work at a university?"
> Alberta pulled out her university identification card and her driver's license.
> The desk clerk smiled and handed her cards back to her.
> *"You can't always tell by looking,"* he said.
> "How true it is", said Alberta. *"I could have been a corporate executive."*
> (emphasis mine) (174).

Another Native female character who not only shuns stereotyping but also manipulates it to her advantage is Latisha. Latisha's comically named Dead Dog Café is a play on the White idea of the Native. It simultaneously pokes fun at the offensive term "dog-eater" used for the Natives and makes the whites literally "pay" for the joke. The name "Dead Dog Café," according to Chester, brings to mind "Nietzsche's famous words that "God is dead," or at least contrary in the Blackfoot country" (Chester 55). Latisha serves "authentic" "dog-meat" for the "tourists" coming to her restaurant and makes a parodic mythification of the expected "exotica." When she is questioned about it by some "tourists" she very forthrightly declares it as a "treaty right" (132) and goes on to add that the "idiots" love it. Her subversion of a colonialist joke has transformed her restaurant to a "nice local establishment

142

with a loyal but small a tourist trap" (emphasis original) (108). Her menu boasts of Dog du Jour, Houndburgers, Puppy Potpourri, Hot Dogs, Saint Bernard Swiss Melts, with Doggie Doos, and Deep fried Puppy Whatnots for appetizers (109). The restaurant wall is also done up with "photographs like those you see in the hunting and fishing magazines" but the white hunters are replaced with "Indians and dogs" (109). The waiters at her restaurant dress up to complete the picture and the "dressing up" is more about variety than authenticity. Latisha's exploitation of the white perception /imagination of the Native counter-appropriates and confronts the dominant discourse by poking fun at its own constructs. Cheryl Lousley remarks that, *"The Dead Dog Café* disrupts and disturbs the racist tourist gaze by playing with and profiting from the tourist's own cultural narratives and assumptions" (Lousley 33).

King's portrayal of the "Dead Dog Café" thus confronts the ideas generated and propagated by the dominant colonial discourse and counters it by comical subversion. In the process, he also "capitalizes" on the "commodification" of the Native by reversing the offense of "dog-eater" on the whites. By his "Dead Dog Café" Joke, King also shatters another myth that Natives are not capable of humor. The joke in fact stems from a tragic experience from the past of the Native peoples. Margery Fee and Jane Flick comment that "Native Americans turn the sad reality of near-starvation for the Sioux around the time of Little Bighorn, when they had to eat dogs after the buffalo disappeared, into a joke" (Fee and Flick137).

Further, Latisha also confronts and discards canonical patriarchy by ending her marriage to a white, abusive husband. Latisha is initially attracted to the American George Morningstar because his name "sounded slightly Indian" (131). But the marriage crumbles down with George's increasingly violent physical and emotional assaults. Latisha avoids her own "thingification" by her white husband by abandoning the abusive relationship.

The brain behind Latisha's "Dead Dog Café" is her auntie Norma. Norma is a guide to her young nieces and nephews and helps them out with their personal and professional lives. Having lived all her life in the reserve, she also commands respect in the community. She is also the one who makes the family members aware of their traditional roles. She understands her own responsibilities quite well. She also punishes Eli for having been away from home for long by not informing him about their mother's funeral. But Norma is also the one who drives Eli to stay at their mother's house, thus giving him a chance to 143 reclaim his family and community identity. It's not strange then that Norma shuns both her brother Eli and nephew Lionel for each one of them trying to be a "white man." She tells disapprovingly of the white man: "As if they were something special. As if there weren't enough of them in the world already" (37).

Norma's worldview is a maternal-matriarchal worldview that denies a superior status to men because as a Blackfoot woman, she debunks the patriarchal, colonial view of women being dependent and subordinate to men. She turns the table by saying it's actually men whose distorted thought processes make them think so. Norma is of the view that it's not actually men but children that women want. Norma's tribal, feminist discourse is further strengthened in the following passage:

> ... Most women want children. Why do you think there are so many human beings in this world? You think women are that crazy about man? You think women are that crazy about sex? Day after we find some other way to get pregnant, you guys will be as attractive as week-old fry bread" (124).

Norma doesn't stop at advising Lionel and guiding him towards a better life. She also expects Eli to do his duty of an uncle who had to "counsel his sister's son, tell him how to live a good life, show him how to be generous, teach him how to be courageous" (264) and it can be derived that its owing to Norma's insistence that Eli takes Lionel to the Sun Dance that subsequently culminates in Lionel's reintegration to his family and community. At the end of the novel, when Eli dies in the earthquake, Norma is happy for him because "he had a good life" and he "lived it right" (420). Norma also demonstrates her sense of familial responsibility by opting to live in her mothers' house after Eli's death. King's female characters thus confront the colonial idea of women and present themselves as assertive individuals who discard submission to victimization and trivialization and who live life on their own terms and conditions. They are no less feminine for being so.

As history is experienced differently by different people often depending on the power/powerlessness of the people who experience it, Native authors while reappropriating the representation of their own selves also reappropriate the representation of the colonial forces on Native terms. King's portrayal of the white characters in *GGRW* is in keeping with this aspect of postcoloniality.

The character Buffalo Bill Bursum, named in allusion to the Bursum Bill of 1921 infamous for its hostile proposal to divest Pueblo land to non-Natives and also to William F. Cody whose Buffalo Bill Cody's Wild West Show exploited Indians for entertainment of the whites (Flick148) perhaps engrosses Native and non-Native readers of the text equally well. By being the creator of "The Map" in the text that gives him a sense of "power and control," Bursum represents the colonial gaze. Bursum's contempt and hatred for Natives is evident in the following passage. The passage also reflects on the colonial affinity for naming the Other:

> ...You couldn't call them Indians. You had to remember their tribe, as if that made any difference, and when some smart college professor did come up with a really good name like Amerindian, the Indians didn't like it (187).

Bursum is shell-shocked when the four magical Indians fix his favorite Western and thus enable a Native victory because his "knowledge" would not permit such a reversal. A firm believer of the "map," Bursum "had looked at the topographical map that Duplesis provided" and "picked out the best piece of property on the lake" that was "secluded," "exclusive" and "valuable" (256). By putting him on the spot when the Coyote generated earthquake changes the landscape to its pre-dam avatar, King, in a sense, makes him a witness to experience the geographical appropriation, giving him a taste of what the Natives must have felt when their lands were forcefully taken away from them.

The racist bias inherent in the dominant community is further substantiated by King's portrayal of Clifford Sifton, the dam engineer. The historical Clifford Sifton was a Federal minister of the Interior and superintendent of Indian affairs in 1896 and was an aggressive promoter of the Prairie West movement that resulted in the displacement of a large Native population (Flick 150). Fee And Flick thus comment on the deafness of the historical Sifton, "That the historical Sifton was quite deaf is apt--many characters in this novel don't listen when they should" (Fee and Flick 132) King's Sifton too is a champion of the colonial urges to control and exercise power over nature who discards Native rights as a "barrel load of crap" (138) and dismisses Indians like Eli who "drive cars, watch television, go to hockey games" as not "real Indians"(141). Sifton's short sightedness and the characteristic colonial sense of superiority is evident when he says that the dam will "crack   145 and leak" but "won't break" (143). By the end of the novel, we have witnessed the futility of such claims. Robin Riley Fast thus comments on Sifton:

> King draws attention to ... antihistorical bias in the beneficiaries of white historical varieties; this is most obvious in dam engineer Clifford Sifton, who simultaneously disclaims responsibility for the dam and asserts control (Fast 32).

Sifton's shortsightedness is reemphasized when the missing cars appear on the lake but are "beyond the range" (401) of Clifton's sight and he can only see them as "dots on the horizon" (401) even when he uses "the glasses" (402). The colonial discourses' blurred vision and lack of listening skills are metaphorically alluded to in Sifton's apparent deafness and his unhealthy vision.

Another white character in the text that needs mention is that of George Morningstar, Latisha's abusive American husband. Latisha's initial liking for him notwithstanding, George is a racist to the core. His name alludes to George Armstrong Custer, the famous general. In fact, at one point in the book, he introduces himself as General Custer, thus giving the reader a broad hint of the allusion. George is further related to John Wayne, the star of the Western that gets fixed, by his "fringed leather jacket." If Sifton represented the colonizer's lack of ears, George stands for the colonizer's make-believe, pretentious listening to the Native-"He made you believe that he was listening, made you believe that what you had to say was important, made you believe that he was interested" (133). But reality was far from it. George listens because his colonial mindset is hopelessly clueless about Natives in particular and the world in general. His pretentiousness also manifests itself when from not at all touching Latisha in their first month together, he becomes a terribly abusive wife-beater. George's almost stupid and absurd generalizations about the 'Americans' and the 'Canadians' that always ended up with a superiorization of the American is a parody of the contemporary American neo-colonialism. The colonial affinity towards the non-living and the mechanical finds expression in George's daily procurement of a new kitchen gadget when he briefly takes up cooking at home. George too, like Bursum and Sifton, is dispossessed of his sense of superiority and power when in his final appearance in the novel he is caught by Eli while secretly photographing the Sun Dance. George is interested in the Sun

Dance not because he truly respects the sanctity of the ritual but because it's a "Real Indian" thing "just like the movies" (336). That George's reality is shaped by the movies speaks a lot about the distortion of reality in the hands of the hegemonic forces.

One of the most amazing characters in *GGRW* is Dr. Joseph Hovaugh, his name being an allusion to the biblical Jehovah, and who is now the director of the mental asylum from which the four old Indians escape. Hovaugh's faith in "the book" and "the map" reinforce his colonial perception of the world. Moreover, his constant preoccupation with "the dates," "Occurrences, probabilities, directions, and deviations" (16) emphasize the colonial difficulty with wilderness. His office desk, "a rare example of colonial woodcraft" has been "stripped, repaired and stained blond" and thus is akin to what the Natives have been subjected to in the colonial discourse/rule. Lousley points out thus, "Dr. Hovaugh's "Colonial woodcraft" desk carries the memory of colonial deforestation and the associated persecution, displacement, and forced assimilation of Aboriginal people" (Lousley 19). Hovaugh's obsession with "patterns," his uneasiness with Canada that "seemed slightly wild, more out of hand, disorderly, ever chaotic," his research with "brochures and travel guides" and his chart of the "literal, allegorical, topological anagogic" also connects him to Frye's *Anatomy of Criticism* (Chester 30) as "King's text self-consciously defies categorization in Frye's terms" (Chester 50). Dr. J. Hovaugh in both his first and final appearance in the book takes pleasure in looking out at the wall and the tree and the flowers and the swans on the blue-green pond in the garden" (16). This perhaps points to the fact that the colonizer has not undergone change with time and experience and is in fact the one "wrapped in the past."

King's portrayal of the whites in his fiction thus confronts the hegemonic sense of superiority and provides a more accurate picture of the dominant culture, its peoples and practices. His depiction of the whites in *GGRW* borders on the satiric and thus counter-appropriates the hegemonic discourse.

Simultaneously operating at least two levels of narration, the text deals with the lives and times of a group of contemporary Blackfoot characters and the whites somehow or other associated with them on one level and with the magic realist counter-mythification of canonical stories on the other. The common thread that joins the two narratives is King's appropriation of the master discourse. The structure of the novel, thus, can be described in terms of what George Lipsitz 147 terms as "counter-memory":

Counter-memory looks to the past for the hidden histories excluded from dominant narratives. But unlike myths that seek to detach events and actions from the fabric of any larger history, counter memory forces revision of existing histories by supplying new perspectives about the past. Counter-memory embodies aspects of myths and aspects of history, but it remains an enduring suspicion of both categories. Counter-memory focuses on localized experiences with oppression, using them to reframe and refocus dominant narratives purporting to represent universal experience (Walton 74).

King's narrative style foregrounds the cyclicality central to Native oral traditions. Articulating a Native view of the world with seamless effort, King's plotting of the story challenges the western conventions of storytelling. King's narration juxtaposes cultures, traditions, norms, myths, histories, and all such constructs in a confrontational atmosphere, though it does not necessarily make them oppositional. Louis Owens argues that for "writers who identify as Native (American), the novel represents a process of reconstruction, of self-discovery and cultural recovery" (Rohrbarcher np). King's narration works towards this objective of appropriation and cultural survival. Written in the Native tradition of storytelling, *GGRW* is, as King himself says, an "oral piece" (Gillies 91).

Thus King's narrative technique fuses myth and reality to such an extent that alternative discourses overlap and combine to produce what King calls an "Interfusional" effect. In *GGRW*, "the real, as it were, and the fantastic are so intertwined so as to dovetail into one another that it's hard to draw the line between where one ends and the other begins," King tells us (Andrews 179). As the Four mythical narrators take turns narrating their versions of the canon and the realist Blackfoot characters move on with their stories, a dynamic set of stories comes to circulate and "create a world where the border lines between human, natural, and supernatural are not clear or hierarchized" (Lousley 24).

GGRW is dialogic in more than one sense. Its continuous concern with the oral and the written, the Native and the Alter-Native, the canon and the anti-canon is reflected in King's use of multiple sources and multiple narrations in the book. Linton argues that "the text represents a communal reciprocity" and "a shared consciousness by means of echoes linking one strand of narrative with another" (Linton 224). As King blurs conventions, boundaries, and

148

codes, the text speaks to the readers from a dialogic gap. As he draws alternatives for literary and historical discourses, *GGRW* is narrativized to concurrently present two worldviews as separate from each other as they could be. As the text speaks from within and outside, differences are contextualized by means of dialogic. Drawing from Bakhtin's "dialogism," Chester comments that *GGRW* is a "dialogue between oral and written, between Native and Christian creation stories, and between literary and historical discourse" and "(T)he various written dialogues that are created and carried on throughout *GGRW* suggest a dialogism that reflects oral tradition and First Nations and Native American perspectives of the world" (Chester 45-46). Thus conversations and dialogues abound in the text fulfilling King's purpose of creating a confrontational narrative.

The rich intertextuality, a dialogic mode, multiple narrative modes, a confrontation of pre-established norms, appropriation of the master discourses and the drawing of multiple sources in *GGRW*- all point towards its postmodernist character. Even as *GGRW* draws from the Native oral tradition, it demonstrates the author's grasp of the canonical traditions and devices. That the author is technically sound and at ease with western conventions of writing is evident in his use of allusions, allegory, irony, parody and subversive humour, all elements of a "postmodern Pastichè" (Walton 73). King's postmodern parody in *GGRW* that worked towards representing the unrepresented thus qualifies to be a postcolonial text. His playful fusion of the Native orality with the postmodern mode of self-conscious storytelling along with his use of western literary devices makes *GGRW* a hybrid text of the postcolonial, postmodern variety.

Chapter V:
Building up Myths:
Maria Campbell's *Halfbreed*

Postcolonial writing has enabled the marginals of the world to build up myths of their own peoples, communities and cultural practices. The exponents of the poststructuralist movement have also eased the path for the reshaping of the conventional assumptions and conceptions of language, literature, history and textuality. It is now widely agreed upon that "absolute" is a falsity and truth is what is represented and hence no more single or authentic. With a newfound pride in their ways of life, their culture and heritage, the subaltern communities are becoming conscious of their sense of place and time in the scheme of the universe. Hence, they are debunking the stereotypical terms in which they were defined till now which leads them to a deliberate creation of myths about themselves in an attempt to make others understand who they really are and also as a weapon of resistance. This chapter seeks to investigate such conscious processes of mythicizing at it takes place inside the autobiographical novel of Métis writer, poet, activist Maria Campbell's much acclaimed autobiographical novel *Halfbreed*. This chapter looks into Campbell's craft of negotiating a unique identity for her peoples through her mythicizing of historical times as well as her own childhood memories. It dwells on Campbell's mythicizing of the varied aspects of Métis life including the love for family and community, the relationship between the younger and older generations. It also deals with a Métis representation of the Canadian history and the representation of such historical figures as Louis Riel and Gabriel Dumont as Métis heroes. It will also underline the female hero's journey towards her own identity in the fictional world, which will testify to the reaffirmation of the subaltern in the face of the odds of the hegemonic society.

Postcolonialism, amongst its various functions and agendas, foregrounds the presence of peoples and communities hitherto relegated to the margins of existence. Passed off till recently in the dominant discourse as a bunch of minstrels or buffoons, these marginals are now raising their voices and filling the gap with their stories, their myths, their worldviews and their thought processes. Dismissed and denied an identity in the myths of the dominant cultures/ races/ discourses, these marginals are taking charge to recreate a lost identity and rewrite myths through their writing. Using the very tools that were used against them, the marginals are building up new myths to replace the falsifications they have been subjected to by the dominant forces. By using various techniques of subversion like irony, humor, parody, mimicry etc., the marginals are building up new myths about themselves. Moreover, while writing in the language of the dominant forces, they twist it in such a manner that the indigenous myths and stories are underlined.

This chapter looks into these postcolonial practices of the marginal communities of the world. Taking the framework of a postcolonial, postmodernist, poststructural perspective, this chapter attempts to understand the building up of myths in the writings of marginals with a focus on one such voice from the margin. Taking the Métis Canadian writer storyteller Maria Campbell's autobiographical novel *Halfbreed* into account, this study attempts to analyze the building up of myths in her novel. This study also attempts to recognize the various nuances Campbell uses for mythicizing the stories of her life and her people.

The status of myth has actualized itself in different forms and different domains in the contemporary postcolonial era. In such a scenario, it becomes a herculean task to demonstrate the significance of myth in an effective and equivocal manner. Eric Gould in his brilliant book Mythical Intentions in Modern Literature thus tries to capture the vastness of myth in the following words:

> ... myth is now so encyclopedic a term that it means everything or nothing. We can find in it whatever we want to say is essential about the way humans try to interpret their place on earth- myth is a synthesis of values which uniquely manage to mean most things to most men. It is allegory and tautology, reason and unreason, logic and fantasy, waking thought and dream, atavism and the perennial, archetype and metaphor, origin and end (Gould 5).

Myth, as the quote above suggests, thus, has an inherent power not merely to re-present events through language but also to re-shape the event itself. Myth taps the internal landscape of the collective consciousness of a community by means of giving them a place in the world and mythical time often decides the contemporary understanding of a people about themselves. Quoting Frank Kermode, Sylvia Söderlind emphasizes on the difference between myth and fiction:

> Myth operates within the diagrams of ritual, which presupposes total and adequate explanations of things as they are and were; it is a sequence of radically unchangeable gestures. Fictions are for finding things out, and they change as the needs of sense-making change. Myths are the agents of stability, fictions the agents of change. Myths call for absolute, fictions for conditional assent. Myths make sense in terms of a lost order of time, *illud tempus* as Eliade calls it; fictions, if successful, make senses of the here and now, *hoc tempus* (emphasis original) (Söderlind 17).

Not quite in agreement with the view, this study proceeds to propose through the analysis of *Halfbreed* that myth in fact changes with time and a brilliant writer like Campbell can justifiably modify previous myths to establish new myths through fiction. For myths and fictions reveal the paradox of language itself as a system, defined in linguistic terms as both sequence (syntagm) and schemata (paradigm), observes Gould (Gould 11).

In that sense myth surpasses history and historical records, thus throwing light on what existed before history came into existence. For it is in myth that the human being gains the knowledge of a pre-historic past and it is in myth that she often seeks solutions for the issues of the present. For myth has always existed in human psyche and internal landscape as that which was and which no more is unambiguous. Amidst these conditions, it becomes essential for writers like Campbell to wipe out the ambiguity and confusion so as to establish a clear picture and to take pride in such an act.

It is through myth that reality takes shape and life gathers meaning. It is by means of mythical imagination that a community gains its own significance and identity. It is through myth that a community distinguishes its own way of life, its culture, its rituals and ceremonies, customs and practices, its understanding of the world and its distinction from others. Fiction, thus, dives into mythicity in order to acquire for itself the authority of myth. In the process, 153 however, it demythicises earlier myths so as to replace them with what could be termed *contemporary myths* (emphasis mine). Speaking from a peripheral space of the pariah, the marginalized and the colonized, Maria Campbell is one author who is not once, not twice but *thrice marginalized* in her gender, her race and her Halfbreed descent (emphasis mine). For this purpose, it twists language and events in a manner hitherto unimagined. Hence, Myth and fiction in the postcolonial, postmodern era become interdependent and complementary for mutual survival. And history is often appropriated through mythicizing.

She is a woman, a Native woman and a Métis Native woman all at once. This is not quite an envious positionality to say the least. Holding on to this abstract positionality in a dignified and determined manner, Campbell raises her voice to speak the othered other's story. Darias-Beautell comments:

> It is this cultural split of the Métis subject that is explored and contested in Maria Campbell's autobiographical *Halfbreed* (1973). Away from the either/or Indian/White French choice, Campbell's parodic discourse makes use of well known cultural stereotypes to counteract an exclusive biculturalism and to posit, instead, a third more fluid transcultural position (Darias-Beautell 194).

In its assertive depiction of Métis culture and lifestyle, Campbell's *Halfbreed* demythicizes the earlier notions held of her peoples and her race in the dominant discourse. Colonial writers have often stereotyped the Halfbreed as an amalgamation of the "civilized"/ "savage" dichotomy. One such example is found in William J. Scheick's depiction of the Halfbreed or Half-blood, which is reproduced here: "By his very nature the half-blood epitomized the integration (whether successful or unsuccessful) of the red and the white races, provided a dramatic symbol of the benign possibilities or malign probabilities inherent in their encounter..." (Hobert 5). Maria Campbell, through *Halfbreed*, breaks down these myths about the Métis propagated by the colonial mind to give us a truer and honest picture of what it means to be a Halfbreed in Canada.

Speaking from the margin, Campbell, through her portrayal of her community, their fun and frolic, their stories, their livelihood, their language, their festivals and music, attempts to establish an identity, unique and distinct as it is, of her own people and for the outside world to reckon it. Sylvia Söderlind comments on this

154

postcolonial politics of difference: "... any statement of identity is an assertion of difference ... the postmodern interest in the ontology of difference is central to the postcolonial situation" (Söderlind 5).

Drawing upon the already held notions about the Halfbreed peoples, Maria Campbell deconstructs known moulds to replace them with myths that she builds up through her description of the Halfbreedian ways of life. Alicia Ostriker in "The Thieves of Language" calls this "feminist revisionist mythmaking" (Kent 105).

Taking pride in the pejorative term "Halfbreed," Campbell goes on to write her story interfused with the larger story of her peoples. In the novel, she sprinkles with good measure experiences from her childhood to establish a singular identity of the Halfbreed Community, distinct from both the Whites and the Natives. Toni Culjak writes: "... Maria Campbell's *Halfbreed* ... deals specifically with Métis culture, the only one that presents a 'world in between'"(Culjak 142). For the whites, the Métis were "breeds" and "Road-Allowance people" and for Indians they were "poor relations" "*awp-pee-too-koosoons*" or half-people. Living in between cultures and accepted in neither, Campbell defines the happy times as well as bad times of her people in graphic detail. Straddling between two worlds and deriving their way of life from both, the Halfbreeds represented a unique identity of their own.

Campbell adds to the mythic dimension of her story by depicting several aspects of Métis life, the problem of racism being only one of all. She goes on to give us details of the various socio-cultural practices of her peoples, like marriages, funerals, festivities, dance and music and also fights. Upsetting the stereotypical highhandedness of the so-called "pure" cultures, of which none can truly claim to exist in the postmodern reality, Campbell takes a certain pride in describing the vivid pluralism of her own culture, the Métis.

In her depiction of the gala time (she and her people had on Christmas) and of their attending the Sun Dances (of their Indian neighbors), Campbell shows a people comfortable in, and accepting of, both European and Indian traditions. She recalls with vivid detail the fun she had as a child in going for the midnight Mass, in the Christmas dinner full of delicacies, the dances and the accompanying fights. Campbell also talks about the elaborate weddings of her community thus: "Weddings were something special, and were gay and gala affairs, in which everyone in our area and other communities participated" (52). The beauty of *Halfbreed* lies in that even while describing such   155 happy times as marriages, Campbell subtly reinforces the poverty that was an integral part of Métis life. Here is a poignant quote demonstrating the same:

> Everyone lined up in the procession with their horses decorated as well. *The bride wore a white satin dress which had been worn by many other brides and was altered so many times you could see all the different stitches* (emphasis mine) (52).

The funkiesm of the community is highlighted in all aspects of their lives. Violence, it seems, was also an accepted social behavior, as the Halfbreeds loved good fights as much as they loved dancing and merrymaking. The Halfbreeds, Campbell says, enjoyed fighting with dancing: "We never had a dance without a good fight and we enjoyed and looked forward to it as much as the dancing" (52). Campbell also tells us how the community would have fun in after-wedding parties. She tells us:

> The bride and groom would then move into their new home built by the men in the community. On their first night together the rest of us would collect pans, whistles, drums, anything and sneak over. Then we would all yell and scream and bang the pots and pans together till the couple would both come out and make a speech (53).

Through these descriptions, Campbell builds up myths about her community and its culture, heritage, and ways of life. In her proud reconstruction of her own people, Campbell also celebrates her community. As Penny Petrone observes: "She celebrates community life, capturing the fun-loving spirit of the Métis at weddings, week-end dances with fiddler music, and sports competitions" (Petrone 115). The communal hunting and berry picking trips Campbell describes also emphasize the funkiness and merrymaking nature of the Halfbreeds. Campbell gives a very happy picture of the Métis communal trips in the passage quoted below:

...there were ten or more families in a long caravan....
The evenings were great. The women cooked while the
men pitched the tents and we kids ran about, shouting
and fighting. Parents ... were enjoying themselves ...
the men would wrestle, twist wrists, have target hitting
and there was dancing and singing and visiting. We
kids played bear and *witecoos* ... when we were put to
bed the grown-ups would gather outside and an old
grandpa or granny would tell a story while someone
built up a fire. Soon everyone was taking turns telling
stories, and one by one we would creep out to sit in
the background and listen (emphasis original) (34).

This playfulness of the Métis in "the masks and spaces" in the Métis
could be easily termed as what Mikhail Bakhtin calls as "carnivalesque."
The carnivalesque temperament in Métis people is so strong that poverty
or the lack of clothes, proper food and shelter could never suppress the
vitality of this "unofficial culture" (New 278-279). Campbell expresses it
nicely in an interview with Hartmut Lutz in which she tells us:

We are not poor. We are the richest people in this country.
My people are rich. We might not have lots of stuff, but
we're rich. Anybody that can come through what we've
come through and still be able to laugh and smile is rich
(Lutz 60).

Stories abound in Campbell's *Halfbreed*. Campbell mythicizes her
culture not in vacuum but through a series of stories that mattered in her
childhood. There are stories in the text that tell us about her childhood,
about the community, about elders and leaders, about shame and survival.
It is through these stories that Campbell establishes the prototype of a
Métis childhood and asserts her people's cultural difference from the
other. There are stories about her family, her clan, chiefly depicting the
Métis beliefs and practices.

The stories which Campbell tells in the narrative reveal the
nuances of the Halfbreeds' ways of life. While discussing the different
clans, she takes pride in saying that "they produced the best and most
fearless fighting men and the best looking women" (25). That
doesn't, however, deter her from emphasizing on the special   157
qualities each of her clan people possessed, be it about the

Arcands who were "the music makers" of the community, the St.Denys, Villeneuves, Morrisettes and Cadieux who were producers of home brew and also "ak-ee-top" (pretend) farmers (25).

Through the telling of these family and clan stories, Campbell brings an almost mythical quality to her people. They become mythical characters as we come to know about their very special qualities and powers, and their energy and positivity. Franz Boas, the noted anthropologist points out: "Only when we ourselves are transferred into the realm of mythical beings, that continue to exist somewhere in unknown parts of our world, may myths again become happenings" (Boas 32).

Campbell, by telling us the stories of her people takes the reader into a mythical world where the reader can experience the stories and living through these comes to acknowledge the myths Campbell proposes and propagates.

Not merely that, the very essence of her people and their lives, the fun and frolic, laughter and humor, that is so much a part of Métis life, comes alive through Campbell's generous spread of anecdotal stories in the book. Making ample yet subtle use of techniques like irony and parody, Campbell, through her stories, makes the reader laugh and cry in the same vein. Debunking the stereotype of a serious looking portrait of the aboriginal people sans humor, Campbell portrays the unadulterated picture of Métis life through her signature style of humor.

One such anecdotal story, of the village Joker Alex Vandal is especially interesting for the dual humor it produces. Using the postcolonial practice of subversion, Campbell, through this story, reconstructs the stereotyping her people have been subjected to, only to reverse it and laugh at the dominant culture's perception of her people. She tells us this story that happened on the school registration day:

> The teacher called the roll and parents were to stand in front of her and answer questions. Alex Vandal, the village joker, was at his best that day. He had told Daddy that he was going to act retarded because the whites thought we were anyway, so when his son's name was called he shuffled over. The teacher asked for the first name. Alex replied, "Boy." Then he looked dumbly around and finally yelled at his wife in French and Cree. "Oh, the name is

Paul." The teacher then asked whether Paul knew his ABC's? "No." "Does he count?" "No." "Does he know his prayers?" "No." "Does your son believe in Jesus Christ?" "No." "Don't you believe in Jesus?" "I don't know, I never saw the god" (45).

The depiction of Alex as a dumb person is deliberately done in order to show how the whites foolishly believed in such decrepit notions. Maria, the narrator is very conscious of the reactions of her people in such scenes and, hence, she rightly adds:

> Our people looked straight ahead *trying not to laugh* and the whites were tittering. Alex and Paul returned to their seats all smiles (emphasis mine) (45).

By mimicking the colonizer's idea of the Métis, the Halfbreeds, as a community, and Maria, as a representative of the community, could intentionally poke fun at the master narrative in order to upset the stereotypes. But, unfortunately, the white race sometimes did not have the ability to notice the pranks of the Métis, while at other times, did not relish the same, bitter as it was in nature. Kate Vangen, one of the noted Canadian critics, has rightly observed:

> ... indigenous peoples have undoubtedly been using humour for centuries to 'make faces' at their colonizers without the latter being able to retaliate; however, Native humour has escaped most historical and literary accounts because the recorder did not perceive the gesture as humorous or because he did not appreciate the humour (Grant 127).

There are various other stories in the book, stories that entertain as well as educate the reader about the Métis way of life. One particularly enjoyable story is that of the "ghost" Wolverine that Maria recalls from her childhood days:

> One grave in particular, right beside the fence, had a horrible story associated with it. Grannie Campbell used to tell us that the old man buried in it was called "Ke-qua-hawk-as," which means wolverine in Cree....Whenever I had to go to the store in

159

the evening I would jump the fence and run as fast as
I could, feeling sure that Wolverine was behind me....
Daddy's youngest brother, Robert, was a terrible tease
and was never afraid of ghosts. He would lie beside
Wolverine's grave and when I came back from the store
he would make scratching noises and talk in low gruff
tone...I would pee my pants from fear while running up
the hill, and he would pound the ground to make a sound
of footsteps right behind me" (57-58).

Likewise, the story of witecoos, the white monster who eats
children at night, is not only humorous but is also a subtle strategy to
laugh at the hegemonic forces.

By thus intermingling subversion and laughter, irony and parody,
Campbell, while laughing at herself and her peoples, also laughs at the
white other. Humor, for her, is not merely to entertain but also to resist.
By using humor and by the telling of stories, Campbell not only mythicizes
her childhood experiences but also highlights the importance of these
elements in Métis life, especially stories. Much learning takes place
through the stories and community myths that Métis children listen to
from family members and community elders. It's through these sessions
that the transfer of knowledge takes place and children learn about various
aspects of Métis cultural heritage.

Emphasizing the importance of stories for the very survival of her
culture and peoples, Campbell, in an interview with Hartmut Lutz, opines
that "if we lose the stories, we've lost the people" (Lutz 56). To take it
further, it is in mythicizing that the present and future of the Métis can
be aspired for and it is in mythicizing that the past can be reconstructed.
By her use of humor, pathos, resistance, courage and defiance, Campbell,
through the stories of her childhood, has mythically recreated a community
that is suffering from degeneration through the imported problems of
alcoholism and loss of pride and thus reestablishes the history of her
peoples through her own history.

By telling the "truth" of the other side, Campbell creates new
myths and shatters many previously held notions about her peoples. By
reconstructing her childhood through humour and stories, Campbell
thus defies the convention. Through this Campbell attempts to gain an
identity that asserts "a feeling of rootedness of belonging to a time and
place" (Bastien 128).

Campbell adds to the mythic dimensions of her story by the portrayal of such graceful and gigantic figures of her race like her great grandmother. Cheechum, as she calls her, is at once her teacher, confidante, philosopher, all rolled into one. Firm and determined throughout her life, it is Cheechum who is the pathfinder for Maria. In her childhood as well as later in life, when she is lost in the bylines of alcoholism and exploitation, its Cheechum's teachings that help her recover. Maria learns the lessons of life, social, cultural as well as political from her various conversations and interactions with Cheechum. Early on in the book, we are introduced to the daring attitude and ferocity of Cheechum. Married to a jealous and suspicious Scottish man, Cheechum however does not accept a silent sufferer's destiny. Her husband pays for his brutality with his life, apparently killed by her kinsfolk. Again, when the white government tries to dispossess her off her house, she fiercely defends herself and her home, never to be troubled again.

Thoroughly disapproving of the colonizer's ways of life, Cheechum, "refused to sleep on a bed or eat off a table." It's through Cheechum that Maria gathers her knowledge of Métis history and tradition. Through Cheechum Maria reappropriates the history of the Northwest Rebellion. Never accepting their defeat at Batoche in the hands of the white Canadians, Cheechum would always say, "Because they killed Riel they think they have killed us too, but someday, my girl, it will be different" (15). Two things are important here: first, the historical Riel Rebellion which will be dealt with later in the chapter; secondly, the role of Cheechum, acting as the towering figure in the shaping of Maria's life.

Cheechum infuses the sense of community pride and what could be termed as Métis consciousness in young Maria, She is the one who instills in Maria the confidence and courage to "walk with your head up" (36). Cheechum awakens Maria to the dominant forces' divide and rule policy and warns her not to fall into a trap of self-hatred and a hatred of her own people.

Eternally waiting and continually becoming optimistic, Cheechum hopes for a better future for her peoples. When Maria's Daddy becomes the butt of jokes in his community for being a part of a new political movement for the Métis, it's only Cheechum who supports him wholeheartedly and defends his stance. Later on when the movement fails again due to the divide and rule policy of the whites, and Daddy returns home a defeated man, Cheechum is still persistent with her hope of a brighter future. She tells Maria, "It will come, my girl, someday it will 161 come" (67). Cheechum asks Maria to stay unperturbed and wait for that one real leader to come. But when Maria's father signed up for the war and got rejected, Cheechum was happy, as she was opposed to the white man's war. She would say: "The war was white business, and was just between rich and greedy people who wanted power" (24).

Cheechum stands for the Métis community, consciousness, political dream, and socio-cultural preservation of tradition in the book. The narrative almost moves through her voice and Maria's search for an identity concretizes with Cheechum's teaching. Commenting on this aspect of *Halfbreed*, Helen M. Buss points out: "Through her use of Cheechum as a paradigm, and through the writing of her autobiography, Campbell attempts to restore an archetypal image of woman as powerful and good" (Buss 165).

Not only her political and communal sense but also Maria's spiritual sense of the world is shaped by Cheechum. Not quite in agreement with the church, a young Maria's view of the world and all its beings is constructed by Cheechum. Sprinkled with practicality of the Métis life and worldview, Cheechum's philosophy comforts Maria. Maria learns the Métis idea of truth and beauty through Cheechum's teachings. Cheechum's practical wisdom, which almost echoes oriental Karmic philosophies and worldview also subtly links the past to the present, a past supported by quite a good amount of anthropological evidence that the Orientals were perhaps the founding ancestors of the Natives of the U.S and Canada. Campbell tells us about Cheechum's philosophy that teaches her to see and respect life in all creation and to understand the continuity of the soul:

> Her philosophy was much more practical, soothing and exciting and in her way I found comfort ... She taught me to see beauty in all things around me; that inside each thing a spirit lived, that it was vital too, regardless of whether it was good or bad; that heaven and hell were man-made and here on earth; that there was no death, only that the body becomes old from life on earth and that the soul must be reborn, because it is young; that when my body became old my spirit would leave and I'd come back and live again (72).

When Qua Chich, Maria's wealthy Indian grandaunt tells Maria not "to look at animals or people when babies were being made" or else "go blind," Cheechum tells her about the beauty of procreation – "No one goes blind from seeing animals make babies. It is a beautiful thing" (23). Cheechum is the symbol of Campbell's sense of cultural identification and it is her influence on Campbell that helps the great granddaughter seek "her sense of place, self, and community," Culjak rightly observes (Culjak 142).

Maria Campbell carefully weaves a myth about the engaging activities of the Halfbreed children in the early stages of their life when they are surrounded and protected by their parents and grandparents. Such mythicizing not only goes against the downsizing of the Halfbreeds by the mainstream whites, but also celebrates the inner strength of the Halfbreeds and their culture. It is also in Cheechum's stories that Maria gets her primary training in the telling and understanding of stories. The narrative of *Halfbreed* perhaps would not have been as lucid and moving without Maria's childhood experience of listening to stories Cheechum told. Campbell has talked about several storytellers in her community, their use of language and their power to convince. To quote her from the interview with Lutz: "... With the family, the storytelling, its just rich ... The way they use the language, the way they say things. Writers would kill to be able to do that" (Lutz 55).

Keeping intact the oral tradition of the Native peoples which taught the children about "who they were, where they came from, and what they had done" (20), Cheechum tells the story of the little people in which she "believed with heart and soul" (20). In this mythical tale, there are little people who "are so tiny that unless you are really looking for them you will never find them; not that it matters, because you usually only see them when they want you to" (21). Cheechum would also tell about one meeting she had with the little people "dressed in beautiful colors" who, "sat with her until the sun had gone down and then said good-bye and disappeared into the forest" (21). So smitten was the young Maria with the tale that she "would lie by the waters for hours hoping to see the little people" (21).

While dilating the power of the Métis to the mythic dimension, Maria also shows how as peoples, the Métis are endowed with the rare power to know the future through their intuitive sense. Many a time, it had been seen that Cheechum also had a second sight, a mythic vision, an intuitive mind with which she would often correctly predict the death of a loved one or some such tragedy. This capacity to see through the reality into the unknown was not merely the privilege of Cheechum.

163

It was a grand characteristic of the Métis as peoples, Nation. Maria, too, was no exception to it. That Maria too enjoyed such a rare privilege could be proved when she could foresee her mother's death.

Apart from and along with all these, a very important metaphor of the book, that of the blanket, is also created through Cheechum's conversations. On her path to recovery from the vices of the city that had gripped her and taken away her sense of self-worth and dignity, Maria is reminded of the blanket Cheechum used to talk about:

> My Cheechum used to tell me that when the government gives you something, they take all that you have in return—your pride, your dignity, all the things that make you a living soul. When they are sure they have everything, they give you a blanket to cover your shame ... She used to say that all our people wore blankets, each in his own way. She said that other people wore them too, not just Halfbreeds and Indians, and as I grew up I would see them and understand (137).

Victimized by the strategies and policies of the government, the Natives thus lose their sense of a separate entity. Cheechum, through this metaphor of the blanket, is asking them to come out of their cocoons/blankets and speak and stand for themselves. And it is in her ultimate success of throwing off the blanket that Maria fully regains her own place and identity in the world.

Cheechum, thus, is one role model other than her childhood hero, her Dad that Maria tries to emulate. There are many Grandmothers in *Halfbreed*. There is Granny Campbell and Granny Dubuque but none like Cheechum. With her liveliness and ferocity and by expressing the Métis view on politics, social life, tradition, culture, spirituality and religion through her Halfbreed Great Grandmother, Maria gives Cheechum a mythicality she truly deserves. Being a niece of Gabriel Dumont, one of the heroes of the 1885 Rebellion, Cheechum's link to the mythical past is evident.

It is this special, intimate bond that Maria shares with Cheechum and the same bond teaches her all that she would need to sustain and survive in the world, Métis or otherwise. And Cheechum, in a way, is the last link between the thriving past and the present when 164 the Native culture is at the brink of extinction/destruction. Johnson rightly observes:

> *Halfbreed* is bound by the spirit of Cheechum...While Campbell's father taught her to set traps, shoot a rifle and fight like a boy and her mother taught her how to cook, sew and knit like a lady, Cheechum taught her all she knew about life. Cheechum's strength became her confidence (Johnson 3).

By narrating her experiences at school, Maria Campbell, first of all, deconstructs the official, government-sponsored myths of schools, commonly thought to be being the Native people's way to a better life; By her portrayal of the residential and day schools where the Métis children went to "study," Campbell cracks open long-denied pictures of the "mixed school." Campbell's first brush with school comes at the age of seven when she gets a gift from her Indian maternal grandmother, Granny Dubuque, in the form of an admission in a residential school in Beauval. She remembers the unpleasant smell of the school, something akin to "soap and old woman" and of her "footsteps echoing through the building." The prayers at that school, Campbell remembers, were endless.

Maria's second stint at school starts with a new mixed school that came up in Spring River. However, this mixed school, Campbell describes, was heaven in comparison to the residential school. She also tells us her gradual coming of self to protect her siblings in school. She remembers one particular brutal incident that happened to Robbie, her kid brother and though a little late, her firm protection of her brother:

> Robbie was always getting x's as his fingernails were never clear and his hands were chapped and dirty. One day, the teacher found his ears dirty again and told him that if he wasn't clear tomorrow, she would clean him up properly. Robbie washed well the next morning but forgot to do his ears. So she took him to the cloakroom and with a scrub brush- the kind you use on floors- started scrubbing his hands, neck and ears... Soon I heard Robbie whimpering and became alarmed... I went into the cloakroom. She had him bent over the basin, his poor little neck was bleeding and so were his wrists. She was starting on his ears with the brush when I snatched it away and slapped her (77).

She also remembers how her sister Peggie would be insulted by the white teachers at school for her pronunciation of English words. What Peggie and Robbie and their kin face at school is an attempt by the white colonizer to dominate by fear, which Adams calls "the school's network of fears" (Adams137). Discriminated against and marginalized in the school, the Métis children however did not always suffer in silence. Poking fun at the white other in school was their way of punishing the colonizer. Humor being an integral part of the Halfbreedian ways of life, the Métis children enjoyed their share of fun and frolic by othering those who looked down upon them for the colour of their skin or the community they belonged to. She vividly recalls how the Métis children would tease the white children:

> ...they acted very authoritarian and superior towards us...
> In the winter they drove to school in a small caboose...
> We would hide by the side of the road and scare their old
> horse so bad it would run away. It's a wonder they weren't
> burnt alive. Next morning the teacher would receive a
> letter from the parents and we would be whipped in front
> of the class, but in the afternoon we would make it just as
> bad for them until they learned to shut up (48).

These stories/events/incidents from her schooldays reinforce Maria's conscious attempt to break previously held notions and beliefs and construct new myths that represent the Métis reality. In spite of the school negating the Native children their culture, their ways of life, their social practices and deliberately working towards the gradual degeneration of the Native communities, the Native peoples always found ways to survive and thrive. Being disapproved in their behaviour, dressing and food habits, and religious practices did not stop Maria and her kin from leading a truly Métis life.

Contempt for the colonizer's institutions has been an important postcolonial practice. In her scathing attack on the white religion and its symbol, the church, Maria Campbell has not only debunked the missionary and government ideologies but also has reestablished, in the process, a respect and dignity for her people's spiritual and religious orientation that has been denied to them by the oppressor. Showing little respect for the church or for Christianity as such, Campbell tells the reader that she often thinks of "Christians and old clothes together" (28) because of her childhood experiences with the church and its followers. Maria remembers her unpleasant memory of going to the church only once with her mother and her mother being insulted there.

Maria, in a tone of irony, tells that her people were "good Catholics" (31) who believed that "missing Mass was a mortal sin" (31) and then adds that breaking commandments was easy as a few "Hail Mary's" was all that they needed to say in confession. In her imagining the nuns with their black robes and swinging crosses as "The Lady of Shallot," Campbell shows early glimpses of an imaginative mind but in equating the nuns with an Euro-Western figure of pining love, she underscores scant regard for the colonizer's religion. She would rather draw inspiration from her visits to a Church of England in the Sandy Lake Reserve, her maternal grandparents' place, because this church, the catholic nuns would say "was founded by fornicators and adulters" (32) and she is even disappointed to know that an "exciting figure" like Henry VIII "belonged to the Indian instead of the Halfbreeds." In an interview with Lutz, Campbell tells us what she thinks of the church:

> My personal opinion is that when it comes to Aboriginal people in Canada, we have the church 'to thank' in all areas, whether we are Métis, non-status or whatever, for the dilemma that we are in now! Certainly the church has always been the 'man coming in front of' the oppressor, the colonizer (Lutz 47).

Maria's hatred for the church is also manifested in her grave dislike of the priest who would eat "all the choice food" her mother cooked when he came to hold masses in the community and knowing her hatred, "he would smile at me." Parodying the Christian practice of condemning something in public and doing it in private, Maria recalls the "luscious strawberries" of the church which they were not allowed to eat because the Father would say that "it would be stealing form God" and the same father would conveniently steal things from the "Indian's Sun dance Pole" which belonged to the "Great Spirit" (30). Maria's alienation from the church is complete when some years later in an act of counter-hatred, the same Father refuses "to give Momma a Mass because of all the torment I'd caused him" (70). As Franz Fanon distinctly points out: "The Church in the colonies is the white people's Church, the foreigner's Church. She does not call the native to God's ways but to   167 the ways of the white man, of the master, of the oppressor"

(Gallagher 24). Even when Maria gets married she refuses to marry in church saying that "if it would not take my mother, it would never be good enough for me" (105).

Much of Maria's idea of religion and her scorn for Christianity are shaped and influenced by her Great Grandmother Cheechum. Convinced in her knowledge that having married a Christian she has lived in hell and "nothing after death could be worse!" (15), Cheechum has never converted to Christianity. Poor as they were, money paid to church collection was disapproved by Cheechum. She would often say that the Catholic God took more money from her peoples then the Hudson's Bay Store. Even when the whole family would visit the Church for the midnight Mass on Christmas, Cheechum "stayed at home and kept the fire going."

Cheechum's philosophy of life and her approach to religion made more sense to young Maria than the Church could ever have. Discarding the binary vision of Christianity in terms of good/bad, God/evil and such like, Cheechum's spirituality has been Maria's religion:

> She said God lives in you and looks like you, and not to worry about him floating around in a beard and white cloak; that the Devil lives in you and all things, and that he looks like you and not like a cow. She often shook her head at the pictures I gave her of God, angels and devils and the things they did. She laughed when she saw the picture of the Devil turning people over with a fork in the depth of Hell's fire, and remarked that it was no wonder those people looked so unhappy, if that's what they believe in. Her explanation made much more sense that anything Christianity had ever taught me (72).

The Halfbreeds are mythicized as a Nation of another kind, entirely different from the majority culture that encircles them, through their unique love for family in particular and community as a whole. *Halfbreed* reaffirms this integral aspect of Métis life through several anecdotes and instances of Maria's love for her family as well as community. Her early memories of family and community life are a proud and happy one. She fondly recalls early memories of her mother thus:

Mom laughed in those early years, but I remember mostly the clean, spicy smell when she held me close and sang to me at night. She had a soft voice and sang and crooned the babies to sleep (18).

Maria also recalls festive days like Christmas Eve that was full of laughter, good food, "gifts for everyone" and family visits. Maria's depiction of her bonding with her Daddy can be a point of envy for many who belong to the white world. She remembers the exciting hunting trips she had with her Dad. In her loving remembrance of her brothers and sisters, Maria also builds up the myth of what a Halfbreed family is like. Maria nostalgically recalls one communal family trip they had had in the early days of her life:

Summer was always a great time ... We would leave our houses early in the morning and head for the bush to pick Seneca root and berries ... By dinner time three or four wagons of Halfbreeds had joined us along the way and everyone was talking and yelling and joking, excited at seeing one another... What a sight we must have been, each family with one or two grannies, grandpas, anywhere from six to fifteen children, four or five dogs, and horses trimmed with bells. (33-34)

Maria's love for her family becomes even more evident when her mother dies and in an attempt to keep the family together and raise the children, she has to assume the responsibility of being both a father and a mother to her younger siblings. With her mother's death, Maria suddenly becomes a woman with the responsibility of the whole family. She remembers with fondness the close bond her parents shared with each other and how her mother's death completely breaks down her father.

The close bonding between the parents and the children has also an impact on the siblings themselves. The closeness of the family and love for each other manifests itself in her younger brothers who willingly took up work to lend Maria a helping hand. With a new job as a farm hand for Daddy, her family shifts twenty-five miles away from home where the only consolation they had was of being out of the clutches of the relief man. Having lived amongst their people and community, Maria feels lonely; but being a dreamer she also hopes of making friends with the people in her new surrounding and

169

of finishing high school. Further, her friendship with Karen, a white girl, breaks some of the boundaries both were supposed to stay put in. Maria's friendship with Karen is in fact a treatise of crossing the borderline and blurring the binaries of the dialectical world. In the process, old myths like colonizer and the colonized can never be friends stand broken.

The closeness and intimacy Maria feels for her family is again manifested when in spite of dire poverty and having been offered the adoption of her infant siblings by Bob and Ellen, her kindhearted friends, Maria as well as her father reject the idea of parting with them. Proud of their own family and culture and unwilling to accept sympathy even in difficulty, Maria recalls how she felt about the offer:

> Those little ones were mine and part of me. I could
> not give them away. We were very close, all of us, and
> protected and loved each other (92).

Being such a close-knit family, Maria also disapproves her father's idea of remarrying to manage the house. He, too, on his part brings a woman named Sarah home and they stay together for quite some time but ultimately he declines marriage to Sarah because "Mom was the only woman he had ever loved" (103). Thus, the responsibility of the family falls back once more on Maria. Maria is fifteen by that time and with the danger of the relief man lurking hard, she knows she has to decide what to do to keep the family intact.

Having discussed several plans that would help keep the family together, Maria along with advice from her brother Jamie decides that the only option they have is for her to marry. That looks like the only way to keep the relief people at bay. In spite of her fondness for the Halfbreed boy Smoky, she decides against marrying him because "he had nothing" that would help her sustain her family and hence marries Darrel, a white man, at the age of fifteen. Cheechum disapproves of the Match and is almost prophetic in her prediction that "nothing good ever comes from a mixed marriage" (105).

The marriage does not sustain for long. Maria's husband soon starts showing his original racist self and physically and emotionally abuses her. The birth of Maria's firstborn coincides with her husband's betrayal of reporting her family to the welfare. Maria poignantly recalls the ultimate loss of her family:

Darrel was in Prince Albert the day the welfare people came. We were all home and the children were eating lunch when a station wagon pulled up. I looked out the window and I knew that this was it. It was all over. The kids started to cry and hang onto me, but they were pulled away and were in the wagon within a few minutes. I couldn't move. I felt like a block of stone. The wagon drove away with six little faces pressed to the windows, crying for me to help them. I walked around in a daze. Everything went to pieces inside (107).

Lambasting the Canadian government's policy of foster homes for Native and Métis children M.F. Salat comments:

For after all, it is part of the Canadian Government's policy to safeguard the interests of Canadian children. However, the policy does not take cognizance of the human element involved in this separation of parents and children. That the child who is taken away is deprived of natural parental love and bonding in the process is never thought of as being of any consequence. The fall out of the affirmative action in terms of emotional distress is not even acknowledged (Salat 133-134).

Maria Campbell's mythicizing comes to an apotheosis while she deifies the fictional female hero, i.e., Maria struggling through a series of obstacles in her life's journey. She endows on the female hero grandeur through a tragic dignity which she achieves in course of her life. While doing so, Campbell attests to the fact that a Halfbreed is more than a mere stereotype, and could have as many selves as is possible for a real individual. Thus the fictional Maria could never be dismissed as a limited self-suffering from reduction, rather a versatile self-having as many selves as there are occasions. Thus, Maria, very consciously, and rightly so creates a halo around the Halfbreeds who are usually spurned by the whites. Having already lost her siblings to the welfare, Maria soon disintegrates to lose her own self too. Her marriage to Darrel slides down even further. She moves to Kristen, Alberta with her husband to his sister Bonny's house. Darrel's sister does not hide her dislike for her Halfbreed sister-in-law and often taunts Maria with racist remarks. Bonny makes sure Maria does not have any

171

peace of mind and, like the oppressor threatening the subjugated Native, threatens her with taking away her daughter. Not much after, Maria is taken to Vancouver by her husband and deserted there. With a young child, no money, no groceries and no knowledge of skilled work, Maria isn't left with too many choices. This is when she steps into a vicious cycle of physical and emotional abuse. This is also the time when she knows that all her dreams with the white ideals of success have been shattered. She also knows now that even dreams ought to be followed cautiously. She reckons: "Dreams are so important in one's life, yet when followed blindly they can lead to the disintegration of one's soul" (116).

Maria's dreams of keeping her family together, of toothbrushes, milk and cookies, bowls of fruit for her brothers and sisters and a beautiful home instead of a mud shack are gone forever. She no more dreams of any future for her child either. In such a scenario, she takes onto drugs to "forget about yesterday and tomorrow." She almost becomes a being sans emotions. Living in denial of her Native identity is what seems to her to be the solution of her problems. Moreover, she doesn't want to go back and admit that she has failed herself and her family and community. She doesn't want to face the ugly reality stalking on her face:

> How could I go home and say ... I'd failed?
> *My home and my people were a part of my life that*
> *I wanted to forget*, and if calling myself French or
> Spanish or anything else would help I would do so
> (emphasis mine) (120).

Home, family, community- all these are the pillars on which the Native conceives her/his identity. Living communally, listening to the stories of the land, practicing the rituals and customs of the community, contributing to the family's needs, and taking responsibilities of one's own people- this is how the Native person's sense of being is shaped. Maria's loss of self-dignity and identity are a result of her having lost her family and community.

However, drawing strength from her great grandmother Cheechum, Maria starts towards a path of recovery. Cheechum's voice echoes throughout the novel giving Maria strength and courage at the ugliest times. In a sense, she wants to become as firm and determined as her Cheechum has been. This relationship of the old and the young generation too is a virtue of the Native peoples.

172

Living in hostility and a daily fight for survival also toughens up an individual. Thus, Maria, in spite of having fallen to the vices of the colonizer's world, strengthens herself to come out of all these. And many a times its Cheechum's voice that guides her and a feeling of Cheechum's presence that helps her fight her loneliness. The first time she quits drugs is to make a clean break from her own haunting past and to live only for her own sake, even at the cost of letting go of her Native identity. But this break period is short-lived because she does not acknowledge her own identity and hence continues to live in negativity. The second time she goes through withdrawal, however, is because she wants to look forward to future. This time, because her reasons are in keeping with her true self, she realizes that her "Cheechum was with me (Maria) the whole time" (124). She leaves Vancouver for Calgary and tries her hand at different jobs, without much success. She also enrolls for a hair dressing course and in spite of being pregnant midway into it, she finishes the course and gives birth to her second child. Holding her newborn in her hands, she knows that she has to survive so that her children survive. Meanwhile, she befriends Marion, an Indian girl who tells her about welfare and being a "Whiteman's Indian," ideas which Maria categorically rejects because of her strong sense of a Métis identity. Soon afterwards, she gets to know about the AA meetings.

But she doesn't go to attend the AA meetings until after her nervous breakdown sometime later. In between, she meets David, a twenty-eight year old truck driver who loves her, makes her laugh and it almost seems like Maria's problems are over forever. They have a son together too. But Maria's own insecurity of David catching up with her past bothers her from within and leads to her nervous breakdown. She is admitted to Alberta hospital and one night at the hospital she tells about her past to David, which leads to a break-up of their relationship. She starts attending AA meetings on the doctor's advice. It is here that we can see Maria gradually healing and regaining her own sense of identity. Having lived communally since her childhood, Maria returns to her own self only when she belongs back to a community, even if it's a community of the pariahs of the society. And having been educated through the stories of the community, Maria's healing takes place through the stories she listens to. Her regeneration occurs not from an individualistic perception of the world but by learning through the stories and experiences of the members of Alcoholics Anonymous.

173

It's also in these meetings that she is initiated to the Native Movement in Alberta. Reminded of her Cheechum's lessons once more, Maria realizes what she ought to do with her life and the objective she must work towards. She befriends Edith, a part Indian woman who awakens her to the importance of leadership and change. She is now able to reinterpret Cheechum's lessons.

Campbell's mythicizing comes to an acme as she upholds the Halfbreed's sacrifice for the community above everything. To the Halfbreeds, the individual is a part while the community is a whole. In her reinterpretation of Cheechum's lessons, Campbell acknowledges that as a Métis woman and as a Native person, she will only be content with a communal identity, not an individualistic one advocated by the western tradition. Hence, the solution to her personal problems will also be found by getting herself involved in the community. As Helen M. Buss rightly observes: "...the ego-shaped journey of individual 'fortune' is not suitable for a mixed-blood woman; hers must be a journey towards 'leadership,' towards relationship" (Buss 166). That the Métis can be taken for granted is disproved by the constant changing of the self. The self is not something that can be taken for granted. Maria rejects the Whiteman's idea that the Métis are stereotypes. Her picaresque journey from one self to another and her gathering of changing shelves are a proof to this. Maria's tricksterism is postmodern- thereby fact of her changing shelves.

In her search for the "brothers" and "sisters" her Cheechum had talked about, Maria comes across several Native leaders, some of whom she mentions in the book. She talks about her "brothers" like Eugene Steinhauer, a fearless and outgoing leader of the Native movement of Alberta; Stan Daniels, a Halfbreed leader from Alberta and Kay, whom Maria thinks of as one of the leaders Cheechum forecasted. These leaders fill her with hope of a better tomorrow.

Whereas *Halfbreed* starts and continues unto a point about Métis way of life and Métis upliftment, towards the end of the book Campbell's voice becomes more and more inclusive as she talks beyond racism. While talking about the rejuvenation and reemergence of dormant Native organizations, Campbell talks about a "united voice" that would speak for all the people who need a voice, including poor whites.

In her ambition to speak for all the voiceless of Canada, irrespective of their gender and skin colour, Maria Campbell creates the myth of a nation that goes beyond the exclusivist paradigms in which "nation" was hitherto defined. Campbell also accepts the fact that in the contemporary context, armed revolution is not an option for the Native peoples because it would not culminate in bringing the change necessary for survival and sustenance of the Native communities.

While being distinctly proud of her own Halfbreed identity, Campbell however no more limits her dreams to the Métis world. She would rather work towards and advocate for a better future for all the downtrodden peoples of the society. In this sense, she goes beyond Cheechum's lessons and thinks for humanity as a whole. As Julie Cairnie points out:

> While Cheechum's position is understandable, Campbell is unwilling to limit coalition to Halfbreeds, even after her own marriage fails. She explores unity in far more diverse and creative ways than Cheechum: in her identification with both the Chinese Canadian family in Kristen and the "Chinese ... part Indian" prostitute in Vancouver; in the lingering possibility of coalition between Indian, poor whites, and Halfbreeds; and in the tangible success of her relationship with a white girl (Cairnie 100).

As she used to protect her siblings in her school days from the racist teachers, she now knows that she has to again start speaking for the "brothers" and "sisters" of the community. Her sense of community too, now, is more widespread. As she becomes driven to raise her voice for her peoples and for others like her, Campbell becomes more and more optimistic. Campbell knows that she can now discard the blanket of identity she had been forced to live with:

> Cheechum said, "You'll find yourself, and you'll have brothers and sisters." I have brothers and sisters, all over the country. I no longer need my blanket to survive (157).

Halfbreed neither paints the picture of a rosy future nor does it end on a grim note of dreamlessness. The novel ends with Cheechum's death, Maria's only link to an older generation. But she understands that she herself is one of the leaders Cheechum had waited for and she knows that there are many others who will realize Cheechum's dreams. In an optimistic ending, Campbell asserts that Native life and cultures will continue to survive, irrespective of what the colonizing forces dream of or plan for. Ending her story with

175

a hope of survival thus affirms the continuity of Métis life and culture. In the process, it becomes a part of a larger story, the story of survival and endurance that many Native peoples are writing about.

Maria's journey from being a Métis girl to a more accepting Native activist underlines the point that for survival, if for nothing else, the communities must look forward to strength in unity. As Julie Cairnie points out: "In *Halfbreed* Maria Campbell acknowledges the importance of differences...but regards division (personal and social) as a world that needs to be healed" (Cairnie 99).

Halfbreed establishes the Métis culture as a distinct culture on its own. Campbell, through her life story, deconstructs known myths about the Métis to replace them with new perceptions, an insider's point of view. But that's not all. Through the retelling of the events of 1885, Campbell also challenges the "official history" and presents the Métis version of the story. Going beyond the western convention of "myth," Campbell rewrites history from a Métis perspective.

By changing the content and the construct of Métis history, Campbell reclaims a place for her peoples in the history of the nation as well as in Canadian Imagination. In the process, Campbell shatters the notion that myths can only take shape in the hands of the elite and the elite can hegemonically control the "authority" of mythmaking. Commenting on the power myths can exercise over history and their various functions, Daniel Francis in his seminal book *National Dreams: Myth, Memory, and Canadian History*, tells us:

> ... myths are not lies ... Rather, they express important truths... *myths idealize*. They select particular events and institutions which seem to embody important cultural values and elevate them to the status of legend. In Canadian history that would be the Mounties, to take an example, or the transcontinental railway, or the North. Conversely, *myths demonize*. They villify, or at least marginalize, anyone who seems to be frustrating the main cultural project- Indian, for example, or communists, or Quebec separatists ... Myths are echoes of the past, resonating in the present (emphasis mine) (Francis 11).

By fighting off the falsifications promoted by official versions of history, Campbell breaks down the universality of accepted norms and perceptions leading to a revision of history and the way it has been constructed. In the process, Barbara Godard suggests: "What is foregrounded is history as narrative, history as telling, history as a process of unfolding of local stories, or provisional truths- narratives that make no claims to universal Truth" (Godard 200). It's in the creation and presentation of a historical tradition, often through tales from the past, that the identity of a community is constructed. Keeping with this, Campbell remythicizes the historical and political legends concerning her peoples so as to reaffirm a district identity for her peoples.

Early on in the book, before she starts her life story, Campbell starts with a reconstruction of the 1869 Red River Rebellion leading up to the 1885 Northwest Rebellion and the execution of Louis Riel. Giving us the unrecorded side of the story, Campbell cites the reason behind the 1869 Red River Rebellion. She tells us:

> The fear of the Halfbreeds that their rights would not be respected by the Canadian Government when it acquired the land from the Hudson's Bay Company, along with the prejudice of the white protestant settlers, led to the Red River Rebellion of 1869 (9).

This, Campbell says, was followed by the establishment of a provisional government by Louis Riel that was dismantled by the arrival of troops from eastern Canada and Riel's subsequent escape to the United States in 1830.

Discarding the white account of history that portrays Louis Riel, Gabriel Dumont and other Métis leaders as evil personified, Campbell, with facts and figures to support her version, reincarnates them as the heroes of her peoples. Louis Riel especially, has been represented in the mainstream Canadian imagination as an escapist traitor and even a lunatic (Bumstead 26). Campbell's portrayal of Riel establishes exactly the opposite. It reconstructs Riel's actions and in doing so establishes him as the mythical heroic figure of the Métis who wanted peace and dignity for his people at the cost of his life. Campbell reckons the Battle of Duck Lake from where started the Riel Rebellion as a "Victory for the Halfbreeds" (11). Campbell also hints at the contemporary construction of anti-myths regarding Métis heroes in the popular culture 177 such as movies.

Thus presenting a counter discourse of the Canadian History, Campbell not only gives a new story and an altered history but also subverts the myth of the dominant discourse. The Mounties often hailed as generous heroes and benevolent protectors of the powerless in the Canadian myth are shown from the other side of the mirror. Lambasting the oppressive policies of the white colonial power, Campbell rewrites the history of the crushing of the Riel Rebellion.

In wholesome rejection of the "official" history, Campbell tells us that "*The History books say* that the Halfbreeds were defeated at Batoche in 1884" (emphasis mine) (11), suggesting that the history books have never been fair in their account. She tells us that Louis Riel was hanged with a charge of "high treason" which nevertheless was as false as the Ottawa government's peace plans. In the process, she presents the reader with her own account of Métis history, a Métis "history book." Myth connects the past to the present. Campbell's account of the Halfbreed history similarly connects her own life story with the hi/story of her peoples, thus creating a link between yesterday and today. It's important to note here that the very act of executing Riel which was supposedly conducted by the colonizing forces to create a sense of awe and fear in the mind of the Native serves as a symbol of Native resistance and glory, even after a century. Albert Braz rightly observes: "... by killing Riel, his foes do not destroy the Métis Nation but rather provide it with a vital symbol of national resistance" (Braz 57). However defenseless they might have been during the Rebellion of 1885 and however the oppressor might have treated them, Campbell's account tells that the spirit of her people has not been defeated.

While talking about leadership for the Native peoples, Campbell often highlights another rarely recorded tactics of the colonizer. In the early part of the book, when Campbell gives a Métis account of the Canada of 1880's, she speaks about the divide and conquer policy adopted by Ottawa to weaken the rebellion which ultimately led to the failure of the movement.

Much later, while giving an account of her own experience as a Native activist, Campbell again laments that the divide and rule policy of the dominant forces still operates and operates as successfully. In her preface to *Halfbreed*, she thanks Stan Daniels "for making me angry enough to write it." Campbell portrays Stan Daniels as a charismatic Halfbreed leader who understands and is concerned about the problem of the community, who could have found out solutions for many malaises and implemented them, but who like many others prior to him, falls to the trap of the white system.

178

On her visit from the city back home, Campbell realizes that "something had changed" (148). She laments the problems of alcoholism, physical and emotional abuse and a gripping sense of loss that has engulfed her people. She herself has come to terms with life the hard way. But she is still not desperate. She is optimistic and its with optimism that she rekindles the stories of her people, the culture, the livelihood, the happy times, the communal life and in the process builds up a mythic people.

Campbell's *Halfbreed* has been variously described as an autobiographical narrative, a confessional narrative, a testimonial, a representative text as well as a narrative of resistance and recovery. Arnold Krupat in his essay "Monologue and Dialogue in Native American Autobiography" observes that Native American Autobiography offers "dialogic models of the self" (Krupat 133). This holds true in the context of a Native Canadian autobiography like *Halfbreed* as well. *Halfbreed* records Campbell's "dialogic self" in the sense that it documents her dilemma with her own self, the dilemma of her peoples as well as that of the larger society/white outside world. Moreover, as a voice from the margin, Campbell records not only her individual life story but also the communal story of her peoples as well so as to ensure sustenance and survival for both.

Indigenous cultures have often looked up to their women as the forbearers of tradition, the teller of stories and the nurturer of life. In her role as a writer, storyteller, and activist, Campbell assumes all these responsibilities traditionally demarcated for women in Native societies. By foregrounding her own life story as an experience to be shared, though not necessarily as a model to be emulated, Campbell dons the cap of a community healer. As she has pointed out: "I don't think of myself as ... a writer because I really don't know what that is ... I know what a storyteller is. A storyteller is a community healer and teacher" (Lutz 41-42). By foregrounding her collective roles as storyteller and activist, she thus makes *Halfbreed* a testimonial narrative. As Cairnie comments on Campbell: "She prioritizes her collective roles as storyteller and activist, similar to the narrator of a testimonial narrative." (Cairnie 103)

One can hardly ignore the fact that Campbell's is a "postcolonial voice," a voice that is heard from a site where the "post" is not yet over for the Native communities. In that sense, Campbell writes her novel from a site of resistance, as a writer who is not only shaped by the politics of the "post" but in the very act of writing also shapes or rather affects the political process. Julia Emberley points out: "Texts   179 by Aboriginal women demand to be read in the context of *resistance*, in particular, resistance to the structure of internal colonialism in Canada" (emphasis original) (Emberley 91).

One of the major practices of Resistance Literature is a scant respect for literary traditions or established genres. By blurring the boundaries of truth and untruth, fiction and non-fiction, these writings not only resist in theme but also in the actualization of the text itself. Treading between the lines of fiction and non-fiction, *Halfbreed* thus confuses the colonial mind and resists attempts for categorization in moulds derived from the mainstream.

In this sense, hybridity goes beyond being a biological or socio-cultural construct confining the author within its own fold and is practiced as a means to creativity, thus making *métissage* both the theme of the text and the text itself (emphasis mine). Even while appearing in the language of the dominant discourse, the text thus maintains its own indigenousness.

Campbell believes in what Margaret Laurence says: "Myth is reality." It is this which spurs her mind to use a sheaf of myths to uplift the image of the Halfbreeds. Both Campbell and Laurence do not bifurcate the myth from the reality. They are interchangeable. The barrier between the reality and the myth, fact and fiction disappears; they rather complement with each other in their writing. Campbell writes *Halfbreed* to upset stereotypes of her peoples, to present an alternative version of history, to discard fake ideas, to blur established genres and thus generate new myths- Métis myths. She writes as a Native voice, as a Métis member of her community and also as a woman victimized by the double-edged sword of internal and external colonialism. In that sense, her autobiography, like that of her "Sisters," becomes a "mimetic response" to her experiences of racism and sexism (Kent 102). By being the representative voice of Native women and their experiences, Campbell thus elevates *Halfbreed* to the status of a representative text, a text that in its telling becomes the story of Native women all over Canada and even beyond. Maria Campbell's life story is a story of the people from the lowest rung of Canadian social structure, a story of loss and deprivation, of trauma and degeneration, of hopelessness and despair; it's not a "happy book" as Campbell herself asserts at the very outset of the text. But hers is nevertheless also a story of regeneration and recovery, strength and endurance, and most tellingly, optimism and dream. This is what makes *Halfbreed* a unique experience, in text, theme as well as narrative and places it on the top of the literary scale.

Conclusion

The study of the four texts discussed in the four chapters foregrounds certain commonalities between these, traits that can be assumed as representative of Native literatures as a whole. Rejecting the colonizer's illusory "world of wealth, promise and fabulous disease" (Welch 27), these Native writers are producing their texts from a site of cultural resistance and appropriation and in doing so, they are recreating Native identities in the contemporary atmosphere of postcolonial plurality. Native literature, as is evident from this reading of four representative texts by four Native authors, thus functions with the purpose to highlight and "to transform themselves from marginalized cultures to emergent cultures capable of challenging and reforming the mainstream" (Patel 3). From a position of voiceless invisibility, Native writers are "speaking' and "showing" their cultures, thus redefining the dimensions of society and culture of the margin and the centre. What Fleck observes in the context of Native American novelists holds true for Native Canadian writers as well: "Contemporary Native American novelist's contribution toward a definition of American society is invaluable in that they present a third world view from within" (Fleck 3).

As they deconstruct the distorted versions of Native philosophies, stories, myths, legends, histories and images in the hegemonic discourse, Native writers like Erdrich, Silko, King and Campbell reject the exoticization of the Native cultural, historical, and political identities. By telling their own stories in their own ways, Native writers resist generalizations and universalized versions of "truth." Writing with a postmodernist purpose of righting the wrongs of the past and a contemporary formation of identity, Native writers, including the ones we have discussed in the chapters, have been accused of being political in their textual productions. But as Native poet Beth Brant comments, "our very survival is a political act" (Rani 48). Through their writings, Native writers thus emphasize the point that it is time to reject the Whiteman's view of the Native, thus it is in fact essential to understand and perceive Native culture on its own terms. By giving the reading audience an insight into the Native worldview, the Native writers discussed in this study demand cultural recognition. As Cederstorm suggests: "We desperately need to focus upon Native culture as Natives themselves perceive that culture and to develop a vocabulary with which to assess the contributions of Native authors" (Cederstorm 145).

A common factor in all the four texts discussed here is their respect for and practice of orality in the textual production. Criticizing the modernist view of textuality as superior to orality, Krupat comments:

> Textuality was new, advanced, and male; orality was old, backward, and female. Not only female, of course, for the backwardness of the oral encompassed the "primitive" as well: the unlettered red savage or black slave (Krupat 46).

However, as one reads through these textual productions by Native authors, one witnesses an oral expressiveness that is neither primitive nor backward. Rather, paradoxically, this very orality of these texts assign a postmodernist quality to them, suggesting that Native authors are very much aware of the power of language and orality, not only from a Native perspective but also from the sophisticated stance of postmodern discourse. As they manipulate oral into written, the Native world emerges from the English texts and manifests a Native consciousness and a postmodern representation.

Orality is both theme and technique in *Tracks*. As the novel structures itself on the "stories" of the two alternating narrators, it oralizes the trauma of displacement and destruction of the Native culture and communities. In the same vein it also celebrates the power of orality and its contribution to the upkeep of tradition, continuity, and survival. As it holds a mirror to the society as a whole, both Native and white, Erdrich's craft essentially duplicates community experience and collective history.

In Silko's *Ceremony*, Tayo's healing occurs through his regaining the faith in the stories of the land. As language is continually assessed and reassessed, Tayo's sense of identity reemerges from the reconstruction of storied events. From a state of speechlessness that fragments him from inside, Tayo graduates to become a Laguna man at the end of the novel with a knowledge of stories, stories that connect him to the land through Ts'eh and A'moo'ooh and gain him a respectful entry into the Kiva. As Arnold observes about Silko's orality in *Ceremony*:

> Silko translates the oral tradition and experience into the
> literary form of the dominant culture to keep the tradition
> alive by recreating it ... at the same time she recreatesthe
> written word, translating it into a new form that makes
> the patterns of ongoing creation visible and thus provides
> a map for the future (Arnold 88).

Thomas King's *Green Grass, Running Water* territorializes the hegemonic discourse by engaging in the production of orality in the textual world. As King's four mythical trickster spirits tell stories, the "master narrative" and the "mainstream culture" are renarrativized in terms of a Native understanding of the world. In their parodic subversion of the "official" versions of "truth" and "myth," "history," and "politics," King's mythical spirits become Native figures of resistance and reappropriation and thus construct a postcolonial, postmodern version of Native past and present.

Campbell's *Halfbreed*, in spite of its deceptively simple way of presentation, is shaped through and through by the grandmother figure Cheechum's stories. It's through Cheechum's stories that a young Maria views the world within and without and much later its again through her conversation with Cheechum that Maria regains her lost sense of identity and personhood. Hanging from a precarious position owing to her race and gender, Maria reemerges from the path of destruction to recovery and survival through her belief and continual inspiration from Cheechum's stories.

Native culture and religion has been systematically denigrated and vilified by the colonizers as this denial of cultural ethos served the colonizer's cause of snatching away Native land and amputating the Native spirit. The erasure of the remnants of Native culture and ways of life has been continually achieved by the superimposition of Christianity on Native religious practices. By portraying the Native as "a quintessence of evil"(Gallagher 7) and their religion as "pagan," the hegemonic forces have accentuated the process of cultural annihilation of the indigenes. This colonial agenda has been exposed and the propagated religion of Christianity stands rejected in the postcolonial productions of the Native authors discussed here.

Louise Erdrich outlines the devastating effects of Christianity on Native culture and personhood through her delicate portrayal

184   of the fanatical Pauline in *Tracks*. The reader is simultaneously exposed to the consequences of a transplanted Christianity

on the identity formation of a Chippewa female and also to the author's parodic mockery of the practices of Christianity. Further, it's in their rejection of religious imposition and continuance of Native religious and traditional practices that characters like Nanapush and Fleur narrativize a contemporary Native presence.

While Aunt Thelma's regular church visits in *Ceremony* add to her "burden" of pain and fail to save her son from being a victim of the evil witchery, Tayo's trust in the Native ritualistic purgation heals his body and spirit. By rejecting to pray to the "plaster Jesus" (155) Tayo finds his own ground on the Native land. Tayo finds his spiritual pursuit in the ancient order of the feminine, the constellation of stars and in the tracks of the mountain lion whose path he covers with yellow pollen, thus ensuring the continued fertility of the Native world.

In King's *Green Grass, Running Water*, the four mythical spirits not only reject Christianity but also re-place the colonizer's patriarchal worldview with a retelling of the cosmic stories. By counter-appropriating Christianity and its "little god," the four mythical Native spirits construct a postcolonial, postmodern Native discourse and thus reinscribe the hegemonic worldview. Christianity is further appropriated in the realist plot where characters might have "English" names and contemporary lifestyles but who continue to participate in and draw their spiritual strength from Native rituals and ceremonies like the Sun Dance.

Influenced and inspired by her grandmother Cheechum, Campbell in her autobiographical novel *Halfbreed* rejects the church and Christianity as a whole and draws her strength to endure the hardships of life from Cheechum's philosophy of the presence of God or evil in all things and beings of the universe. Campbell's disregard for Christianity is manifested throughout the text in her narration of her early experiences with the church, the church's denial of a burial for her mother, the gluttony of the Father, the Father's habit of condemning certain practices in public and practicing the same in private and such like. Campbell repeatedly underlines the point that if she ever prayed it was meant for a divine spirit and not for Christ or Mary or any such proclamation.

The Native literary productions discussed above also share a common debunking of the colonizer's offer of assimilation or annihilation. Offered in the guise of cross-cultural communication and a "better" life for the Native, the choice of assimilation often brings with it a sense of self-hatred, a loss of identity and culture and ultimately the loss of the Native community self, history and memory. Native   185
authors write from a space to reclaim a Native way of life and

rejuvenate Native philosophy and thus reject the choice of assimilation that leads them to self-contempt, alcoholism, violence and suicide. As Jeanette Armstrong tells in an interview with Janice Williamson:

> The process of writing as a Native person has been a healing one for me because I've uncovered the fact that I'm not a savage, not dirty and ugly and not less because I've brown skin, or a Native philosophy ...The suicide rates and problems our people are having are a result of being told you're stupid, ignorant, a drunk, you'll never amount to anything-just because you're Indian. To me, that's the biggest lie of all that needs to be dispelled (Williamson 10).

As Nanapush in *Tracks* lives the life of a traditional Chippewa, hunting, gathering and practicing magic and medicine, Pauline, the torchbearer of assimilation in the text loses more and more of her own self with her almost insane passion to manifest her loyalty to the oppressor other. By her rejection to learn the "quillwork" and "beadmaking," Pauline metaphorically rejects to learn the intricacies of Native culture and ways of life. However, her interest to learn "lacemaking" like the white girls results in her sweeping and cleaning the floors of the colonizer's institutions. Erdrich's disapproval of Pauline's assimilationist stance is complete when Pauline ultimately re-names herself in the colonizer's discourse and thus gets "lost" from the Native picture of the world.

Emo, Harley, Leroy, Pinkie, Rocky, Helen Jean, and Laura are lost in the bylines of assimilation in Silko's *Ceremony*. Their devastation is a consequence of their belief in the hallucinatory dreams of the white ideals of success and happiness. Rocky pays with his life for his constant desire to move out of the reservation and succeed in the white world. Emo, Harley, Leroy and Pinkie lose themselves to alcoholism and thus destroy their own selves as well as their communities. Laura and Helen Jean pay with their modesty and dignity of life for their myopic dreams of high heels and made-up appearances. Silko thus foregrounds the point that *the choice offered to the Native is not actually to assimilate or get lost but to assimilate and get lost* (emphasis mine).

King's realist characters in *Green Grass, Running Water* demonstrate another aspect of the choice of assimilation and the rejection of it. Whereas the assimilated Charlie starts off as a well-to-do corporate lawyer in the text, by the end of the book one witnesses his "failure" as he loses both his job and his beloved Alberta. On the contrary, Eli, in spite of his death, shines as a Native person in the text. Latisha is successful in both worlds-she runs a packed restaurant serving "dog-meat" and still lives her life the Blackfoot way. Alberta is a "University Professor" who could have been a "Corporate Executive" but she is impregnated by Coyote, the Native trickster and is willing to help rebuild Eli's cabin, the symbol of Native resistance and presence.

Campbell's dreams of "toothbrushes" and a "bowl of fruit" on the dining table for her family drive her to exploitation, drugs and alcoholism. Though fiercely protective of her Halfbreed identity throughout her schooldays, Campbell commits the blunder of marrying a white man to fulfill her hopes of a life away from the log houses and good food and education for her siblings. But it's only when she realizes the futility of such dreams which lead to hatred of one's own self, one's family and community that she comes back to life and identity. It's in the rejection of the path to assimilation that Campbell finds a way back to the Native world.

Postcolonial fiction all over has witnessed an appropriation of the colonizer's language and Native literature is definitely postcolonial in this context. Using the colonizer's language for a telling of their own stories, Native authors like the ones discussed here have rewritten the language of English and contextualized it to the Native perspective. Their use of English for their cultural/literary production however does not bind them to the assimilationist advocates of the dominant cultures. Nor do they fall into the trap of the nostalgic recreation of a bygone past. Rather, truly postmodern as they are, these Native texts reflect on the here and now, the contemporary trials and tribulations of Native peoples and towards this objective, English as a language is a means and not an end. With a postcolonial mastery of the colonizers' language, Native authors discussed in this study thus manipulate and twist English to describe Native experiences. Historically misrepresented and subjugated by the colonizers' language, Native writers subvert the colonizers' discourse in their own language. Further, the use of English connects the vast number of Native communities across North America and helps create a pan-Indian sense of identity. As W.H. New points out: "... the challenge is to use the existing language, even if it is the voice of a dominant "other" – and yet speak through it: to disrupt... the codes and forms of the dominant language in order to reclaim speech for itself" (New 81).

Nanapush's adaptation to change, to the colonizer's   187
language, his ability to speak and use "good English" as and

where necessary helps him survive the onslaught of alien discourses and government papers in *Tracks*. Contrarily, Pauline's unquestioning acceptance of the superiority of English provides her a place in the convent but her spirit is split and she gains no inner peace whatsoever. As a poststructural work of art, *Tracks* emphasizes on the breaking down of boundaries and the creation of layered meanings. English becomes a Native tongue through Nanapush's storytelling and Nativeness finds expression in English.

Similarly, while the traditional old medicine man Ku'oos'h fails to cure Tayo primarily because of his inability to communicate in English, Betonie's adaptation to the changing realties of the Native world helps him create a living tradition that has place for Tayo in it and that has cure for the fragilities of mixed-bloods like Tayo. Silko spins the Native creatrix Spiderwoman's webs in the text of *Ceremony* through her intricate patterning of the language so as to highlight a Native perspective of the world. But Rocky's unprecedented faith in the English textbooks also warns the reader about the tragic consequences of submerging oneself in the others' language.

In *Green Grass, Running Water*, all the realist characters in the plot can speak and write English. But they go a step further as they exhibit their ability to twist the language for a Native advantage. If Alberta's classroom presentation, Eli's court injunctions and Latisha's restaurant menu are any hint, then the Native person has not only gained mastery over the language of the colonizer but can also resist, as in case of Eli, or dupe, as in case of Latisha, the colonizer in their own tongue. Further, by nativizing the names of Christian mythological figures while still naming them in English, King demonstrates the "savage" Native's sophistication of thought.

Halfbreed does not explicitly deal with the issue of English and its effects on the Native peoples. But Campbell does not forget to emphasize that her family spoke "Cree" at home and her sister faced discrimination and humiliation at school for her inability to "pronounce" English words. However, by her very act of writing her life story in English, Campbell succeeds to reach an audience she would not have been able to gain had she written in Cree and thus uses English for the furtherance of Native brotherhood and sisterhood. As Campbell herself comments:

> For a long time I wouldn't write anything, because I didn't know how to use English...When I was writing I always found that English manipulated me...then I was able to manipulate English, and once I was able to manipulate English, I felt that was personal liberation (Rani 45).

This constant engagement with the language of English to foreground Native experiences makes the texts discussed here inherently dialogic. As postcolonial fiction encourages a dialogic interpretation of history, myth and memory, these Native authors inform their texts with a dialogism that concerns itself with the poststructural creation of multiplicity of meanings and realities. Without falling into the trap of ethnocentrism, these four Native writers engage in dialogue at different levels and form different perspectives in their writings that highlight the heterogeneity of Native communities and life experiences and their oppositionality with the Euro-American discourse. As writers born into Native communities and still exposed to a world outside, these Native writers continually reflect on and cancel the authorities of the two worlds they inhabit. This paves the way for the creation of a postmodern polyphonic discourse in the texts. As Rohrbacher observes:

> Native American authors infuse their writing with utterances that deliberately draw on two sets of ideologies: Euro-American and Native American. In effect, they write to two audiences with opposing viewpoints. The effect of this dialogic writing is an atmosphere of heteroglossia and carnival (Rohrbacher np).

Dialogue creates layered structures of meaning in *Tracks*. While the two warring, alternating narrators' simultaneous and continual questioning of each other's authority, authenticity and reliability raises the postmodern quotient of the text as a whole, their dialogic storytelling techniques reflects on the author's clever manifestation of her experiences as a mixed-blood treading between two worlds, both of which inform and illuminate each other. In doing so, Erdrich achieves to present the novel "the Indian way" (Sergi 279). Further, by keeping both her narrators inside the Chippewa reservation, Erdrich is able to depict the details of the conflicts rising within Native communities as a result of the colonial experience.

189

In Silko's *Ceremony*, Tayo is at a constant dialogue with his own sense of tribal identity. Brought up in the Laguna land, though not born in it, and exposed to the bloodcurdling violence of the "civilized" peoples' war, Tayo starts his dialogue at a point where neither world has a promise to comfort him. Neither White nor fully Native, Tayo fails to fit into either side of the two warring discourses. But unlike in *Tracks*, Tayo's conflict arises from within his own self and hence he must look within for a dialogue. By guiding Tayo to the story of the Laguna land, Betonie helps Tayo resolve his internal conflict. Tayo does not reject dialogue; rather by recognizing and being a part of the changing and living tradition, Tayo emphasizes the need for dialogue to foster survival and continuity in the postcolonial world.

Rohrbacher's observation of the creation of "heteroglossia and carnival" through dialogue perhaps suits best to King's *Green Grass, Running Water*. *Green Grass, Running Water* is a funny book with serious undertones that facilitates dialogues between race, gender, religion, history and textuality. King's Cherokee lineage, almost white upbringing and his affiliation to the Canadian Blackfoot create the field for a dialogic discourse and his constant play with language, orality and storytelling creates multiple layers of meaning and challenges all authority, thus generating a poststructural, postmodern delight. Both the mythical and realist characters in *Green Grass, Running Water* constantly weigh the various "options" available to them and thus engage in dialogue with themselves. Moreover, by commenting on and appropriating the white versions of history, culture, politics and so on, King's fiction also creates a dialogue between the oppressed and the oppressor.

Campbell's *Halfbreed* deals with dialogue on a different level. Writing with a Halfbreed consciousness, Campbell reflects on the lack of and the need for dialogue between Halfbreed communities, between halfbreed and full blood Natives, between the marginalized and the powerful, between men and women and so on. As a Halfbreed person, Campbell does not initially recognize herself or her community as Natives and in fact describes the differences between halfbreeds and Indians at great length. However, as the novel comes to an end, Campbell is comfortable enough to describe herself as a Native person working for the recognition and betterment of all marginalized peoples, including poor whites and encouraging dialogue among these people to ensure a better future for all.

As minority voices writing from a postcolonial space and reflecting on postcolonial conditions, these Native authors make use of the available forms of representation from the dominant culture's sociopolitical and literary paradigm. Thus, their textual productions while engaged in the assertion of a definitive construction of a Native identity, also become textually intercultural. Simultaneously, these Native writers also reconstruct indigenous modes of presentation and contextualize in the contemporary production of a postcolonial discourse. Krupat categorizes indigenous literature as "that type of writing produced when an author of subaltern cultural identification manages successfully to merge forms internal to his cultural formation with forms external to it" (Krupat 214). Native writers thus represent their individual identities and cultures through the use of the colonizer's language and through the creation of a participatory dialogue in the text. But they also draw from their own cultural ethos the forms and techniques of storytelling. Thus while they do not hesitate to use the novel form to tell their stories, the stories are however told in the Native pattern of a circle. All the four novels discussed here manifest this trait of Nativeness in the narrative form and progression. In a way all these novels start where the story ends and end where the story begins.

Tracks begins at a point where Nanapush is telling stories to his young granddaughter Lulu about her family and the Turtle mountain Chippewa. As the author incorporates her vision into a Native framework, the tribal aesthetics of a circular form comes to play. Lulu, distanced from her mother and the Chippewa land, has moved out of the sacred circle of a tribal identity, Nanapush's narrative as well as the text end at a point when Nanapush has succeeded in bringing the girl back into the Chippewa circle of identity, both personal and communal. If Chippewa life is to continue, Lulu and her generation of Chippewa youth must reconnect to the tribal way of life and thus ensure a revitalization of Native culture.

Silko's *Ceremony* has been often described in connection with the Laguna Spiderwoman's web of stories. Interestingly, in spite of her use of novel form and her brilliant handling of the colonizer's language, Silko's text is not divided into neat chapters-thus structuring the novel on layers and layers of meaning, creating a narrative like that of a spring, each circle connected to and capable of influencing another. As Silko weaves the story of a Laguna mixed-blood's search for identity to that of a Laguna creation story and further to the ontology of violence in postcolonial times through the uranium bomb story, a Native pattern of 191 circle becomes evident and integral to the interpretation of the text. Through her cyclical flow of narrative, Silko creates a unifying, holistic vision of the Native world that would sustain itself in spite of the westernized/anglicized discourse.

Green Grass, Running Water integrates the circle to both its theme and structure. Through his extraordinary use of Native storytelling devices like repetition and parallelism, King alludes to the circle as both sacred and essential for a Native expression. In *Green Grass, Running Water*, language and creation themselves are storied into the sacredness of Native cyclicality. *Green Grass, Running Water* also starts and ends at the same point-when the story starts, there is already a sense of continuity demonstrated through the use of the word "so." Likewise, when the narrative comes to an end, the reader gets a feeling that the text might have ended but the story continues- thus reinforcing the circularity of Native vision. Characters often refer to stories previously told, left untold, or narrativized through another character, thus ensuring continuity as well as circularity.

Campbell's *Halfbreed* perhaps looks the most westernized of all the four books. Like a western autobiography it has clear-cut chapter breaks, a progression of plot from the author's childhood and ignorance to her present state of youth and understanding, and an almost linear narrative. But as soon as one scratches the surface of the text, one finds that the narrative of *Halfbreed* too respects the tribal circular pattern. The author starts at a point where she wants the readers to know the challenge of being a Halfbreed woman in contemporary Canada and at the end of the text the reader comes to an understanding of the trials and tribulations of the Halfbreed in the postcolonial era. However, the author who laments the loss of home, love and family has also reintegrated herself to the Native society, her fragmented existence having given way to a wholesome experience of life and identity. Her life thus has come full circle, from happiness and content to loss and fragmentation and back to a meaningful Native personhood.

As Postcolonial writers, these Native authors are concerned with providing a kaleidoscopic picture of the Native world. Towards this objective, they exhibit a Native sense of time in their texts that denies being defined and slotted in the colonizer's understanding of time. The Western chronological time fragments life and experiences by dividing it into slots of past, present and future. This fragmentary view stands irrelevant for the telling of Native stories. A Native consciousness is created in these texts through the use of the tribal ceremonial time. Connecting colonization and chronological time, Allen remarks:

> There is a connection between factories and clocks, and there is a connection between colonial imperialism and factories. There is also a connection between telling Indian tales in chronological sequences and the American tendency to fit Indians into the slots they have prepared for us (Allen 151).

By rejecting the western concept of time, Native writers thus refuse to be defined and constructed in terms of the dominant discourse. All the four texts discussed here create a Native consciousness in their texts by confirming to the Native perception of time. As Allen points out:

> Ultimately Indian time is a concept based on a sense of propriety, on a ritual understanding of order and harmony ... The right timing for a tribal Indian is the time when he or she is in balance with the flow of the four rivers of life (Allen 154).

If one goes by the chapter headings in *Tracks*, time appears on a chronological plane where the events in the novel take place in between 1912 to 1924. But both Nanapush and Pauline tell stories that debunk chronology, or at least the western version of it. While Nanapush claims to have seen times his listening audience i.e. Lulu or the reader will never know, he not only reflects on a Chippewa past but also on his own timelessness as well. As the Chippewa trickster transformer culture hero, there is enough evidence in Chippewa tribal lore that Nanapush or Nanabozho existed before the beginning of time. Paradoxically, Pauline, too, in her graphic description of the lake monster Missipeshu who has not been sighted by any of her contemporaries, amusingly hints at the possibility of having existed at a time prior to this.

In Silko's *Ceremony*, myth and reality intertwine and fuse together thanks to the presence of a mythical timelessness in the text. Stories happen simultaneously in a mythical past and a contemporary plane in *Ceremony*. As Silko weaves stories upon stories creating a plethora of meanings, she also stops in between stories, jumps from one ontological and epistemological plane to another

193

with the swiftness and delicacy of a spider and thus creates a sense of the simultaneous presence of past, present and future. The reader journeys with Tayo to a mythical Laguna past and then seamlessly into some of the most significant moments in chronological history like the WW II or the first atomic bomb explosion experiment at Jemez. As Tayo unlearns the violence of the Western linear narrative, he is reintegrated to tribal time and harmony.

The four mythical spirits in King's *Green Grass, Running Water* travel back and forth in time as they unravel stories starting from a point before time. In their mythical re-creation of the beginning of the world, these Native spirits predate the Native framework of universe to that of the chronological view of Christianity. As the Native trickster figure Coyote permits "the little god" to become an upper case Christian GOD, Native time occurs before the Christian time. Further, the four mythical spirits allude to four directions of life and thus confirm to the sacred flow of life in tune with Native time. With their power to enter all times at all moments, these Native spirits can "fix" a western classic, the life of a contemporary Blackfoot, stories from history and popular culture as well as Christian cosmologies and thus create a Native timelessness in the text.

Campbell's *Halfbreed* does not allude to this Native sense of timelessness. As the novel proceeds from her early years to her contemporary age, it definitely draws from a western linear understanding of time. However, it also has its own moments of timelessness- when a young Maria would lie by the riverside to see the "little people" and time would pass by, when she would draw her inspiration from Cheechum's teachings from the past or when she dreams of a future that is free from racism, sexism and poverty. As a Halfbreed, Campbell believes in past, present and future but the Native in her also helps her recreate a life in the text as realistically as if it all happens in front of the reader's eyes.

One of the purposes of postcolonial fiction is to demolish the stereotypes created by the centre of the margin. Conscious of their postcolonial agenda of debunking stereotypes, the Native authors discussed here deconstruct the myth of the "serious savage." That humor is an integral part of Native life is demonstrated amply in these textual productions. Humor, for the Native person in the postcolonial context, becomes not merely a tool of entertainment but also serves as a strategy for survival and resistance. As Hernadez rightly claims: "Indeed humour is very much a part of living and 'fighting back' as an Indian in today's world" (Hernandez 15). As writers speaking from cultures hitherto unheard of, their humor comes out aloud in the texts. Laughter becomes a healing medicine and humor is the ritual revival of Native spirit in the texts discussed here. Terming humour as "one of the most important parts of American Indian life and literature," Erdrich renames it as "Survival humour." To put it in her words:

> ... Indian people really have a great sense of humour and when it's survival humour, you learn to laugh at things ... it's a different way of looking at the world, very different from the stereotype, the stoic, unflinching Indian standing, looking at the sunset. It's really there, the humor, and I really hope that ... people would see the humour (Coltelli 46).

Much of the humor in *Tracks* falls into the category of survival humor. While the consumption takes away the lives of the powerful Pillagers, Nanapush survives because as the Native trickster he can laugh with others, make others laugh and laugh at himself too. If the Pillager clan continues, it is also due to Fleur's frequent flashing of the Pillager smile. If young Chippewas like Pauline are to be brought back to the Native universe, it has to be through humor as well. In fact, Nanapush's water story is deceivingly humorous and hence succeeds, though temporarily to break Pauline's ridiculous "Christian" practice of controlling her "low functions." Pauline, paradoxically, fails to survive in the Native world because she has developed the stoicity of a convent nun and thus has disassociated herself from humor.

Ceremony does not have many humorous scenes. But as a writer from and for a Native perspective, Silko creates her own style of humor in the novel. While Nanapush in *Tracks* survives because of humor, the likes of Emo, Pinkie, Leroy and Harley are destroyed in *Ceremony* because of their derisive laughter. Possessed by the witchery, these young Laguna men draw their laughter from violence and death and hence succumb to violence and death themselves. Further, in her pink blouse and her ever smiling face, the Gallup prostitute Helen Jean tries to wear a mask of happiness and laughter that has been denied to her as a Native person. Left without a home and land, the Utah girl remains alive perhaps only because she can laugh off her terrible state.

Survival is also the motif for humor in *Green Grass, Running Water*. While the four mythical Indians re-tell stories from the past and present and counter-appropriate the hegemonic   195 record of history, politics, memory and myth, their funny revisions are meant to create laughter that would further Native culture and mythology. The Native trickster spirit's "shameless" "Hee Hee's" not only amuse the reader but also deconstruct the image of the stoic Indian. By laughing at the oppressor's idea of them, the Natives thrive and survive to tell their stories. In the process, they construct an identity of difference and foreground their unique cultures.

Halfbreed also has many episodes in it that exemplify survival humour. When a young Maria and her Halfbreed siblings and friends trouble some of her white classmates, it is to survive the rampant racism practiced at school by the bossy white children and the biased and equally racist teachers. When Alex Vandal acts dumb and naive in front of the white officials at school, it is to conform to the white's idea of the "foolish savage" so as to prevent a racist onslaught and thus survive. To take it a step further, when the halfbreeds laugh at the comic portrayal of their heroes in the popular culture, it is perhaps because they recognize their own powerlessness and laugh at it so that they would survive to see another day.

As these Native texts use humor for the representation, survival and continuity of their cultures and communities, they also work with a purpose to create a postmodern parody of the hegemonic discourse and thus revise their colonized pasts. With intent to highlight the political and ideological formations of a Native worldview, Native authors thus engage in a play of language that builds a postmodern tendency to avoid or refuse closure of their narratives. And as their stories start before and continue after the textual productions, Native writing moves beyond the confines of textuality to foreground a postcolonial, postmodern perspective of the Native as well as the outside world. In the process, colonial tradition and language are "used" but not "confirmed" in the Native texts. As W.H. New rightly puts it:

> Parodic forms are attempts to achieve self-expression without resorting either to actual violence or to the familiar techniques of social representation; they occur most frequently within a frame of reference involving received language and tradition but are themselves gestures against passive surrender to such traditions (New 284).

196

Along with the various Native themes it highlights, *Tracks* is also a postmodern counter appropriation of the practices of Christianity, and a parodic text mocking the so-called saintly practices of the Catholic nunnery. The figure of Pauline in *Tracks*, her bizarre practices towards the self-devised goal of a Christian salvation and their exceedingly horrible consequences make the text a Native manifesto exposing the duality of the patriarchal religion of the colonizer. Pauline's Christianity drives her from self-abnegation to murder and in the picture of Pauline Erdrich shows us the devastating consequences of embracing an essentially alien discourse; in the process, she parodies and renegotiates the narratives from the centre.

Parody is not as explicitly employed in Silko's *Ceremony*. However there are many instances in the text that draw from parody. The character of Rocky in *Ceremony*, as an assimilationist voice, assigns complete trust on the productions of the hegemonic discourse. Whilst Rocky believes that the white writers of the texts on cattle breeding know everything about it, such belief is parodied when Joshia, even after death, succeeds in creating a new breed of cattle that would survive in the parched land of Laguna and about which there is no mention in Rocky's textbooks. In doing so, the author not only parodies the hegemonic narrative but also underlines the center's "ignorance" and "lack of knowledge" about Native land and ways of life- thus reversing the adage of "ignorant savage" unto the colonizer. Further, Aunt Thelma's belief that to be Christian is to be burdened and vice-versa also functions as a parody of the colonizer's religion.

As a postmodern text, King's *Green Grass, Running Water* employs parody as a major technique to resist and counter the colonizer's view of the culture, community and identity. In its creation of multiple realities and authorities, the text parodies the monolithic view of the colonial discourse and encourages a polyphonic narrative point of view. As the four mythical spirits involve in and reconstruct held notions from all planes of time, they make it a point to parody the colonizer's version of history, myth, and religion. Further, in assigning Alberta's pregnancy to coyote trickery, King ultimately mocks at and parodies the idea of virgin birth central to Christian mythology.

In Campbell's *Halfbreed*, it is parody at work when the halfbreeds are renamed as CCF horses by their colonial masters. The naming demonstrates the colonizer's sub-human understanding of their fellow peoples. Alex Vandal's dumb act at school registration day is a parody of the colonizer's expectation of the stereotype; the   197 "welfare coat" Campbell had to wear for getting welfare from the government, the mention of the Calgary Indian stampede where the Native has to act as the "White man's Indian," all these point to a parody of the colonizer's distorted perception of the Native.

By employing parody, Native writers thus engage in creating a postmodern meta-narrative of their past, present and future. Most North American (United States and Canadian) Native societies regard the feminine and her powers as sacred and potent. Like the trickster that appears in different forms and shapes among different tribes, the powerful figure of the ancient feminine too is commonly found in her various avatars among Native communities. Writing with this sense of tradition, Native authors discussed here portray the women in their texts as assertive, bold and courageous persons with a fierce desire for survival of their children, their families, their communities and their cultures. Simultaneously they also reflect on the steady erosion of the power of their women in contemporary Native societies as a direct result of colonization and its patriarchal antecedents. The importance of the feminine in traditional Native thought pattern and the growing marginalization of contemporary Native women from both within and outside their communities thus becomes two faces of the postmodern reality and are aptly described in the writing of these authors. To quote Patricia Chuchryk and Christine Miller in this context:

> While the literature calls attention to the serious problems existing in many Aboriginal communities, colonialism has resulted in an attenuation of women's roles in tribal societies, endangering women both within the larger society and within their own communities (Chuchryk & Miller 4).

In Erdrich's *Tracks*, Fleur is the epitome of Native feminine strength. Drawing her powers from the Chippewa mythical being Missipeshu, Fleur commands an aura of awe and mystery. Born to the Pillagers and nursed by Nanapush, Fleur is also empowered by the Native elders. In *Tracks*, both narrators are occupied with telling Fleur's story and Fleur's last act of magic in the book is meant to punish the offenders of the Chippewa land, the white colonizers and their killer technologies. It is through Fleur that Erdrich suggests survival of the Native spirit and culture in the postcolonial times. Further, it is again through a female figure, Lulu, Fleur's daughter that Native culture can look forward to future.

198

Ceremony is a web of stories woven by the Laguna feminine spirit Thought Woman. It is through her various manifestations as Night Swan, Ts'eh, Tsi'tisi'nako, Grandmother Spider and A'moo'ooh that Tayo unlearns the colonizer's stories of violence and comes to an identity of his own. While Betonie tells Tayo the stories of a changing Laguna and the need for a dynamic tradition, Ts'eh is the one who makes the stories happen. As myth and reality are fused through the feminine connection to land and the beings of universe, Tayo is blessed with understanding the importance and relevance of stories. The ones who perish in *Ceremony* are the ones who fail to connect with the feminine.

In *Green Grass, Running Water*, the patriarchal, hierarchical Christian stories are appropriated and put in a Native context so as to demonstrate that the creation is the work of an ancient feminine spirit who precedes the Christian god. King's emphasis on the Earthdiver creation myth foregrounds the role of the feminine in bringing the world into being. As First Woman, Changing Woman, Thought Woman, and Old Woman move around the contemporary Blackfoot world and 'fix' things, they emphasize the power of the feminine that can create and transform, repair and destroy, and in the process topsy-turvy the colonizer's ways of perception.

Halfbreed, written as it is by a woman and a survivor of social and cultural genocide, recites the power of the feminine. Maria, being a woman of grit and determination survives the violence of her body and spirit and in fact draws strength from the worst kinds of experiences life has given her. Cheechum, Maria's great grandmother, in her long life has shown what it takes to be on the other side of the story. At her lowest moments, Maria draws her inspiration from Cheechum's teachings.

It is interesting to note here that the women who die or lose their identities in these texts are women eager to conform to the colonizer's ideal of women. Pauline in *Tracks*, Laura, Helen Jean and Auntie in *Ceremony*, Maria's mother, and to some extent Maria herself in *Halfbreed* suffer, die, or lose their identities because they fall prey to the colonizing discourse that depicts women as powerless, secondary, and vulnerable.

Writing with a nationalistic impulse to highlight and appropriate the hard colonial experiences, these Native writers deconstruct the "appropriate" and "legitimate" versions of hegemonic history. In their deliberate undermining of the dominant version of history, they signify their sense of cultural specificity and communal identity. By discarding the absolute and exclusivist versions of history, 199 these Native writers rewrite histories from a postmodern point of view. As they subvert the authoritarian narrative, history is configured from a time previous to the arrival of the Euroamerican forces. Further, by retelling portions of their experiences with the colonizer, these Native writers produce cultural and historic counter narratives. Native writing, thus "moves to decenter the imperialist basis of these discursive constructions when it directs attention away from the traditionally privileged signifier to that which is consequently marginalized in the signifying practice" (Walton 73).

Tracks reappropriates the contemporary history of the Turtle Mountain Chippewa. Nanapush tells us the story of the large-scale death of the Chippewa people in the colonizer's diseases. Set in early twentieth century, *Tracks* also highlights the ever-encroaching greed of the colonizers and the Anishinabe's loss of home and livelihood resulting from this. As Nanapush shapes Lulu's Nativity and paints her fabric of experience with colours from a Native past, he also reflects on the colonizers' early practices of division and fragmentation that continues till date. Pauline's stories, contrarily, do not have any historicity in them as she herself is in a process to ensure complete erasure of her own history from the Native world.

In *Ceremony*, Silko reapproarpiates history with her retelling of the colonizer's dualistic, opportunistic policies. The hegemonic forces' dualistic policies stand exposed when hordes of Native youth like Rocky and Tayo get drafted to the war with a promise of equality and a better future and are abandoned to oblivion soon after their utility is over. While the hegemonic discourse would have us believe that it was an act of compassion to distribute blankets among the Natives, Silko's *Ceremony* points out that the blankets were infected with smallpox and thus served as the colonizer's tools for annihilating tribes and furthering their agenda of genocide. Further, by giving us the story of the uranium mine and the atomic bomb experiment, Silko connects history to present as she links the Japanese faces to Laguna faces and the dryness of the land to the violence inflicted on Mother Earth.

King's *Green Grass, Running Water* in a pejorative take on the official versions of history, recreates history from a Native context. In a quasi-comic recounting of events from the colonial past, *Green Grass, Running Water* highlights facts about Native history, art and cultural practices that have gone unrecorded in the colonizers' discourse. Native history ranging from the incarceration of Native chiefs in the nineteenth century to the American Indian movement of the twentieth are all raeppraorpiated to signify the marginalized other's version of events and happenings. Further, through his retelling of Melvilles's *Benito Cereno*, King also comments on the plight of marginals from another part of the globe and connects them to a single thread of exploitation and dehumanization by the colonizers.

Campbell's *Halfbreed* begins with a reappropriation of Métis history before it sets on the history of Campbell's life and experiences as a Métis woman in contemporary Canada. By portraying Louis Riel and Gabriel Dumont as Métis heroes and denying defeat at the Battle of Batoche, Campbell makes a postmodern alteration of the authoritarian discourse. Through her retelling of the events of 1880's, Campbell textualizes a version of history other than what the "history books say." And in doing so, she frees herself and her peoples from the captivity of the master narrative-thus redefining Native community and history from a Native point of view.

Writing with a postcolonial, postmodern consciousness, these Natives writers do not conform to categories and hence border crossings and boundary blurrings are commonly manifested in their works. The colonial categories of race, sex, nation, and such binary divisions are disregarded, subverted, parodied in the four texts discussed here. The authenticity and originality of all sorts of demarcations are questioned and challenged in the Native literary productions. The personal and the communal, myth and history, story and reality, male and female are all mixed up in a heady cocktail of postmodernist discourse. While these writes write from the gap of a postcolonial space, they also bridge the binaries of past and present, oppressed and oppressor and such like and thus challenge the reader to change from a dualistic to a holistic perception of the universe. Truly postcolonial in their sense and content, these Native texts thus qualify to be called hybrid texts. As they reject the idea of clear-cut boundaries, these Native authors simultaneously dislocate the hierarchical and binary thought patterns of Western master-narratives. As Petrone observes regarding Native Canadian authors:

> Canada's native writers have borrowed from Western traditions the forms of autobiography, fiction, drama and the essay. Their use, however, judged by Western literary criteria of structure, style and aesthetics, do not always conform...Like the archetypal figure, the trickster, native writers easily adopt a multiplicity of styles and forms to suit their purposes, and in so doing they are giving 201 birth to a new literature: a written literature that is

> finally and gratefully being given to us by the first peoples
> of our country-enabling us to hear voices most of us
> have not heard before, bringing to life people, places,
> experiences and problems that are uniquely Canadian,
> yet universal too (Petrone 183-184).

In *Tracks*, boundaries blur at multiplicity of levels and meanings change continually. While both Nanapush and Pauline blur the boundaries of male and female through their actions and stories, Native time co-occurs with linear time. Nanapush exists not only as the trickster Nanabozho in a mythical Chippewa past but also in the context of a contemporary reservation life. Pauline's denial of motherhood and the brutal killing of her one-time lover are acts that foreground her masculinity, though, paradoxically, she becomes Sister Leopolda at the end of the text. Magic, medicine, shamanism and Missipeshu coexist in *Tracks* with land allotment, government papers, community conflict and the missionaries. In her clever transgression of boundaries, Erdrich thus creates a postmodern text.

Silko's *Ceremony* is a novel; but it has no chapter names. There is no linear progression of plot and growth of character in the western sense of novel writing. Rather, things happen simultaneously on different planes of reality. Myth affects the process of identity formation of a contemporary Laguna youth and a mixed-blood man like Tayo can foresee what other full-bloods fail to. Betonie's medicine includes both deer-hoof clackers as well as English newspapers. While Tayo is racially ousted by the majority community, he is also equally troubled by the Natives' non-acceptance of the colour of his eyes. Though Ts'eh is the mythical feminine spirit of the Laguna land, Tayo can make love to her and thus heal his own wounded identity.

Green Grass, Running Water blurs boundaries through both theme and technique. A novel written in English, *Green Grass, Running Water* has chapter names in Cherokee, thus privileging the Native reader over the non-Native. Conversely, its self-reflexive storytelling technique foregrounds the author's mastery of the sophisticated western literary aesthetic. The four mythical Indians are simultaneously male and female, both in their stories as well as in reality. The 'animal' Coyote impregnates the 'human' Alberta. George Morningstar is an abusive white whose name sounds Indian. Latisha's restaurant menu is and is not authentic. Alberta loves two men but won't marry either of her two lovers. All these contradictions heighten the postmodern

202

tension in the text and thus foreground a contemporary Native existence and experience. In their continuous to and fro journey between U.S. and Canada, King's characters also fuse the borders of the two nations.

Campbell's *Halfbreed* treads between fiction and non-fiction. While she signs her book as Maria Campbell, her 'real' name is June Stifle. Though most of the experiences Campbell recounts in the book are real, she changes the names of people and places at various points in the text. Thus her textual production is both an autobiography and a novel. Campbell further blurs boundaries in her identification with the Natives as a whole rather than only the community of Halfbreeds. As a young girl too, Maria is equally adept at hunting and trapping as her brothers and father. In such blurring of boundaries and demarcations Campbell's text becomes a postmodern work of literature.

Native fiction, written from the point of view of the marginalized thus offers a site for resistance. In their conscious subversion of the master narratives, rejection of assimilationist discourse, retelling of the Native past, assertion of cultural uniqueness, creation of a community identity, blurring of form and technique and moreover a reformation of their very existence on earth, Native writers resist the power of the dominant discourse and counter it with Native strength and steadfastness. In the process, they as a community and entity achieve decolonization and thus alter their hitherto marginal status. As Emberley points out:

> Resistance is itself a process ... In a deconstructive analysis, the intolerable hierarchies of race, class, sexuality, and gender contained in binary oppositions such as colonizer/colonized, inferior/superior, Indian/White, woman/man are overturned when these class oppositions, in which subjects are contained by a revolving notion of being either one or the other, are displaced. The point to displacing this opposition, taking an indifferent position toward either side of the opposition, is to rearticulate open, or alternate, subject positions (Emberley 102).

Nanapush and more than him Fleur are the figures of resistance in *Tracks*. Though Pauline flows with the wave of assimilation and ultimately loses her own self, Fleur resists the current of assimilation by keeping her connection intact with the Lake Matchimanito, the source of both life and death for the Chippewa. While Nanapush is proud of his "good English" and in spite of the fact that he is 203 telling his stories in English, he often draws words and phrases from the "old language." *Tracks* as a text concerns itself only with the lives and experiences of the Anishinabe and resists the intrusion of the white others into the text.

Ceremony rejects as well as resists the violence of the colonial discourse. While Tayo's problems start with his participation in the war, the manifestation of imperialistic violence, his healing results from his resistance to the temptation of indulging in Emo's bloody ritual and hence as a Native text, *Ceremony* foregrounds the futility and destructiveness of violence. In Tayo's resistance to violence and welcoming of love lies the future of a Native world as well as the world beyond it. Betonie, too, in his role as a mixed-breed medicine man who draws from two traditions, emphasizes the need for change and thus resists a slow death of the Laguna.

In *Green Grass, Running Water* Eli resists the taking away of Native resources such as land and water. While his act of staying put in his mother's cabin obstructs the colonizer's dreams of capture and control, this act of resistance frustrates the representatives of the hegemony such as Clifford Sifton. Further the retellings of stories from multiple fields and discourses not only provide a postcolonial, postmodern appropriation of the dominant narrative but also resist the Native's being defined and constructed in an-Other's discourse. Though resistance involves risk and loss as is evident from Eli's death, it seems to be a dignified choice as it gives the Natives a chance to live their lives with respect and honor.

Halfbreed is a text of resistance. At the very outset of the text, the reader knows that it is a tale of survival and resistance. As Campbell tells us the story of her life, various episodes in the text, starting from her schooldays to her mother's death to her rebellious teenage and her rejection of welfare, point to the author's sense of dignity and her immense desire to resist from being robbed off her dignity. In her fictional recreation of a difficult life, Campbell resists being relegated to the margin and makes her voice heard, and that voice is not only a voice of resistance but also of hope.

Coming as they do from cultures that have been muted and hidden by the hegemonic discourse, Native texts often reflect on their own invisibility and voicelessness. Pauline's unnoticed presence behind the walls of town shops, and Lulu's 'invisibility' in *Tracks*, Tayo's feeling of becoming white smoke in *Ceremony*, the four mythical spirits' invisibility and Coyote's unseen existence in *Green Grass, Running Water*, Maria's astonishment at seeing her

204

own face in the mirror and not recognizing it in *Halfbreed*, all these point to the absent presence of the Native in the Colonial Landscape. Likewise, Fleur's voicelessness in the narrative of *Tracks*, and Tayo's equating his tongue to the carcass of a tiny rodent in *Ceremony*, Coyote's not getting a turn to tell his story in *Green Grass, Running Water* and Maria's jabbed tongue in front of Darrel's sister or her white masters in *Halfbreed*, all these experiences foreground the plight of the unheard Natives. Unseen and unheard in the colonizer's scheme of things, these Native texts have to shout and speak aloud so as to show others that they exist and cannot be anymore trampled under the feet of the apparently civilized mainstream. Texts rising from this postcolonial consciousness of marginality hence have challenged the conventional notions of aesthetics and canon. In a pluralistic, heterodoxical, postcolonial world, the scope of canon needs to be revised and reconstructed so as to include the realities of the contemporary world and come out of the cocoon of an exclusivist paradigm. As Rodney Simard suggests in his seminal essay "American Indian Literatures, Authenticity and the Canon":

> Pluralism does not mean a diffusion of quality; it means a redefinition of quality...I propose that our national literature, as a single entity, must be viewed as the text of the country in its multifaceted, multicultural, multiethnic, multiexperential reality (Simard 244).

To further extend Simard's remark, it is both essential and desirable to work towards including these Native texts in the canon and thus resist segregation of these landmark texts in the narrow definitions of minority/ethnic or tribal literature. Some Native scholars like Allen and Armstrong argue for Native paradigms to assess and analyze literary productions of Native authors. To this, it can be contended that while Native paradigms of understanding would certainly help broaden the perception of indigenous writing, it is also advisable that one looks at these texts from a postcolonial, poststructual, postmodern perspective so as to gain further insight to understanding these texts. This is because colonization having been a part of the life experiences of the Native peoples has affected their worlds, values and perceptions in a multiplicity of ways and without taking a postcolonial perspective into the reading of these texts, these perceptions cannot be facilitated. With their reassessment of the history and politics of their land and communities, these Native texts are definitely postcolonial in both tone and character. The new orality and historicity these texts produce do not merely promise a nostalgic recounting of past nor do they conventionally conform to a future based on fictionality. In their honest re-creation of a past and a practical tone for the future, these Native texts thus rise to create the opportunity for a sincere understanding of the marginal's chances in the contemporary scenario. As they write, they evolve and with evolution comes survival. It's hence apt to conclude with a remark by McGrath and Petrone regarding Native writing:

> Young natives, increasingly caught between tradition and mainstream culture are writing about and interpreting themselves...While still looking to their traditional oral literature for direction and inspiration, they are exploring new content. With better education, mastery of the language and the craft, and sense of pride and authority in their spiritual roots, they are asserting their uniqueness within a stronger, more diversified literary tradition (McGrath & Petrone 319).

End notes:

1. "Interfusional literature," King suggests, is one that blends oral and written literature and forces the reader to read aloud, thus recreating the performative aspect of oral story telling.

2. King has explained "Associational literature" as that literature which concerns itself with the dialects of Native life- along a flat narrative line. It foregrounds a community-centric worldview and avoids being judgmental or offering any closure.

Works Cited:

Adams, Howard. *Prison of Grass: Canada from a Native Point of View.* 1975. 2nd Ed. Alberta: Fifth House Publishers, 1989.

Akiwenzie-Damm, Kateri. "We Belong To This Land: A View of 'Cultural Difference.'" *Literary Pluralities.* Ed. Christl Verduyn. Ontario: Broadview Press Limited and *Journal of Canadian* Studies, 1998. 84-91.

Allen, P.G. *The Sacred Hoop: Recovering the Feminine in American Indian Traditions.* Boston: Beacon Press, 1986.

Allen, P. G. "The Feminine Landscape of Leslie Marmon Silko's *Ceremony." Studies in American Indian Literature: Critical Essays and Course Designs.* Ed. Paula Gunn Allen. New York: The MLA of America, 1983.127-133.

Allen, P. G. "Introduction." *Spider Woman's Granddaughter: Traditional Tales and Contemporary Writing by Native American Women.* Ed with Intro. P.G. Allen. New York: Fawcett Columbine, 1989.1-25.

Andrews, Jennifer. "Border Trickery and Dog Bones: a Conversation with Thomas King: *SCL/ELC* Interview." *Studies in Canadian Literature* 24.2 (1999):161-185.

Anonymous. "Postmodernism". http://www.pbs.org/faithandreason/gengloos/postmodernism_body.html. 9April 2007.

Anonymous. http://www.qub.cu.uk/en/imperial/canada/surfacing.htm. dt 6 July 2004.

Armstrong, Jeannette. "Invocation: The Real Power of Aboriginal Women." *Women of the First Nations: Power, Wisdom, and Strength.* Ed. Christine Miller et al. Manitoba: The U of Manitoba P, 1996. IX-XII.

Arnold, Ellen L. "An Ear For the Story: An Eye For The Pattern: Rereading *Ceremony." Modern Fiction Studies* 45.1 (Summer 1999): 69-92.

Ashcroft, Bill; et al.; Ed. *The Postcolonial Studies Reader*. London: Routledge, 1995.

Atwood, Margaret. "A Double-Bladed Knife: Subversive Laughter in Two Stories by Thomas King." *CLC 89*. Ed. Christopher Giroux. Detroit: Gale Research Inc., 1996. 75-79.

Babcock, Barbara. "'A Tolerated Margin of Mess": The Trickster and His Tales Reconsidered." *Critical Essays on Native American Literature*. Ed. Andrew Wiget. Boston: G.K. Hall & Co., 1985.153-185.

Bakhtin, Mikhail M. *The Dialogic Imagination*. 1981. Ed. Michael Holquist. Trans. Caryl Emerson and Michael Holquist. Austin: U of Texas P, 1991.

Barak, Julie. "Blurs, Blends, Berdaches: Gender mixing in the Novels of Louise Erdrich." *CLC 120*. Eds. Jeffery W. Hunter and Timothy J. White. Detroit: Gale Group, 1994.184-190.

Bastien, Betty. "Voices through Time." *Women of First Nations: Power, Wisdom and Strength*. Ed. Christine Miller et al. Manitoba: The U of Manitoba P, 1996.127-129.

Beirder, Peter G. "The facts of Fictional Magic. John Tanner as a Source for Louise Erdrich's *Tracks* and *The Birchback House*." *American Indian Culture and Research Journal* 24: 4 (2000): 37-54.

Belsey, Catherine. *Poststructuralism: A Very Short Introduction*. New York: OUP, 2002.

Benediktsson, Thomas E. "The Reawakening of the Gods: Realism and the Supernatural in Silko and Hulme." *Critique* 33:2 (1992): 121-132.

Bennani, Benjamin and Catherine Warner Bennani, "No Ceremony For Men in the Sun: Sexuality, Personhood, and Nationhood in Ghassan Kanafani's *Men in the Sun*, and Leslie Marmon Silko's *Ceremony*." *Critical Perspectives on Native American Fiction*. Ed. Richard F. Fleck. Washington D.C.: Three Continents Press, 1993. 246-255.

211

Bennet, Donna. "English Canada's Postcolonial Complexities." *Essays on Canadian Writing* 51-52 (1993-1994): 164-210.

Bhaba, Homi K. "Representation and the Colonial Text: A Critical Exploration of Some forms of Mimeticism." *The Theory of Reading*. Ed. Frank Gloversmith. Brighton (Sussex): Harvested Press, 1984. 93-122.

Blair, Barbara. "Textual Expressions of the Search for Cultural Identity." *American Studies in Scandinavia* 27:1 (1995): 48-63.

Boas, Franz. "Mythology and Folk-tales of the North American Indians." *Critical Essays on Native American Literature*. Ed. Andrew Wiget. Boston: G. K. Hall and Co., 1985. 28-50.

Braz, Albert. "The Absent Protagonist: Louis Riel in Nineteenth Century Canadian Literature." *Canadian Literature* 167 (Winter 2000): 45-67.

Brehm, Victoria. "The Metamorphosis of An Ojibwa *Manido*." *American Literature* 68.4 (December1996): 677-706.

Brown, Dee. *Bury My Heart at Wounded Knee: An Indian History of the American West*. Lincoln: U of Nebraska P, 1967.

Bruchac, Joseph. "Whatever is Really Yours." *CLC 120*. Ed. Jeffrey W, Hunter and Timothy J. White. Detroit: Gale Group, 1999.134-139.

Bumstead, J.M. "Louis Riel and the United States." *American Review of Canadian Studies* 29.1 (1999): 17-41.

Buss, Helen M. "The Different Voice of Canadian Feminist Autobiographies." *Biography* 13.2 (1990): 154-167.

Cairnie, Julie. "Writing and Telling Hybridity: Autobiographical and Testimonial Narratives in Maria Campbell's *Halfbreed*." *World Literature Written in English* 34.2 (1995): 94-108.

Campbell, Maria. *Halfbreed*. Toronto: McClelland and Stewart Limited, 1973.

Canton, Jeffery. "An Interview with Thomas King." *CLC 89*. Ed. Christopher Giroux. Detroit: Gale Research Inc., 1996. 98-101.

Cardinal, Harold. *The Unjust Society: The Tragedy of Canada's Indians.* Edmonton: M.G. Hurtig Ltd., 1969.

Césaire, Aimé. *Discourse on Colonialism.* 1972. Trans. Joan Pinkham. New York: Monthly Review Press, 2000.

Cederstorm, Lorelei. "Introduction to the Special Issue on Native Literature." *The Canadian Journal of Native Studies* (Spring 1987): 145-149.

Chester, Blanca. "*Green Grass, Running Water*: Theorizing the World of the Novel." *Canadian Literature* 161-162 (Summer/Autumn 1999): 44-61.

Chuchryk, Patricia and Christine Miller. "Introduction." *Women of the First Nations: Power, Wisdom, and Strength.* Ed. Christine Miller et al. Manitoba: The U of Manitoba P, 1996. 3-10.

Clutesi, George. *Son of Raven, Son of Deer: Fables of the Tse-shant People.* Sidney, B.C.: Gray's Publishing, 1967.

--------------------. *Potlatch.* Sidney, B.C.: Gray's Publishing, 1969.

Coltelli, Laura. "Louise Erdrich and Michael Dorris." *Winged Words: American Indian Writers Speak.* Lincoln: U of Nebraska Press, 1990. 40-52.

Concannon, Kevin. "Deer-Hoof Clacker and Coke-Bottles: The Construction of the Postcolonial Nation in Leslie Marmon Silko's *Ceremony*." *ariel* 5.2-4 (July- October 04): 183-200.

Cooper, James Fenimore. *The Leatherstocking Saga.*1826-1841. Ed. Allan Nevins. New York: Modern Library, 1966.

Copeland, Marion W. "*Black Elk Speaks* and Leslie Marmon Silko's *Ceremony*: Two visions of Horses." *Critique* 24:3 (Spring 1983): 158-172.

Cruickshank, Julie. *The Social Life of Stories: Narrative and Knowledge in the Yukon Territory.* Vancouver: U of British Columbia P, 1998.

Culjak, Toni A. "Searching for a Place in Between: The Autobiographies of Three Canadian Métis Women." *The American Review of Canadian Studies* 31.1-2 (2001): 137-157.

Cutchins, Dennis. "'So That the Nations May become Genuine Indian': Nativism and Leslie Marmon Silko's *Ceremony.*" *Journal of American Culture* 22.4 (1999): 77-90.

Cuthand, Beth. "Transmitting Our Identity as Indian Writers." *In the Feminine: Women and Words* (Conference proceedings 1983). Ed. Ann Dybikowski et al., Edmonton: Longspoon Press, 1985. 53-54.

Darias-Beautell, Eva. *Contemporary Theories and Canadian Fiction: shifting sands*. Queenston: The Edwin Meller Press. 2000.

Dasenbrock, Reed Way. "Forms of Biculturalism in Southwestern Literature: The Works of Rudolf Anaya and Leslie Marmon Silko." *Genre* 21.3 (1988): 307-319.

Defoe, Daniel. *Robinson Crusoe*. The Life and Strange Surprising Adventures of Robinson Crusoe, of York, mariner. 1719. Oxford: Oxford Classics, 1981.

Delicka, Magdalena. "American Magic Realism: Crossing the Borders in Literatures of the Margins." *Journal of American Studies of Turkey* 6 (1997): 25-33.

Deloria, Vine, Jr. *Custer Died for Your Sins: An Indian Manifesto*. Norman: U of Oklahoma P, 1988.

Disch, Thomas M. "Enthralling Tale: Louise Erdrich's World of Love and Survival." *CLC 84*. Eds. Daniel G. Marowski and Roger Matuz. Detroit: Gale Research Inc., 1989.

Donaldson, Laura E. "Noah meets Old Coyote, or Singing in the Rain: Intertextuality in Thomas King's *Green Grass, Running Water.*" *Studies in American Indian Literatures* 7.2 (1995): 27-43.

Downes, Margaret J. "Narrativity, Myth and Metaphor: Louise Erdrich and Raymond Carver Talk About Love." *MELUS* 21:2 (Summer 1996): 49-61.

Dvorak, Marta. "The Discourse Strategies of Native Literature: Thomas King's Shift from Adversial to Interfusional." *ariel* 33.3-4 (July-October 2002): 212-230.

Emberley, Julia. "Aboriginal Women's Writing and the Cultural Politics of Representation." *Women of the First Nations: Power, Wisdom, and Strength*. Ed. Christine Miller et al. Manitoba: The U of Manitoba P, 1996. 97-112.

Erdrich, Louise. *Tracks*. New York: Harper & Row Publishers, 1989.

------------------. *Jacklight*. New York: Holt Rinehart Winston, 1984.

------------------. *The Beet Queen*. New York: Bantam Books, 1986.

------------------. *Love Medicine*. New York: Perennial, 2001.

------------------. *The Last Report on the Miracles at Little No Horse*. New York: HarperCollins, 2001.

------------------. *Four Souls*. New York: HarperCollins, 2004.

Farwell, Martin. "Necessary Fictions: The re-visioned subjects of Louise Erdrich and Alice Walker." Order Number DA 9125214, *Dissertation Abstracts International* 52. 4 (October 1991): 1327 A.

Fast, Robin Riley. "Babo's Great-Great Granddaughter: The Presence of *Benito Cereno* in *Green Grass, Running Water*." *American Indian Culture and Research Journal* 25.3 (2001): 27-46.

Fee, Margery and Jane Flick, "Coyote Pedagogy: Knowing Where the Borders are in Thomas King's *Green Grass, Running Water*." *Canadian Literature* 161-162. (Summer/Autumn 1999): 131-139.

Ferguson, Suzanne. "The Short Stories of Louise Erdrich's Novels." *Studies in Short Fiction* 33.4 (Fall 1996): 541-556.

Ferrari, Rita. "'Where the Maps Stopped': The Aesthetics of Borders in Louise Erdrich's *Love Medicine* and *Tracks*." *style* (Spring 1999) 20 Dec 2001. <http://findarticles.com/p/articles/mi_m2342/is_1_33/ai_58055909>.

Findley, Timothy. *Not Wanted on the Voyage*. Toronto: Viking, 1984.

Fleck, Richard F. "Introduction." *Critical Perspectives on Native American Fiction*. Ed. Richard F. Fleck. Washington D.C.: Three Continents Press, 1993.1-11.

Flick, Jane. "Reading Notes for Thomas King's *Green Grass, Running Water*." *Canadian Literature* 161-162 (Summer/Autumn 1999): 140-172.

Francis, Daniel. *National Dreams: Myth, Memory, and Canadian History*. Vancouver: Arsenal Pulp Press, 1997.

Frideres, James S. *Native Peoples in Canada:*

215

Contemporary Conflicts. Ontario: Prentice Hall Canada Inc., 1988.

Frye, Northrop. *Anatomy of Criticism, Four Essays*. Princeton, NJ: Princeton U P, 1957.

Gallagher, Susan VanZanten. "Introduction: New Conversations on Postcolonial Literature." *Postcolonial Literature and the Biblical Call for Justice*. Ed. Susan VanZanten Gallagher. Jackson: UP of Mississippi, 1994. 3-33.

Garcia, Reyes. "Sense of Place in *Ceremony*." *MELUS* 10:4 (1983): 37-48.

Gillies, M.A. "Temporal Interplay." *CLC 89*. Ed. Christopher Giroux. Detroit: Gale Research Inc., 1996. 90-93.

Godard, Barbara. "The Politics of Representation: Some Native Canadian Women Writers." *Native Writers and Canadian Writing*. Ed. W.H. New. Vancouver: University of British Columbia Press, 1990. 183-225.

Goldie, Terry. "Semiotic Control: Native Peoples in Canadian Literature in English." *Studies on Canadian Literature: Introductory and Critical Essays*. Ed. Arnold E. Davidson. New York: The Modern Language Association of America, 1990. 110-123.

Goldman, Marlene. "Mapping and Dreaming: Native Resistance in *Green Grass, Running Water*." *Canadian Literature* 161-162 (Summer/ Autumn 1999): 18-41.

Gould, Eric. *Mythical Intentions in Modern Literature*. Princeton: Princeton UP, 1981.

Grant, Agnes. "Contemporary Native Women's Voices in Literature." *Native Writers and Canadian Writing*. Ed. W.H.New. Vancouver: University of British Columbia P, 1990. 124-132.

Gross, Konrad. "Survival of Orality in a Literate Culture: Leslie Silko's Novel *Ceremony*." *Native North American Literature: Biographical and Critical Information on Native Writers and Orators from the United States and Canada from Historical Times to the Present*. Ed Janet Witalec. New York: Gale Research Inc., 1994. 579-81.

Gzowski, Peter. "Peter Gzowski Interviews Thomas King on *Green Grass, Running Water*." *Canadian Literature* 161/162 (Summer/ Autumn 1999): 65-76.

Hassan, Ihab. "Towards a Concept of Postmodernism."

Postmodern American Fiction. Ed. Paula Geyh et al. New York: W.W. Norton & Company, 1998. 585-594.

Hassan, Ihab. *The Postmodern Turn: Essays in Postmodern Theory and Culture.* Columbus: Ohio State U P, 1987. 91-92.

Healey, Joseph F. *Race, Ethnicity, and Gender in The United States: Inequality, Group Conflict and Power.* California: Pine Forge Press, 1997.

Hernandez, Inès. "Foreword." *Growing Up Native American: An Anthology.* Ed. with Intro Patricia Riley. New York: William Morrow and Company Inc, 1993.

Hobbs, Michael. "Living In-Between: Tayo as Radical Reader in Leslie Marmon Silko's *Ceremony.*" *Western American Literature* 28.4 (1994): 301-312.

Hobert, Cornelia. "A review of *Halfbreed.*" *CLT 85.* Ed. Christopher Giroux. Detroit: Gale Research Inc, 1995.

Horchbruck, Wolfgang. "I have spoken: Fictional 'Orality' in Indigenous Fiction." *College Literature* 23.2 (1997): 132-141.

Hughes, Sheilla Hassell. "Tongue-Tied: Rhetoric and Relation in Louise Erdrich's *Tracks.*" *MELUS* (Fall-Winter 2000). 22pp. 8 July 2006. <http://findarticles.com/p/articles/mi_m2278/is_2000_Fall-winter/ai_74483361>

Hutcheon, Linda. *Splitting Images: Contemporary Canadian Ironies.* Toronto: OUP, 1991.

Hutcheon, Linda. *A Poetics of Postmodernism.* New York: Routledge, 1988.

Jahner, Elaine. "An Act of Attention: Event Structure in *Ceremony.*" *Critical Essays on Native American Literature.* Ed. Andrew Wiget. Boston: G K Hall & Co, 1985. 238- 246.

Johnson, Brian. "Plastic Shaman in the Global Village: Understanding Media in Thomas King's *Green Grass, Running Water.*" *Studies in Canadian Literature* 25.2 (2000): 24-49.

Johnson, Valerie Miner. "Dad was Always Drunk, Mom Always Pregnant." *CLT 85.* Ed. Christopher Giroux. Detroit:

Gale Research Inc, 1995. 2-3.

Johnston, Basil. *Indian School Days*. Norman: U of Oklahoma P, 1989.

Karem, Jeff. "Keeping the Native on the Reservation: The Struggle for Leslie Marmon Silko's *Ceremony*." *American Indian Culture and Research Journal* 25.4 (2001): 21-34.

Kent, Alicia. "Native American Feminist Criticism in the Contact Zone." *Northwest Review* 35.3 (1997): 100-114.

King, Thomas. *Medicine River*. Toronto: Penguin, 1989.

------------------, ed. *All My Relations: An Anthology of Short Fiction by Native Writers in Canada*. Toronto: McClelland & Stewart, 1990.

------------------. *A Coyote Columbus Story*. Toronto: Douglas & McIntyre, 1992.

------------. *Green Grass, Running Water*. Toronto: HarperCollins, 1993.

------------------. *Truth and Bright Water*. Toronto: Harper Flamingo Canada, 1999.

------------------. *Dreadful Water Shows up*. New York: Scribner, 2003.

Konkle, Maureen, "Indian Literary, U.S. Colonialism, and Literary Criticism." *American Literature* 69.3 (Sep 1997): 457-487.

Korkka, Janne. "Resisting Cultural Domination: Thomas King's Canadian Mosaic." *The Atlantic Literary Review* 3.2 (April-June 2002): 143-154.

Krupat, Arnold. *The Voice in the Margin: Native American Literature and the Canon*. Berkeley: U of California P, 1989.

------------------. "Postcolonialism, Ideology and Native American Literature." *Postcolonial Theory And The United States: Race, Ethnicity, and Literature*. Ed. Amarjit Singh and Peter Schmidt. Jackson: U P of Mississippi, 2000. 73-94.

LaRocque, Emma. "The Colonization of a Native Woman Scholar." *Women of the First Nations: Power, Wisdom and Strength*. Ed. Christine Miller et al. Manitoba: The University of Manitoba Press, 1996. 11-18.

Larson, Sidner. "The Fragmentation of a Tribal People in Louise Erdrich's *Tracks*." American Indian Culture and Research Journal 17.2 (1993): 1-13.

Lamont-Stewart, Linda. "Androgyny as Resistance to Authoritarianism in Two Postmodern Canadian Novels." *Mosaic* 30.3 (September 1997): 115-130.
Lee, A. Robert. "Ethnic Renaissance: Rudolfo Anaya, Louise Erdrich and Maxine Hong Kingston." *The New American Writing: Essays on American Literature since 1970*. Ed. Graham Clarke. London: Vision Press, 1990. 139-164.

Lincoln, Kenneth. "Native American Literatures." *Smoothing the Ground: Essays on Native American Oral Literature*. Ed. Brian Swann. Berkeley and Los Angeles: U of California P, 1983. 3-38.

--------------------. "Grand mother storyteller: Leslie Marmon Silko." *Native American Renaissance*. Berkeley: U of California P, 1983. 222-250.

Linton, Patricia. "'And Here's How It Happened': Trickster Discourse in Thomas King's *Green Grass, Running Water*." *MFS Modern Fiction Studies* 45.1 (Spring 1999): 212- 234.

Lousley, Cheryl. "'Hosanna Da, Our Home on Native's Land': Environmental Justice and Democracy in Thomas King's *Green Grass, Running Water*." *Essays on Canadian Writing* 81 (Winter 2004): 17-44.

Lutz, Hartmut. "Maria Campbell." *Contemporary Challenges: Conversations with Canadian Native Authors*. Saskatoon: Fifth House Publishers.1991. 41-65.

-----------------. "Thomas King." *Contemporary Challenges: Conversations with Canadian Native Authors*. Saskatoon: Fifth House Publishers, 1991. 107-116.

-----------------. "Contemporary Native Literature in Canada and The Voice of the Mother." *O Canada: Essays on Canadian Literature and Culture*. Ed. Jørn Carlsen. Oxford: Aarhus U P, 1995. 79-96.

Lyotard, Jean- Francois. "Answering the Question: What is Postmodernism." *Postmodernism: A Reader*. Ed. Patricia Waugh. London: Edward Arnold, 1992.

Maracle, Lee. *Bobbi Lee: Indian Rebel. Struggles of a Native Canadian Woman*. Richmond, B.C.: Liberation Support

Press, 1975.
----------------. *I am woman.* Vancouver: Write-on, 1988.

McGrath, Robin and Penny Petrone. "Native Canadian Literature." *Studies on Canadian Literature: Introductory and Critical Essays.* Ed. Arnold E. Davidson. New York: The Modern Language Association of America, 1990. 309-322.

Melville, Herman. *Moby Dick.* 1851. New York: Barnes and Noble Books, 1993.

----------------. *Benito Cereno.* *"Billy Budd, Sailor" and Other Stories.* New York: Penguin, 1986.
Momaday, N.Scott. *House Made of Dawn.* New York: Harper & Row Publishers, 1969.

----------------. "The Man Made of Words." *Indian Voices.* San Francisco: Indian Historian Press, 1970.

Moodie, Susanna. *Roughing It in the Bush.* London: Richard Bentley, 1852.

Moore, David L. "Myth, History and Identity in Silko and Young Bear: Postcolonial Praxis." *New Voices in Native American Literary Criticism.* Ed. Arnold Krupat. Washington D.C.: Smithsonian Institution P, 1993. 370-395.

Morgan, Thais. "The Space of Intertextuality." *Intertextuality and Contemporary American Fiction.* Ed. Robert Cow Davis and Patrick O'Donnell. Baltimore: John Hopkins U P, 1989. 239-279.

Morse, Bradford W. "Aboriginal Peoples and The Law." *Aboriginal Peoples and The Law: Indian, Métis, and Inuit Rights in Canada.* Revised 1st ed. Ed. Bradford W. Morse. Ottawa: Carlton U P, 1991.

New, W.H. *A History of Canadian Literature.* London: MacMillan Education Ltd. 1989.
Encyclopedia of Literature in Canada. Ed. William H. New. Toronto: U of Toronto P, 2000.

Oandson, William. "A Familiar Life Component of Love in *Ceremony.*" *Critical Perspectives on Native American Fiction.* Ed. Richard F. Fleck. Washington D.C.: Three Continents Press, 1993. 240-245.

Orr, Lisa. "Theorizing the Earth: Feminist Approaches to Nature and Leslie Marmon Silko's *Ceremony*." *American Indian Culture and Research Journal* 18.2 (1994): 145-147.

Ortiz, Simon J. "The Historical Matrix Towards A National Indian Literature: Cultural Authenticity in Nationalism." *Critical Perspectives on Native American Fiction*. Ed. Richard F. Fleck. Washington D.C.: Three Continents Press, 1993. 64-68.

Owens, Louis. *Other Destinies: Understanding the American Indian Novel*. Norman: U of Oklahoma P, 1992.

Perreault, Jeanne; and Vance, Sylvia; Eds. *Writing the Circle: Native Women of Western Canada*. Edmonton: Newest Press, 1990.

Patel, Cyrus R. K. "The Violence of Hybridity in Silko and Alexie." *Journal of American Studies Turkey* 6 (1997): 3-9.

Peterson, Nancy J. "History, Postmodernism, and Louise Erdrich's *Tracks*." *PMLA* 109.5 (1994): 982-994.

Petrone, Penny. *Native Literature in Canada: From the Oral Tradition to the Present*. Ontario: OUP, 1990. 113-137.

Rainwater, Catherine. "Reading between Worlds: Narrativity in the Fiction of Louise Erdrich." *American Literature* 62.3 (September 1990): 405-422.

Rani, Suneetha. "What is Writing? Native Canadian Women Speak." *Multiculturalism: Canada and India*. Ed. R.K. Dhawan and D.K. Pabby. New Delhi: Prestige Books. 2005. 44-57.

Reck, Alexander. "To tell a Story: Time and Memories in *Beloved* and *Ceremony*". 4pp. 8 March 2007. http://www.q.georgetown.edu/faculty/bassr/218/projects/reck/alr.htm#beloved.

Reid, E. Shelley. "The Stories We Tell: Louise Erdrich's Identity Narratives". *MELUS* (Fall- Winter 2000). 14pp.24 Jan 2005. http://findarticles.com/p/articles/mi_m2278/is_2000_Fallwinter?ai_74483360/pg_1

221

Ridington, Robin. "Coyote's Canon: Sharing Stories with Thomas King." *American Indian Quarterly* 22.3. (1998): 343-362.

Rohrbacher, Wendy J. *(Re)Invention and Contextualization in contemporary Native Fiction*. M.A. Thesis. May 1999. np. 10 October 2003. http://towerofbabal.com/sections/tome/nativeamericanfiction/

Rosen, Kenneth, ed. *The Man to Send Rain Clouds: Contemporary Stories by American Indians*. New York: Viking, 1974.

Ruoff, A. LaVonne Brown. *American Indian Literatures: An Introduction, Bibliographic Reviews, and Selected Bibliography*. New York: The MLA of America, 1990.

Ruppert, James. "Mediation and Multiple Narratives in *Love Medicine.*" *CLC 120*. Eds. Jeffrey W. Hunter and Timothy J. White. Detroit: Gale Group, 1999. 145-151.

Salat, M. F. "Subversions and Contradictions: Postmodernism and Canadian Literature." *Postmodernism* and *Feminism: Canadian Contexts*. Ed. Shirin Kudchedker. Delhi: Pencraft International, 1995. 23-38.

Salat, M.F. "Reading Native Women Writing." *Feminist Spaces: Cultural Reading from India and Canada*. Ed. Malashri Lal. New Delhi. Allied Publishers Limited, 1997. 127-138.

Sanders, Karla. "A Healthy Balance: Religion, Identity, and Community in Louise Erdrich's '*Love Medicine*'." *MELUS* (summer 1998). 20 February 2006. http://findarticles.com/p/articles/mi_m2278/is_2_23/ai_54543101

Savage, Jr. William W. "Editor's Introduction." *Indian Life: Transforming an American Myth*. Ed. with Intro William W. Savage, Jr. Norman: U of Oklahoma P, 1977. 3-16.

Scheick, William J. "Grace and Gall." *Canadian Literature* 138-139 (Fall-Winter 1993): 155-156.

222

Schweninger, Lee. "Writing Nature: Silko and Native Americans as Nature Writers." *MELUS* 18:2 (1993): 47-60.

Seiler, Tamara Palmer. "Multi-Vocality and National Literature: Towards a Post-Colonial and Multicultural Aesthetic." *Literary Pluralities*. Ed. Christl Verduyn. Ontario: Broadview Press Ltd., 1998. 47-63.

Sergi, Jennifer. "Storytelling: Tradition and Presentation in Louise Erdrich's *Tracks*." *World Literature Today* 66.2 (Spring 1992): 279-282.

Sequoya-Magdaleno, Jana. "Telling The Difference: Representations of Identity in the Discourse of Indianness." *The Ethnic Canon: Histories, Institutions, and Interventions*. Ed. David Palumbo-Liu. Minneapolis/London: U of Minnesota P, 1995. 88-116.

Silko, Leslie Marmon. *Laguna Woman: Poems*. New York: Greenfield Press, 1972.

------------------------. *Storyteller*. New York: Seaver, 1981.

------------------------. *Ceremony*. New York: Penguin Books, 1986.

------------------------. *Almanac of the Dead*. New York: Penguin, 1992.

------------------------. "Landscape, History and Pueblo Imagination." *The Woman That I am: The literature and Culture of Contemporary Woman of Colour*. Ed. D. Soyini Madison. New York: St Martins P, 1994. 498-511.

Simard, Rodney. "American Indian Literatures, Authenticity and the Canon." *World Literature Today* 66.2 (Spring1992): 243-248.

Söderlind, Sylvia. *Margin/Alias: Language and Colonization in Canadian and Quebecois Fiction*. Toronto: U of Toronto P, 1991.

Stratton, Florence. "Cartographic Lessons: Susanna Moodie's *Roughing It in the Bush* and Thomas King's *Green Grass, Running Water*." *Canadian Literature* 161-162 (Summer/Autumn 1999): 82-102.

Strouse, Jean. "In the Heart of the Heartland." *CLC 54*. Eds. Daniel G. Marowski and Roger Matuz. Detroit: Gale Research Inc., 1989. 171-172.

Swan, Edith. "Laguna Prototypes of Manhood in *Ceremony*." *MELUS* 11.1 (Spring 1991- 1992): 39-62.

------------. "Feminine Perspectives at Laguna Pueblo: Silko's *Ceremony*." *Tulsa Studies in Women's Literature*11.2 (Fall 1992): 309-328.

Tanrisal, Meldan. "Mother and Child Relationships in The Novels of Louise Erdrich." *American Studies International* 35.3 (October 1997): 67-79.

Taylor, Drew Hayden. "How Native is Native if You're Native?" *Expressions in Canadian Native Studies*. Ed. Ron F. Laliberte et al. Saskatchewan: U Extension P, 2000. 57-59.

Tharp, Julie. "Women's Community and Survival in Novels of Louise Erdrich." *CLC 120*. Eds. Jeffrey W. Hunter and Timothy J. White. Detroit: Gale Group, 1999. 162-168.

Towery, Margie. "Continuity and Connection: Characters in Louise Erdrich's Fiction." *American Indian Culture and Research Journal* 16: 4 (1992): 99-122.

Vangen, Kate. "Making Faces: Defiance and Humour in Campbell's *Halfbreed* and Welch's *Winter in the Blood*." *CLT 85*. Ed. Christopher Giroux. Detroit: Gale Research Inc, 1995. 9-11.

Vautier, Marie. "Comparative Post colonialism and the Amerindian in English Speaking Canada and Quebec." *Canadian Ethnic Studies*. 28.3 (1996): 4-15.

Velie, Alan R., *Four American Indian Literary Masters: N. Scott Momaday, James Welch, Leslie Marmon Silko and Gerald Vizenor*. Norman: U of Oklahoma P, 1982.

Vescey, Christopher. "Revenge of the Chippewa Witch." *CLC 120*. Eds. Jeffrey W. Hunter and Timothy J. White. Detroit: Gale Group, 1999. 139-145.

Vidgerman, Patricia. "A Review of _Tracks_." _CLC 54_. Ed. Daniel G. Marowski and Roger Matuz. Detroit: Gale Research Inc, 1989. 171.

Vidmar, Shawn. "The Bear and The Owl: Finding the Imagery in Louise Erdrich's novel _Tracks_." (1997). 9pp.19 Sep 2002. http://www.wdog. com/svid/writing/essays/erdrich_1997.htm.1997.

Wallace, Karen L. "Liminality and Myth in Native American Fiction: _Ceremony_ and _The Ancient Child_." _American Indian Culture and Research Journal_ 20.4 (1996): 91-119.

Walton, Percy. "'Tell Our Own Stories': Politics and the Fiction of Thomas King." _World Literature Written in English_ 30.2 (1990): 77-84.

Walton, Priscilla. "Border Crossings: Alterna (rra) tives in Thomas King's _Green Grass, Running Water_." _Genre: Forms of Discourse and Culture_ 31.1 (Spring 1998): 73-85.

Welch, James "The Man From Washington." _The American Indian Speaks_. Ed. John R Milton. Vermillion: Dakota Press, 1969.

Whitson, Kathy J. _Native American Literatures: An Encyclopedia of Works, Characters, Authors and Themes_. Oxford: ABC-CLIO, 1999.

Wiget, Andrew. _Native American Literatures_. Boston: Twayne Publishers, 1985.

William, David. _Confessional Fictions: A Portrait of the Artist in the Canadian Novel_. Toronto: U of Toronto P, 1991.

Williamson, Janice. "What I intended was to connect ... and it's happened." _Sounding Differences: Conversations with Seven Canadian Woman Writers_. Janice Williamson. Toronto: U of Toronto P, 1993. 7-26.

Young, Robert. _Postcolonialism: A very short Introduction_. New York: OUP, 2003.

Young, Robert. *Postcolonialism: An Historical Introduction.* Oxford: Blackwell Publishers, 2001.

Zamir, Shamoon. "Literature in a National Sacrifice Area: Leslie Silko's *Ceremony.*" *New Voices in Native American Literary Criticism.* Ed. Arnold Krupat. Washington: Smithsonian Institution Press, 1993. 396-415.

Index

230

231

www.ingramcontent.com/pod-product-compliance
Lightning Source LLC
Chambersburg PA
CBHW070347090426
42733CB00009B/1323